A Dakini's Counsel

A Dakini's Counsel

Sera Khandro's Spiritual Advice and
Dzogchen Instructions

Sera Khandro Dewai Dorje

TRANSLATED BY
Christina Lee Monson

FOREWORDS BY
Dzongsar Jamyang Khyentse and
Sogan Tulku Pema Lodoe

SNOW LION

Snow Lion
An imprint of Shambhala Publications, Inc.
2129 13th Street
Boulder, Colorado 80302
www.shambhala.com

Cover art: From a handwritten manuscript of Sera Khandro's teachings in the private collection of Kyabje Chatral Rinpoche
Cover design: Daniel Urban-Brown

9 8 7 6 5 4 3 2 1

First Edition
Printed in the United States of America

Shambhala Publications makes every effort to print on acid-free, recycled paper.
Shambhala Publications is distributed worldwide by Penguin Random House, Inc., and its subsidiaries.

LIBRARY OF CONGRESS CATALOGING-IN-PUBLICATION DATA
Names: Bde-ba'i-rdo-rje, 1892–1940, author. | Monson, Christina Lee, translator.
Title: A Dakini's counsel: Sera Khandro's spiritual advice and Dzogchen instructions / Sera Khandro Dewai Dorje; translated by Christina Lee Monson.
Description: Boulder: Shambhala Publications, 2024. | Includes bibliographical references and index. |
Identifiers: LCCN 2023027913 | ISBN 9781611808841 (trade paperback)
Subjects: LCSH: Rnying-ma-pa (Sect)—Doctrines. | Rdzogs-chen. | Spiritual life—Rnying-ma-pa (Sect)
Classification: LCC BQ7662.4 .B28 2024 | DDC 294.3/444—mdc23/eng/20230727
LC record available at https://lccn.loc.gov/2023027913

For Yangchen Lhamo and dakinis everywhere

NOTE TO READER

Due to the precious and secretive nature of the teachings found within this book, it is best read only by individuals possessing a pure attitude and genuine devotion toward the approach of Dzogchen, the Great Perfection. Ideally, readers will have already connected with authentic Great Perfection lineage holders capable of explaining the subtler points of instruction found here within Sera Khandro Dewai Dorje's spiritual advice. In particular, according to the wisdom intent of Kyabje Chatral Rinpoche, readers also will have been immersed in the preliminary practices of the Tibetan Vajrayana path. Keeping the book as an object of faith and respect on one's shrine until such a time that a relationship with a Dzogchen teacher is established and Vajrayana practice is engaged is an acceptable way to relate to this text as well.

Contents

Foreword by
Dzongsar Jamyang Khyentse

It is with great delight that I welcome the publication of Christina Monson's translation of Sera Khandro's *shaldam*—instructions and advice. The Land of Snows has produced many great and accomplished women teachers, saints, and scholars; of this there is no doubt. But let's face it—Tibet has always suffered from systemic male domination to the detriment of Tibetan women whose achievements have never been celebrated enough, especially in the spiritual world. Yet, in spite of their lack of encouragement, even their active discouragement, remarkable women like Sera Khandro have somehow spilled out.

The twentieth century bore witness to how much the wisdom and greatness of such unique women are so necessary and so missed. As a result, many voices are now calling for the achievements of Tibetan's highly accomplished women to be recognized and made more widely available. Yet, were Sera Khandro here today, she would not approve of my saying any of this if it were understood merely in the context of feminism, gender equality, and similar political agendas. As you will see from many of her teachings, she considered such worldly endeavors to be futile. Instead, she tells us that we should pursue activities that will lead us to transcend the endless entanglement of distinctions.

Nevertheless, every single word of wisdom uttered in this world must be treasured and not wasted. Although wisdom itself is beyond words and conception, the words each individual uses in their attempts to articulate that wisdom and the nuanced experiences and insights they describe in the process of discovering and acquiring it are of paramount interest and importance to their followers. Like all communication in this world, when various people speak exactly the same words, those listening hear them differently, and the impact they make is also different. Sera Khandro's distinctive voice cannot merely be put down to her being a woman—although that certainly brought a richness to her words. Everything she went through in her life and everyone she associated with added a depth of color and taste to all her words. And it is this unique voice of hers that should now be treasured.

We tend to assume that where there's smoke, there's fire. Likewise, it's safe to say that those who lack the merit to have been born at the same time as Sera Khandro can nevertheless assess her greatness by examining her illustrious apprentice, Kyabje Chatral Rinpoche. Now that he has passed away, in addition to his reputation for unparalleled scholarship and vast spiritual achievement, his lack of any trace of hypocrisy and his uncompromising, even stubborn, attitude toward the preservation of the Dharma and how it is taught have become legendary. Even among Tibetan Buddhists, stories about how far he went to demonstrate his unwillingness to compromise in any way at all could not easily be swallowed. Such reverence for and loyalty to wisdom does not appear out of the blue. I had the great good fortune not only to have met Kyabje Chatral Rinpoche but to have received teachings from him. When I think about Kyabje Chatral Rinpoche's own unyielding attitude, I see that it can only have come from his teacher, the great lady, Sera Khandro, whose courage and refusal to compromise I have heard so much about.

In addition to receiving teachings, abhishekas, and guidance from many great Mahasandhi masters—for example, Tulku Urgyen Rinpoche—Christina Monson also received decades of teachings from Kyabje Chatral Rinpoche. Therefore, I do not think of her as yet another mildly curious Dharma student but as a seeker after the truth who was blessed and strongly influenced by many great masters, Chatral Rinpoche in particular. As such, I have no doubt that Christina made many good aspirations as she translated Sera Khandro's words, and, as a result, now that this great lady's words are being made available in English, there is far less chance of the meaning getting lost in translation. For this reason, my aspiration for this translation is that it will be widely read. May those who read this book not only come to know Sera Khandro and her teachings but may the reach of her buddha activities extend to infinity.

Dzongsar Jamyang Khyentse

2023

Foreword by
Sogan Tulku Pema Lodoe

I bow from my heart to the great treasure revealer Dewai Dorje,
a dakini who intentionally came into the world
as a magical emanation of Noble Tara,
the manifestation of the great love, wisdom, and activity
of all triumphant buddhas.

The powerful intentions and karmic aspirations of the buddhas
and bodhisattvas throughout the ages bring myriad wisdom ema-
nations in rupakayas, bodies of form, that accord with the wishes
and minds of the ones who are to be tamed by them. Specifically,
many inconceivably great beings, who are Dharma holders both
learned and accomplished in practice, have come to uphold the tradition of the Buddhadharma transmitted through the three great
masters, Khenpo Shantarakshita, Guru Padmasambhava, and
King Trisong Deutsen, in the snowy, mountainous land of Tibet.

The actions of these noble beings serve the doctrine of the Buddha and sentient beings. They have brought forth many collections
of teachings that clarify the wisdom intent of the profound and
vast sutras and tantras. Among those who are propagating these
teachings, which are allocated per the fortunate shares of future
disciples, came a lady in a body of form born in the twentieth century in Lhasa, whose wisdom activity blossomed in the lands of
eastern Tibet: the great treasure revealer Khacho Wangmo Dewai
Dorje, or Sera Khandro, Kunzang Dekyong Wangmo.

Coming from the vast, exalted sky-repository of treasures of her
enlightened mind are a long autobiography and other versions of
her noble deeds in extensive and concise presentations. In addition,

there are many commentarial explanations of development- and completion-stage practice and Dzogchen. Finally, there are numerous sadhanas focused on the three root wisdom deities and the Dharma protectors, as well as incredibly blessed direct spiritual songs, instructions, and advice. All are contained within seven volumes of her Collected Works.

Here are brought together in one place some of this sublime lady's songs of realization and spiritual instructions as a book. The eminent, richly faithful, and pure-intentioned American woman, Sangye Gyalmo, or Christina Monson, who knows both Tibetan and English languages, translated these into her native English. I deeply rejoice in this and offer her a great thanks.

I would like to offer the readers a few reflections. The whole point of survival, for those of us in this world, is to be of benefit to ourselves and others. Likewise, everyone needs physical and mental well-being. Taking care of ourselves physically and, especially, mentally, I see as being paramount. When we consider Sera Khandro as an example, while her realization was equal to that of a buddha, she manifested on the level of relative perception in the form of a human lady. Amid the events of her life, she withstood great hardship to be of service to the Buddha's lineage and sentient beings. She gave many oral instructions that are unfathomably profound to show her disciples the path in myriad ways. Many of these are contained here in this book.

Therefore, when you read this book, try not to fixate upon just the stories that come out but, with respect and devotion, seize the meaning of what is being revealed. If you can genuinely practice that, you will be led by the luminous blessings of these teachings, and peace and happiness will dawn in your mind like a glorious sun from within. This is certain. I pray it will unfold in this way.

The sixth Sogan Tulku, Sonam Dawai Wangpo, or Pema Lodoe, composed this in Carson City, Nevada, USA, in the Tibetan Wood Rabbit year, on the eighteenth day of the twelfth Tibetan month, February 8, 2023.

TRANSLATOR'S INTRODUCTION

WHAT IS THIS BOOK?

She was a beautiful woman in love, a single-pointed Dharma practitioner, and a realized master and treasure revealer. Welcome to the world of Sera Khandro Dewai (pronounced "day-way") Dorje, the Dakini from Central Tibet (1892–1940). What awaits you in her teachings presented here is nothing short of pristine Buddhist Dharma teaching. What makes it so special is that it comes through the lived experience of a unique Tibetan female teacher. What makes it worth reading is that the heartfelt and intimate advice presented here overflows with lineage blessings that can catalyze transformational change, right on the spot. All that is required is an open heart and mind. Proceed accordingly, secure in knowing that I have taken utmost care to translate accurately and faithfully, to the best of my ability, the meaning of this special woman's sacred speech. It is with deepest respect and devotion to this great master that I offer it to you.

This book contains the translation of selections from Dewai Dorje's *shaldam*. Shaldam refers to a type of spiritual instruction given straight from a master to a disciple.[1] Personal, penetrating, and practical, shaldam bridges an enlightened master's realization with the same potential awakening in the disciple. Whether they are delivered orally and later written or composed first in letter, they often are pithy, encapsulating in few words the most essential key points for that individual's practice. With such power of specificity, the words of shaldam can reverberate with deeper and deeper profundity throughout the entire practice life of students, whether or not they ever meet the teacher who gives them again.

They often release blockages hindering a student's awakening. This is why they're cherished and held with great reverence in the sacred enclosure of guru-disciple relationship. They are, in fact, what is most precious.

Before entering into the individual teachings, an introduction to the person of Dewai Dorje is required. My purpose in offering one next is to employ a big brushstroke to contextualize her world and synthesize qualities that, in my reading of her words and practice of her treasures, essentialize who she was. My understanding comes from many sources. I was first introduced to her and gained a sense of her essence from many conversations with her direct student Chatral Sangye Dorje (1913–2015) as well as other lineage holders. Over time, I deepened my understanding through greater familiarity with her seven volumes of Collected Works, including her long and short autobiographies, her biography of her lama and treasure-revealing consort Drime (pronounced "dree-may") Ozer (1880–1924), personal letters and advice, and four volumes of treasures. Additionally, stellar scholarship by Sarah Jacoby on the chronology of her life, her personhood, and sense-making of her world has enhanced my insights into who she was.[2]

Finally, a note about names is needed. Sera Khandro is an identifier given to her by some people because of her residence at Awo Sera Monastery, on the banks of Nyichu river in Golok, eastern Tibet, starting in 1924. It wasn't a name she used for herself. The name with which she signed most of the pieces in this collection is Dewai Dorje (Skt. Sukha Vajra, "blissful vajra"). Most people from Golok refer to her even now as Uza Khandro, the Dakini from Central Tibet. She had, used, and was called by many names including Kunga Wangmo, Kunzang Chonyi Wangmo, Dekyong Wangmo, Dechen Dewai Dorje, Dipam Tare, Pema Dronkar, Kalzang Drolma, and more. Throughout this book, I've chosen to use the name Dewai Dorje, which is the one she most used to refer to herself.

THE ESSENCE OF DEWAI DORJE'S LIFE

Dewai Dorje was born into turmoil. Her birth year, 1892, fell in the middle of competing Chinese, Russian, and British power grabbing efforts in Asia, a great game that had significant impact on Tibet. The Thirteenth Dalai Lama, Tupten Gyatso (1869–1933) was fleeing his country back and forth to Mongolia and to India, where resistance to the British Raj was fomenting and Rudyard Kipling had just spent formative years as a young adult and nascent writer. Indeed, Dewai Dorje was likely in Lhasa or its environs when the Younghusband Expedition invaded on August 3, 1904.[3] These outer global tensions mirrored a closer web of familiar tensions that infused her early years. The daughter of a Mongolian man and Tibetan woman, she was born into Lhasa nobility with two distinct ethnic identities. Whether she should learn Chinese or Tibetan language, live as a nun or householder, be allowed to be independent or forced to run her father's large dominion were real sources of conflict causing significant stress in her childhood.

These factors and more paved a rough but swift road to renunciation for Dewai Dorje almost as soon as she alighted, painlessly, from her mother's womb. To be sure, she was dedicated, single-pointedly, to the Dharma from her earliest years. She remembered past lifetimes as Dharma practitioners and even was able to remember other languages from them, such as Nepali. She spoke of going to pure buddha fields, such as the Palace of Lotus Light, at the tender age of one. As a small child having big and at times incomprehensible experiences, she was alienated from her peers and often hushed into secrecy about the unfolding of her inner world by her own mother. She thus came to eschew ordinary play with other children, preferring instead to recite the *mani* mantra.[4]

Dewai Dorje's determination to live a life of retreat focused solely on Dharma practice was with her from her earliest days, and it never left her. Her most important life decisions were guided by deep faith in the teachings of the Buddha and their Tibetan manifestation through the eighth-century master Padmasambhava, the supreme consort Yeshe Tsogyal, and envoys, dakinis, who conveyed their messages to her. A conviction to stake her life on the Dharma grew within her—influenced ever more so by a visionary journey to the lower realms, an unwanted arranged marriage, and numerous other experiences. It also blossomed through encounters with wisdom phenomena and hearing about the teachings of Dzogchen, the Great Perfection, from her father who shared his training in perceiving everything as the nature of a dream. In fact, it was he who first watered the seed of this unsurpassed path, ready and waiting to sprout inside her. Simply hearing the word Dzogchen from him when she was nine years old caused deep faith to well forth. Her resolve was fixed. Hers must be a life of Dharma.

Determined and fearless yet tender and dependent, Dewai Dorje encountered a broad spectrum of life experience in the first decade and a half of her life. Externally, this included the painful loss of her mother, while, internally, it included being trained by the great Indian mahasiddhas Saraha and Kukuripa in visionary encounters. Though out-of-order from a traditional way of progressing upon the path, Dewai Dorje's spiritual training was exquisitely appropriate for her. This is because it was through gaining proficiency in the inner practices of her body's wisdom channels, winds, and vital essences that she was able not only to heal herself but also heal others in her youth. In addition, these techniques opened the gateways for refining her perception of reality such that her own *termas*, or treasures, became more accessible to her.

Termas are revelations of wisdom teachings. The Nyingma, or Early Translation, tradition holds that the eighth-century Indian mahasiddha Padmasambhava and his consort, the Tibetan lady Yeshe Tsogyal, hid such teachings in actual places in the greater Tibetan environs for their future discovery by prophesized masters, such as Dewai Dorje. Termas are found in form and formless representations. Some are actual material objects. Others are symbolically encoded in the cryptic, twilight language of dakinis, female embodiments of wisdom. Often dakinis tell treasure revealers the what, when, where, and how of their destined revelations, information contained in "treasure inventories" or, as mentioned below, symbolic scrolls. Treasures usually involve a process of decoding and transcription by their revealers.

Dakinis were ever-present in Dewai Dorje's life. They manifested in multiple forms in dreams, visions, and numerous experiences of luminosity to guide her. They conveyed messages and prophecies, often through birds, or "feathered friends," to her and Drime Ozer both, alerting them to conditions of the other when they were apart. Their central role cannot be understated. Constant companions, they witnessed Dewai Dorje's tenuous relationship with living in the world, providing wise and reassuring counsel to her in times of greatest need. They saw to it that she received the pith instructions she needed to progress on her spiritual path and connected her to the treasures that were hers to reveal.

In the shorter of her two autobiographies, Dewai Dorje summarizes a key event of her spiritual life at age thirteen in which she meets Padmasambhava and the dakini Yeshe Tsogyal:

> When I was thirteen,
> due to the power of previously accumulated prayers,
> I met the powerful siddha Kukupa.
> He introduced me to the pith instructions
> on dispelling obscurations in my channels and winds
> and, using the five chakras as a support,
> taught the stages of the paths of outer and inner
>   Mahamudra
> as well as the secret teachings.
> Invoked through the power of my having released
> the knots in my heart channel,
> the mother-dakinis gave me unmistaken symbolic scrolls,
> and I met Padmasambhava and Yeshe Tsogyal in actuality.
> I was empowered as an emissary of these wisdom beings,
> who predicted that the time was ripe to benefit others
> and gave advice on how to gradually benefit myself and
>   others."[5]

Fortified with this internal Dharma experience and confidence, Dewai Dorje built a capacity for self-sufficiency that was to serve her well in overcoming a myriad of challenges, some life-threatening, that ensued after her daring escape from her brother's home and embarkation on a harrowing journey to eastern Tibet in 1907. To say that this was a courageous act is a gross understatement. It was the most important decision of her life. It reflected her incredible inner resilience and outer survivalist strengths. There were absolutely no conveniences on this one-thousand-mile journey by foot from Lhasa to Dartsang Monastery in Serta, Golok. Yet, it began the actualization of Dewai Dorje's blessed and powerful destiny as a young woman fully in love with her prophesized lama and consort Drime Ozer, the eighth child and fifth son of the electric Dudjom Lingpa (1835–1903).

It was one thing to be the daughter of a wealthy and powerful father in Lhasa's exclusive upper political echelons with their shrewd machinations. It was quite another to be an unaccompanied female in the wilds of eastern Tibet in 1908. The contrast could not have been starker. Arriving at the Dudjom family stronghold of Dartsang, four years after Dudjom Lingpa had passed away, Dewai Dorje found herself in a place where she couldn't communicate in the local tongue, lacked people to vouch for her, notably men, and had precious little in the way of livelihood skills. She frequently referred to herself as a beggar because she really was one. Yet, she possessed an unwavering mind of renunciation and a parched thirst for Dharma teaching and practice. She describes the poignant moment after all her fellow pilgrims returned home with their loved ones and she remained behind, alone:

> As I was left there by myself without any place to go, I felt a bit sad and sang this song:
>
> Indivisible with Padmasambhava himself,
> Bodhisattva Drime Ozer, I beseech you—
> please, protect me with your compassion!

In this impermanent and illusory city,
as I think and think some more,
my sorrow grows.
Summer flowers have vanished now,
again becoming grass.
My companions from Central Tibet,
all gathered through karma,
were here last night
but now are gone.
See how I, a child loved by her parents
for the first part of her life,
the daughter of a powerful minister regarded as
     high,
now am left aside like a stray dog,
abandoned by everyone near and far.
I'm absolutely sure
there is no essence whatsoever
in these impermanent and illusory magical
     displays.
If I cannot practice the sublime Dharma
in a heartfelt way in this life,
I will suffer now and later
as a girl without a single source of refuge.
If I can accomplish the sublime Dharma,
I will certainly be happy in this life and the next.

After comforting myself, I went inside the temple at
Drime Ozer's seat.[6]

Indeed, she had come to the right place. Her love for and deep
karmic connection with Drime Ozer brought her right into the
center of the Dudjom world. Though his life had been marked
more by material poverty and hidden-yogi practice than comfort
and fame, Dudjom Lingpa, a householder with twelve children,
had just founded one of the Nyingma tradition's most imposing,

potent, and majestic treasure lineages. When Dewai Dorje arrived in eastern Tibet in 1907–1908, it was alive and thriving through the activity of his children. Her Dharma training thus began with a total immersion into the vibrant world of the Dudjom Tersar. The Dudjom Tersar, the New Treasures of Dudjom, is one of the most widely practiced treasure lineages among Nyingma followers today. Founded by Dudjom Lingpa in the nineteenth century, it greatly expanded through the activity of his incarnation Dudjom Jigdral Yeshe Dorje (1904–1987). The Dudjom Tersar contains over forty volumes of treasures and teachings between the two masters and is reputed as a complete path to awakening, the followers of which have been demonstrating the highest levels of spiritual attainment for almost two centuries. It is, in brief, a fast track to realization in one lifetime.

Dewai Dorje had the fortune to land right in the center of its charged headquarters. Over time, she was trained by three of Dudjom Lingpa's own sons. Tulku Drime Ozer, of course, gave her extensive Dharma and Dzogchen teachings. Tulku Lhatop (1884–1942) taught her the preliminaries, the *ngondro*, and Tulku Dorje Dradul (1892–1959) taught her the different melodies for the practice of Troma Nagmo, the Great Wrathful Mother.[7]

This outer training combined with her early inner accomplishment solidified her for what would come next: navigating what it meant to be a predestined Secret Mantra consort who was to be widely sought after for the rest of her life. Her first summons based on these very special qualities came from an important treasure revealer named Gara Terchen Dudul Wangchuk Lingpa (1857–1911) of Benak Monastery in Golok. She had been invited, as a dakini with longevity powers, by Gara Terchen to prolong his life. However, jealousy and rivalry on the part of Gara Terchen's wife, a woman named Yakza, obstructed their meeting before the treasure revealer's death. Still, her trip there proved fateful for her life. It landed her in a domestic relationship with Gara Gyalse Pema Namgyal (b. 1882/3), a son of Gara Terchen.

Theirs was not a loving relationship. It was fraught with hostilities from the beginning. Gara Gyalse's mother, Yakza, continued to make life uncomfortable for Dewai Dorje and never let her forget her outsider status. Starting out in Golok as a materially poor foreigner, Dewai Dorje had limited options for actual survival. She had to rely on others. The rough and wild landscapes of Golok's high-altitude plains offered no protection from the raw elements. Food and shelter were not easily found alone. To live meant that Dewai Dorje's own freedom and autonomy to go where she wanted and do as she liked was curtailed, a theme that populates her writing.

Furthermore, Golok's male culture impacted the dearth of choices Dewai Dorje had for living an independent life of Dharma practice. Eventually, Gara Gyalse took up with another consort named Saldron and utterly neglected Dewai Dorje and their daughter Yangchen Dronma (b. 1913) and son Rigdzin Gyurme Dorje (1919–1924). Motherhood, while at times encumbering Dewai Dorje, was a core part of her experience and identity. Her two children were with her constantly, and she loved them deeply. They gave her some footing in Gara Gyalse's household. However, this wasn't enough to keep her there. Her own ailing health combined with the recognition, explicitly stated between Gara Gyalse and Drime Ozer, that she was "meant" to be Drime Ozer's consort were principal factors leading to her final separation with Gara Gyalse to join Drime Ozer in 1921.

When this finally happened, it also posed numerous complexities for Drime Ozer to resolve with his other consorts and extended family. It is clear through Dewai Dorje's many descriptions of the years before and after she left Gara Gyalse that she was a practitioner fully adept in taking obstacles as the path. As outer circumstances over the many years of her life, both with Gara Gyalse and Drime Ozer, fluctuated between joy and sorrow, such as is the case for everyone, her inner realization and treasure activity were already maturing.

To be in love and to have that love returned with equal force and depth by its object is one of the great miracles of being alive. Dewai

Dorje and Drime Ozer shared this miracle together. They truly loved each other. She gazed upon him camped outside her father's mansion at age fifteen in Lhasa, and it changed her life. One of the dimensions of their love was the mutual roles of discovering, decoding, and sharing treasures and teaching each other. Well before they began three blissful years together as treasure-revealing consorts in 1921, they were attuned to each other's revelations. On one occasion, they shared a long and heartfelt meeting at Nedro Dorje Dzong, Drime Ozer's retreat cave near his seat at Dartsang Kalzang Monastery. Afterward, Dewai Dorje offered him some of her most precious and profound teachings. She writes,

> Then, as the Sublime One wished, I offered him the oral instructions on *Drinking Vajra Water* from the *Quintessential Secret Mother Tantra*, as my most precious jewel, without holding anything back. Especially, based on the mandala of the *Secret Sky of Unelaborate Great Bliss*, I gave the four essential practice empowerments and the introduction to the state of great connate dharmakaya, and together with those, opened up the hidden naked instructions containing the pith points for the wisdom intent of the practices of union and liberation and more. Without hiding and concealing anything, I taught my most cherished wealth, all the oral instructions that I had been holding in my mind, to my secret consort, Wish-Fulfilling Jewel.

Auspicious indications followed this exchange, and then Dewai Dorje took her leave. Shortly thereafter, she had a dream in which she saw Drime Ozer looking upset along with other portents of obstacles. The following morning, feeling uneasy, she handed teachings given to her from the dakinis on ceremonies to dispel obstacles along with auspicious substances to Tsultrim Dorje, Drime Ozer's close student and scribe, to give to him. Drime Ozer received them, and the auspiciousness continued.

Tsultrim Dorje (Skt. Shila Vajra) turned out to be one of the most important people in Dewai Dorje's own life. After Drime Ozer passed, he accompanied Dewai Dorje to Awo Sera Monastery, a place she called home for the next chapter of her life. He became her scribe and "heart son," as she addresses him in many of the selections here. The excruciating losses in 1924 of both her own dear son, Rigdzin Gyurme Dorje, and her lama and consort, Drime Ozer, within days of each other, slammed Dewai Dorje with such a crushing grief that finding the will to go on seemed impossible at times. Yet, persevere she did. The love that she knew in her bones as a mother radiated over the coming years to her circle of disciples, which, like her fame, continued to grow.

In the sixteen years that followed these two most tragic events of her life, Dewai Dorje stepped into the most important work of her life. This was her role as a writer, teacher, and preserver and propagator of the treasure lineages of Dudjom Lingpa and Drime Ozer as well as her own. In this capacity, she was intimately familiar with the contents of at least forty volumes of dense esoteric Buddhist teachings and practices.[8] She transmitted and taught these both in personal one-on-one interactions and to congregations numbering in the hundreds while sitting on thrones in places such as the great Riwoche Monastery in Kham.

From a protected daughter of wealthy origins to a wandering beggar lady, Dewai Dorje spent her later years as a respected highly realized Dzogchen master and rare female treasure revealer, bestowing empowerment on queens, kings, and commoners alike. Her final year was 1940, which, according to Tibetan counting, was when she was forty-nine. Her easeful passing happened at the town of Riwoche in Kham, where she had been invited and was staying as a guest at the lama residence. Before this, according to her heart son Chatral Sangye Dorje, she said that nothing was left unfinished since she had accomplished the activities of upholding, preserving, and spreading the precious teachings of Dudjom Lingpa and Drime Ozer in a vast way so that she faced death joyfully.[9]

To welcome death joyfully is taught as the measure of the best

Dzogchen practitioner. In taking to heart the key points elegantly elucidated by this exceptional woman in the pages that follow, there is no doubt that such accomplishment lies in the hands of everyone who embarks upon the majestic path she tread. May it be so!

WHAT YOU NEED TO KNOW

Before engaging with this book, there are several important things for readers to know. First is the greater scope of the path of Dzogchen, as this was Dewai Dorje's own practice and what she principally taught her students. Most of the translated material in this book has a Dzogchen flavor. Second, to better understand the contents of the book, a closer look at Dewai Dorje's shaldam is merited. Finally, connected to this second point, I offer a walk-through of my process of making and organizing the selections that are presented.

THE TEACHINGS OF DZOGCHEN

To establish a connection with the personal teachings of Dewai Dorje is to make a connection with the teachings of Dzogchen, the Great Perfection. These two terms are used interchangeably throughout this book. The Nyingma tradition presents a ninefold framework of spiritual progression that culminates in the approach of *atiyoga*, the highest and most exalted of all paths. This is the path of Dzogchen, the Great Perfection. Subsuming all teachings that come before it, it's likened to the pinnacle of all vehicles and the summit from which everything can be clearly seen. Its special techniques enable practitioners to take wisdom as the path from the beginning instead of having to rely on less direct strategies for awakening involving conceptual mind.

The Dzogchen tradition, highly valued by practitioners from the Nyingma tradition especially, but also by many from other Tibetan Buddhist traditions, is replete with special features that define it. Among these, the importance of devotion in the context of a pure guru-disciple relationship is central. For the tradition's alchemy to be fully unleashed, it requires an encounter between a fully qualified student (one whose mind is saturated with faith and pure regard) and a fully qualified teacher (one whose enlightened mind is blazing with the warmth of realization). It is then that the student can receive, internalize, and awaken through the unparalleled instructions of Dzogchen. According to the teachings, this has happened for centuries, is happening now continuously, and will continue to happen until all realms of wanderers are empty. Dzogchen is a tradition that centers upon direct one-to-one transmission between teacher and disciple, which can unfold in actuality, dreams, visions, or otherwise. Devotion is the foundation.

Another defining feature of the Great Perfection tradition is its plethora of *upadesha* instructions. These are direct teachings, most often orally presented, that introduce practitioners to the nature of mind, just as it is, such that a personal experience of it can occur right on the spot. While there are a great variety of upadesha teachings, those that help practitioners differentiate between conceptual mind and its true nature, *rigpa*, or awareness, play a central role. That differentiation is indispensable for students to take wisdom as the path, a process that requires familiarity with the personal experience of awareness. In general, a focus on cutting through the dualistic contrivances of conceptual mind effortlessly is found in Dzogchen's Trekcho (Cutting Through) teachings. A complementary focus both on coming to and enhancing that recognition through special techniques requiring effort is found in Dzogchen's Togal (Leaping Over) teachings. These are the two main paths of the Great Perfection tradition, ones with which Dewai Dorje was intimately acquainted as practitioner and as teacher. The introduction to chapter 2 explores them in greater detail.

Finally, an important quality of the Dzogchen tradition is that its teachings are both secret and self-secret. In the first case, this means that aspiring Dzogchen practitioners must seek out qualified masters from whom they can receive the teachings in a proper way, according to the tradition. In the second case, this means that the teachings themselves can be impenetrable for students until and unless timing and other such circumstances are correctly aligned. Essentially, students cannot access the teachings until they are ready for them. As her earliest reaction to hearing the word Dzogchen attests, Dewai Dorje was born with deep karmic connection to these teachings, from all her previous lives infused with the tradition. It was her personal path, what she taught her students, and is therefore what you will encounter in the teachings presented here.

Given the special features of Dzogchen I have briefly touched upon above, it might be the case that readers of this material meet terms, ideas, and references that are unfamiliar or unintelligible. However, while I have done my best to provide context for each of the chapters, I make no attempt to explain Dewai Dorje's teachings or Dzogchen. Rather, I trust that my efforts to translate them correctly, according to my limitations, will make accessible for readers what is needed. All mistakes found therein are solely of my own doing and are deeply regretted. As you make your way through Dewai Dorje's writing presented here, you are invited to rest easily with what may not be clear upon first glance, secure in the knowledge that what is meant to be clear for you gradually will be.

DEWAI DORJE'S SHALDAM

The particular qualities of Dzogchen, as explained above, lend it to direct one-on-one modes of transmission, such as are exemplified by the tradition of shaldam. Dewai Dorje's shaldam were composed for some of the most renowned lamas and teachers of her time as well as for humble practitioners. Some of the former include Adzom Drukpa Drodul Pawo Dorje (1842–1959) and his son Dungse Gyurme Dorje, Dudjom Lingpa's sons Drime Ozer and Dorje Dradul, Adzom Seymo Chime Wangmo, Dromge Khandro Dawa Dronma, the Dharma King and Queen of Ling Tsang, and of course her own daughter, Yangchen Dronma. No matter the recipient, the flavor of her teachings remains the same:

heartfelt, emotionally rich, stunningly profound, and graciously crafted. Readers will also note humor and playfulness in some of her words, testament to her capacity to be with, but not made of, her struggles.

The entire collection of Dewai Dorje's shaldam encompasses a wide variety of genres and literary styles including narrative poetry in verse, prophecies, spiritual songs, expressions of realization, meditation teachings in prose, personal letters, prayers, visions, and more. Over one hundred and eighty individual pieces are found, gathered principally in two groupings in different volumes of her Collected Works. Their lengths vary, ranging from a single verse to ten or more Tibetan folio pages. The selections chosen for this book come from both groupings and make up approximately half of the entire shaldam collection.

In choosing the pieces in the chapters that follow, I considered the accessibility of the teaching for a wide audience, as well as the degree of esoteric material in it. My aim was to offer as much of her shaldam as I could, without transgressing sacred lines of secrecy, or including extensive material that requires deep knowledge and background understanding of Tibetan Buddhism to be comprehensible. The choices I made are grouped within broad chapter headings, among which is considerable overlap. Personal letters are also pith instructions and proclamations of realization, and the reverse is also true. There are no equivalent one-to-one categories in the Tibetan manuscripts. I employed the ones here simply to order the material for a Western-style book and render it as accessible as possible.

However, my decisions to include individual pieces under these broader categories were not completely random. For example, in chapter 1, I selected pieces that had a distinctive aspirational and devotional tone and that are, in fact, prayers. If Dewai Dorje wrote in a colophon that she composed the piece "as a prayer," I felt it could fit into chapter 1. In selecting poems for chapter 2, I chose pieces that had metaphorical language and its beauty, along with the acrostics. Chapter 3 was easier because the pieces that are prophecy are quite clear in their being unintelligible! There are extensive prophecies in Dewai Dorje's shaldam, and I chose sparingly. Chapter 4 is where more overlap can be found because proclamations of realization, wonder, and despair are often poetically expressed as well as being instructions in and of themselves. This category contains selections that would fall under the more common designation of *doha* (*mgur*), "songs of realization." Chapter 5 includes pieces expressly named as experiential visions by Dewai Dorje, and chapter 6 is largely composed of shaldam that are not identified as being written for a specific recipient, though of course some of them may well have been. In chapter 7, I included only shaldam that are addressed to specific individuals, as these bring the personal flavor to the forefront. Finally, both pieces in chapter 8 are labeled as final testaments by Dewai Dorje.

The reader will also take note that each selection is titled. Most of these titles, with a few exceptions noted in the individual pieces, do not exist in the original Tibetan. I titled them for ease of reader identification. I tried to find the title naturally in the words of each shaldam, which proved quite easy to do. Finally, when possible, I followed the order of the pieces as they come in the original manuscripts. Thus, the book lends itself to jumping in anywhere, though readers may also wish to proceed through the chapters from beginning to end. Either approach is suitable.

ACKNOWLEDGMENTS

Kyabje Chatral Sangye Dorje, whose mere name constantly evokes in me overwhelming tears of faith, gratitude, and love, is the one that made this book possible. That such a master tread upon this earth in times and places that I, by an inconceivable miracle, chanced to live and venture will always be the greatest gift of my life. Words are woefully inadequate to express how indebted I am to him, my root guru. He first introduced me to Dewai Dorje and bestowed transmission of many of her treasures upon me. Later Chatral Rinpoche's heart son, the head lama of Tengboche Monastery, Tengboche Rinpoche Ngawang Tenzin Jangpo, conferred the Dakini's treasures in full on two separate occasions. The first was to the lineage holder and Dewai Dorje's incarnation Saraswati Devi, Chatral Sangye Dorje's daughter. The second was to the lineage holders Sogan Tulku and Dipuk Tulku along with a few fortunate others, a transmission support by his long-term and most loyal attendant Tenzin Norbu. I had the merit to be present for both transmissions in their entirety. I resolved then and continue to hold that the remainder of my life will be dedicated to continued personal practice of Dewai Dorje's treasures, as well as to their translation and transmission, in attempting to repay these kindnesses.

Many Tibetan translation partners and Dharma teachers supported me throughout this project. The challenge of reading Dewai Dorje's teachings was only somewhat overcome by working with native Golok speakers, as well as with other Tibetans and Tibetan language translators. They kindly and patiently explained to me words and meanings I didn't understand. It is only due to their unremitting help and encouragement that this was able to come to completion. They are dear Dharma family members and teachers whom I regularly consulted and include Sogan Tulku Pema Lodoe, Khenpo Yeshe Gyaltsen, Khenpo Tekchok Gyaltsen, Khenpo Tashi Tseten, Lama Chonam, and Lama Sean Price. Sogan Tulku in particular spent hours with me explaining idioms and colloquialisms of his native Golok tongue found in Dewai Dorje's writings. He patiently humored my clumsy attempts to figure these out on my own and then corrected me. Without his continuous assistance, I wouldn't have been able to produce these translations. In addition, my close Dharma brother and friend, Lama Sean Price, went through the entire manuscript prior to publication and gave me the confidence of having had a more senior and skilled lotsawa check my work. I am profoundly grateful to them both.

Other events greatly enhanced my understanding and were indispensable aids to accomplishing this project. The first was Sogan Tulku's careful and clear teaching of Dewai Dorje's shaldam in 2021, 2022, and 2023, for which I served as translator and interpreter, to a small and fortunate group of his own students. Second, Sogan Tulku, at the request of Lama Tsultrim Allione, taught Dewai Dorje's shaldam for the Tara Mandala community in the spring of 2022, and again I was the interpreter. Third, in 2022, both Tsultrim Allione and Yudron Wangmo invited me to give talks to their students about Dewai Dorje, and these helped me clarify my thoughts and my translations. Finally, I also greatly benefited from inspiring "lotsawa yak" sessions spearheaded by Marcus Perman and Gregory Forgues at Tsadra Foundation. I was able to workshop my translation with the very best translators working in this field, among whose ranks I do not fit. Elizabeth Callahan, Wulstan Fletcher, Gregory Forgues, Sara Harding, Gavin Kilty, and Heidi Nevin—thank you for all you've taught me.

Others have walked by my side over these past years as I aspired to complete this yet remained mired in the daunting responsibility and effort of doing so. They read various pieces and chapters of the manuscript along the way, offered feedback, insights, and always helpful advice. Sarah Jacoby, with her deep knowledge of Dewai Dorje, took meticulous care under a time crunch to carefully review the entire manuscript and offered important insights and suggestions to help me refine, correct, and improve it. Her help was immeasurably valuable. Sangye Khandro, a tremendous lotsawa, mentor, Dharma sister, and friend, inspired and encouraged me in myriad ways as I strove to create a beautiful translation. Tracie Keesee, with her keen attunement to Buddhism's language and meanings and her insightful questions, also offered me the great kindness and honor of reading the entire manuscript from beginning to end, helping me clarify it. Sangye Trakpa, my heart companion, listened to many oral readings of rough versions and offered encouragement, and Peter Moran brought his expert knowledge of Tibetan language to bear as well. My cherished sister Elizabeth Monson weighed in at crucial times in the process, bringing her unparalleled gift with language and Buddhist saturation to steward me wisely. Deborah Cohan, Margarita Loinaz, Carol Schlenger, and Daniel Spitzer offered time and care in reading various draft versions of manuscript selections as well. Chhoje Tulku and Yola Jurzykowski continually encouraged and supported me in numerous ways. Most especially, Emeric Yeshe Dorje, watching me flounder for some time in the magnitude of what I bit off, stepped in with laser-sharp precision, skill, and loving care. He supported me in myriad ways including sponsorship, reading, and editing, and enabled me to bring this project to completion. My gratitude to all of you is overflowing.

Eric Colombel, over a lunch in Alameda, California, in 2018, agreed to sponsor my translation of this material. His constant enthusiastic readiness to support the translation and transmission of sacred Buddhist teaching is unbounded and deserves to be celebrated in a spirit of great rejoicing. His immediate "Yes!" to my request for support led to sponsorship from Tsadra Foundation. I thank Eric and everyone at Tsadra Foundation sincerely. As well, the fabulous editing of Anna Wolcott Johnson at Shambhala Publications guided me with skill and great insight. I could not have done this without her.

Last but by no means least, my beloved family, John and Susan Monson, Donald Monson, Elizabeth Monson, Ying Hsu, Christopher Hall, Alex Monson, Eric Monson, and my dear husband Tejendra Basnet, make the strong net of family love that held me in the tumultuous period leading up to finalization of the manuscript. This book comes to completion in no small part due to their unremitting care.

These sacred teachings of Dewai Dorje inspire and sustain me as my spiritual lifeblood. I offer them into the world with the aspiration that they will contribute to a lessening of suffering and an increase in happiness for all forms of life. May the wisdom beings forgive me for whatever mistakes I have made. May this book water the seeds of awakening that permeate all beings wherever its nourishing nectar flows. Through it, may all beings achieve buddhahood by actualizing the ultimate result, the pinnacle of the path of atiyoga, the primordial ground of self-knowing awareness, Samantabhadra!

A Dakini's Counsel

1. Prayers

Sometimes the only thing to do is pray.

In the Buddhist tradition in general, to pray is to surrender to the infinite manifestative potency of interdependence: causes and conditions coming together such that anything and indeed *everything* is possible. In the Great Perfection tradition, prayer often carries a deeply devotional flavor, reflecting the special relationship between teacher and disciple at the core of its authentic transmission. Dewai Dorje's unbounded devotion, love, and joy frequently burst forth through prayers. These sublime portals into her inner world reveal ways she worked with some of the most powerful emotions of her life and experienced their fullest transformative potential. Similarly, she grounded herself in times of bottomless pain, grief, and sorrow through expressions of heartfelt longing and aspiration. Her intimacy with the vast spectrum of human feeling shines through the numerous prayers she composed throughout her biographical writing and treasure revelations.

Chapter 1 welcomes us through prayer into Dewai Dorje's sea of deep love as seen for and through the eyes and heart of her lama and consort, Drime Ozer. We are treated to a glimpse of their relationship through this first piece, "An Offering from the Vulture to the Cuckoo," a poetic letter authored by Drime Ozer himself. While all other selected translations here were penned by Dewai Dorje, this unique prayer is a rare piece of his original writing. Little of the bulk of Drime Ozer's treasure collection, unlike that of his father Dudjom Lingpa, appears to have survived the turmoil of post 1959 Tibet. However, some selections of his writing, ritual practice compositions, and profound instructions are included in Dewai Dorje's Collected Works. A notable exception is his longest known existent work, an as-yet untranslated commentary on the meaning of his father's seminal teaching *Buddhahood without Meditation*.[1] Drime Ozer's letter to Dewai Dorje takes us into their multidimensional connection as he lauds her special qualities and prays for her longevity. Half prayer, half poem, the language overflows with reverence and love for her. The second half tells the tale of a white vulture and a cuckoo to intimate the connection between Drime Ozer and Dewai Dorje with metaphoric imagery. This unique love language, drawing from the natural world, is found elsewhere in Dewai Dorje's writings. In the poem that directly follows this prayer, seemingly as a response to it, she tells the tale of a "blue lady cuckoo" who perfects Secret Mantra practice and concludes,

> These secret words about secret conduct,
> inspired by the white vulture [Drime Ozer],
> naturally occurred from whatever arose.

She also refers to Drime Ozer as a "white vulture" in his biography.[2] There she recounts a dream where Drime Ozer meets his father Dudjom Lingpa, who instructs him to unite with the magical emanation of Vajravarahi, Dakini Sukha Vajra (Dewai Dorje), to overcome negative circumstances in his life. Dudjom Linga predicts,

> *Hey, hey!*
> When the luminescence of the eastern sky
> is welcomed by the roar of the southern turquoise dragon
> [Dewai Dorje]
> and the triple-skilled white [vulture] soars in space,
> if splendor and thunder come together,
> they are sure to make harmony as one.

The words of the cryptic prophecy continue but clearly refer to him and Dewai Dorje. As further evidence of their prophesized connection beyond the confines of time and space, Drime Ozer makes mention of her connection to his past lives. Some of these specific incarnations are also identified by Dewai Dorje in Drime Ozer's biography where she lists, "At Yarlha Shampo, he was born as Pema Ledrel Tsal. At Dragdra Drogmoche, he was Longchen Dorje Ziji. At Tarpaling in Bumthang, Bhutan, he came as Pema Lingpa. At Yarlung, he was born as Urgyen Samten Lingpa." Such long-term connection stretching across lifetimes defies ordinary notions of relationship. It is a repeated theme between Dewai Dorje and Drime Ozer. The topic of Drime Ozer's past incarnations comes up again in "The Ennobling Deeds of All Buddhas and Their Heirs." There, his past lives as important treasure revealers are emphasized. The Nyingma tradition holds as a core tenet that the activities of realized beings include the revelation of treasures. Myriad in form and modality, treasures are encrypted wisdom teachings. The tradition identifies one hundred masters who are considered great treasure revealers, including five considered to be especially significant.[3] Dewai Dorje's list of Drime Ozer's past lives name at least four with the treasure revealer name Lingpa: Pema Lingpa, Urgyen Samten Lingpa, Dodrul Lingpa, and Rok Dechen Lingpa.

Notable as well in the first prayer is the way Drime Ozer refers to Dewai Dorje using different names. He begins the homage by introducing the three *kayas*, dimensions of wisdom form. These are the dharmakaya, which is connected to mind's empty essence, the sambhogakaya, which is connected to mind's lucid and blissful nature, and the nirmanakaya, which is connected to mind's compassionate capacity.[4] Dakinis, wisdom manifesting through the feminine principle, are present in each dimension. In paying homage to Vajravarahi (Dorje Phagmo), Dewai Dorje's principal tutelary deity, he is revering Dewai Dorje herself as a manifestation of mind's empty and blissful unity. Her special connection with this deity is also further reflected in references to Khacho, the buddha field connected with Vajravarahi.

Dewai Dorje was a practitioner who had mastered the yogic teachings found in the inner tantric approach of *anuyoga*. These are powerful techniques for directly actualizing the potential of the body's subtle network of energy channels, winds, and vital essences to enable realization of primordial wisdom. Relying upon both one's own and another's body, the anuyoga practitioner induces experiences of bliss to swiftly catalyze and deepen recognition of mind's nature. As restrictions to the movement of wisdom winds through the body are lifted, the practitioner's capacity to encounter the entirety of perceptual experience as teacher and teaching and as phenomena of purity is enhanced. In this context, "wind-mind" is a designation used to refer to the mobile aspect of consciousness, refined and rendered pliable through these practices.

Indeed, Drime Ozer himself was a master who had fully perfected the techniques of anuyoga as well. As such, he was a fully qualified consort for Dewai Dorje, her "heruka of great bliss," as she too was for him. *Heruka* is a Sanskrit term indicating a wrathful, "blood-drinking" deity. As a tantric couple, Drime Ozer and Dewai Dorje practiced divine union as a *yab yum* (masculine and feminine) couple, using visualization of the wrathful deities Hayagriva and Vajravarahi and other techniques. Their special relationship thus involved being destined tantric partners for each other, as well as having a mutually reciprocal guru-disciple bond. Dewai Dorje's love and devotion for Drime Ozer as her lama, consort, and treasure-revealing partner are paramount themes throughout her writing.

She celebrates his realization in "The Accomplished Secret Mantra Yogi." Likening him to the primordial Buddha Samantabhadra and the Second Buddha Padmasambhava, the great Indian adept who helped the Tibetan king Trisong Deutsen overcome obstacles to the propagation of the Buddhadharma in Tibet in the eighth century, she lauds his exalted level of realization. To see "the truth of ultimate reality," as he did, is to directly encounter the empty yet luminous nature of mind precisely as it is, within the context of the Great Perfection. This approach—which emphasizes such an encounter and the subsequent training of familiarity with it until stability is achieved—is the only way to untangle the web of dualistic thinking and its mistaken understanding of reality. It's the only place where freedom from the confines of conceptual mind is found. This is what enabled Drime Ozer to "dance" with "wisdom's illusions": to be in the world of relative appearances but not be enslaved by them. This, of course, is made possible through realizing nothing that appears *truly* exists. Rather, according to Dzogchen, phenomenal existence is none other than a manifestation of the ground from which it arises: luminous, empty awareness. For Dewai Dorje, Drime Ozer's realization of this fundamental truth made him a buddha, transcending even the limitation of necessarily appearing in a body made of flesh and blood.

"Prayer of a Crazy, Carefree Lady" uncovers more subtle qualities of his meditative presence, while "The Ennobling Deeds of All Buddhas and Their Heirs" unfolds Dewai Dorje's utter disbelief and joy at having him in her life, as well as her despair at not being with him. This prayer is dated to the Tibetan year of the Dog. This may refer to 1911, according to the Western calendar, a time of intense turmoil for Dewai Dorje as she struggled to find her way without family or support as an outsider in the communities of eastern Tibet, where she had newly arrived.

The remaining prayers in the chapter unfold other dimensions of Dewai Dorje's life in early nineteenth-century Golok. "I Supplicate Pema Totreng Tsal" laments the hypocrisies of fake treasure revealers. Dewai Dorje lived within a world of Dharma communities shaped by beliefs about the continuity of spiritual teachings from Guru Padmasambhava and his Tibetan consort Yeshe Tsogyal in eighth-century Tibet up to her own time and place in early twentieth-century eastern Tibet. These treasures were hidden in the physical world as well as in the intangible domain of the minds of those who were destined to discover them, the treasure revealers. The various mechanisms of their revelation and dissemination made sacred the landscape of Dewai Dorje's life.

Even so, against such a highly sacrosanct backdrop, deceit existed. The degeneration of pure Dharma teachings and traditions for its followers is one sign of what made that time "dark" for Dewai Dorje. While Buddhist cosmology stemming from

Indian sources labels the current age one of dissolution when all things decline, Dewai Dorje identifies in this prayer specific negative characteristics of treasure revealers proximate to her in time and space. To ensure she remains free from such bad behavior, she concludes with an aspiration for the circumstances of her authentic Great Perfection practice to prevail.

Remaining selections include a refined overview of the view, meditation, and conduct of Dzogchen according to her personal experience and practice as well as a synthesized version of some of the most important moments of her life. Much of Dewai Dorje's writing teaches through the way it reflects her own realization. Prayers blend with delicate expressions of insight and wisdom such as the final prayer to Yeshe Tsogyal. This, a supplication to Padmasambhava and Yeshe Tsogyal, presents the progressive unfolding of the visions of pure appearances induced through the Dzogchen practice of Togal. Dewai Dorje's familiarity with the visions of Togal speaks to her stable recognition of awareness, as these appearances of purity both depend upon and enhance a practitioner's authentic experience of it.

An Offering from the Vulture to the Cuckoo

Drime Ozer

Unreachable by word and thought,
the dharmakaya defies all expression.
It's beyond conceptual construct.

Manifesting as great bliss,
it's the sambhogakaya,
present in and of itself.

All the while, its compassionate capacity
appears in the form of nirmanakayas,
such as dakinis who benefit beings.

Homage to Vajravarahi, blissful emptiness!

I offer my body, possessions, and infinite virtue to you
with joyful sincerity and not a single thought of attachment.
Please accept these with your great loving compassion,
and bestow the supreme accomplishment,
the blissful emptiness of primordial wisdom.

Over many lifetimes, you've held authority
over repositories of infinite profound treasures
and released the seals of their vajra messages,
hidden by awareness holders in times past.
Noble White Tara—I'm thinking about you.[5]

Your body is that of a great bliss consort from the Lotus
    family,
and your speech is the voice of the dharmakaya,
the innate nature that can never be articulated.
Your mind is awakened.
It is naturally occurring primordial wisdom.
You're a lady who leads everyone
to the dakinis' buddha field of Khacho.

You are glorious: a precious jewel with inexhaustible noble
    qualities,
but you accept that others consider you to be inferior.
Foremost you are, of dakinis on, above, and below the earth,
but still you thought it best to say
that you don't know when your illusory body will pass away
due to the force of sudden, unexpected causes.

Directly, you converse with Vajravarahi, Noble White Tara,
Yeshe Tsogyal, Mandarava, and hosts of dakinis abiding in
    space,
and they offer you prophecies and empowerments.

Without having had to rely upon progressive training and
    purification,
you experience phenomenal existence
arising as a treasury of signs and instructions
in the spaces left after you released
the knots constricting your central channel.[6]

In particular, through the key points
of the hidden, secret practices of union and liberation,
you've recognized awareness, your true nature,
the primordially secret fundamental nature of reality.
You now establish those connected to you

through karma and pure aspirations
on the paths to maturity and liberation.

Reflecting on all your noble qualities deepens my faith.

Seemingly I'm lost, an ordinary person
controlled by the five poisons.[7]
But the manifestative potency of your great bliss wisdom
automatically connects my body, speech, and mind to their vajra
    essences
and introduces me to undistracted luminosity,
my true dharmakaya nature.
Extraordinary is your great kindness,
Noble Lady, my Wish-Fulfilling Jewel.

The ultimate expanse
is definitely devoid of characteristics to fixate upon.
Yet, from the perspective of disciples who are training,
teacher and retinue seemingly appear.

The fundamental nature of reality
is but a single indivisible sphere.
Yet, those with impure perception
see it as distinct from confusion.

In essence, awareness transcends fears
about birth and death,
but for those who cleave to permanence,
dying and becoming seemingly appear.

Most certainly you have mastery
over the phenomena of samsara and nirvana,
yet you continuously practice
the two stages of development and completion.[8]

Originally, you are truly and completely enlightened,
but you act in ways that exactly accord
with what your disciples can understand.

Great yogini Dewai Dorje, sole hope for all of your followers—
pray, care for us without ever lessening your compassion
and be seated evermore upon the throne of vajra immutability.

Dakini prophecies, delivered through the talk of feathered friends,
have said a few things that cause me to doubt everything.
You, the youthful light of my life, have become weak.
Based on the relative way things look from the outside,
it seems you will depart for the ultimate buddha field of Khacho,
and you've intimated as much through your letters.

Sole Mother, I've a few requests for you.

As the consort who has always induced blissful emptiness
for Pema Ledrel, Dorje Ziji Tsal, Pema Lingpa, Orgyen Tenyi Ling,
Samten Ling, Drodul Ling, and others,
throughout many lifetimes in human and nonhuman forms,
now, when the dangers of illness, old age, and death are at hand,
you must be victorious over the demon of the Lord of Death.

Effortlessly bestowing the wisdom blessings of the inner meaning,
Chief Dakini Lady Tara—
just like bodhisattvas Manjushri and Avalokiteshvara,
who never feel overwhelmed by others' delusion—
for as long you remain in existence, may your enlightened
    aspirations,
and your body of form, be stable as the sun.

Otherwise, if you don't listen to this written appeal,
I, as your spiritual hero, am ready to go together indivisibly with
    you

to the isle of Khacho, for you are my only hope now and in the
future.
How could it be otherwise?

Dakinis on earth, below, and in the sky—
don't lessen your compassion!
Increase the enlightened activity and longevity
of this coemergent, powerful lady,
and with your splendor, subdue attacks from hidden and
malicious spirits
that she may reign victorious over such forces of negativity.

Through the blessed potency of the profound interdependence of
method and wisdom,
may we rely upon each other to open the doors of our profound
treasures.
May limitless rays of our compassion benefit others,
lead everyone we encounter to the buddha fields of awareness
holders,
excellently spread the light of goodness throughout the universe
and to all within,
and cause everything that serves Buddha's teachings and living
beings to flourish.

From now until I reach the heart of awakening,
may I never be separated from you, Dechen Dewai Dorje!
May I revel in your glory through the connate four joys
and fully inhale the fresh breath of your ambrosial wisdom
speech.

May we all benefit ourselves and others in thought and deed
and have no doubts about the path of secret conduct.
May we see everything you do as the activity of a buddha.
Having invoked the blessings of your enlightened mind with
faith and devotion,

may we all become accomplished together
within one, indivisible, exalted state of wisdom.

Appearance as the aspect of supreme method
is the heruka of great bliss,
and emptiness as the aspect of wisdom
is the consort Vajravarahi.

May we perfect their unity
through the conduct of union and liberation
and awaken within the luminous aggregates
of Buddha Vajrasattva,
endowed with the seven branches of union.[9]

With these wholly pure intentions,
I offer an unceasing and infinite amassing of goodness
through the profound practices of development and completion
for your long life, Sublime Lady, Mother of All Buddhas.

May you rest forever upon the throne of vajra immutability,
manifesting as Buddha Amitayus,
and may your wishes all be effortlessly accomplished!

E, E!
An immaculate crystal vase
is the best container for wisdom ambrosia.
Wiped clean of cognitive and emotional dust,
it pours a stream of nectar,
conferring the four empowerments
from the mother's hands.

Once a wish-fulfilling jewel
is mounted upon a victory banner,
it radiates luminescence
as inexhaustible Dharma treasures.

Lighting up the smiling face
of the golden bird from India,
a hidden cuckoo in Lhasa
takes flight, singing sweetly,
and, as though dancing on her legs,
alights upon the meadows of Tsari.[10]

When counsel reveals the unpleasant—
the praise and blame of irrelevant talk—
and warns of ripening karma,
the cuckoo longs to go elsewhere.

But when she dances her little dance
and sings her little song,
the cliff-dwelling king of birds,
the white vulture
cleansed of former habitual patterning
and endowed with all-knowing eyes of wisdom,
arrives before her, his blue lady cuckoo.

He carries a garland of golden letters,
wrapped in divine clothing,
adorned with excellent prayers,
and mounted on his ten-fingered horse.

When he flies with his twofold stride,
the blue lady cuckoo realizes the power
of their auspicious connection and says,

> Blissful, blissful, the dakinis' magical city
> is none other than my own perception,
> and I, a blue lady cuckoo,
> have mastered wind-mind.
> Though I still want to go to that sacred place,
> the white vulture's request

gives me hope for more meaningful things.

Then within the palace of the unchanging emblem,
the avian couple rich with gold
enjoyed the glory of great exaltation
and ate the sweet food of the two stages.
Smaller birds gathered, and they protected them,
staying together and leading everyone to pure buddha fields.

How amazing!

Later the vulture, who had interrupted his flight,
returned to the high rocky cliffs.
He visualized the pure realm of his destined Buddha family
and perfected the accumulations of merit and wisdom
through *ganachakra*, feast offerings.

To fulfill and delight his blue-colored lady with some gifts,
he'll come from time to time
though his magical skills
and offer many things.

In the ultimate expanse, all is but one taste,
yet in the unstoppable rain of relative appearances,
now we are together,
and some wishes have been fulfilled.

How wonderful!

The King of Birds, the Vulture [Ledrel Tsal, Drime Ozer] offered these
words to the Cuckoo [Dewai Dorje].

The Accomplished Secret Mantra Yogi

How amazing!
The accomplished Secret Mantra yogi
no longer appearing in corporeal form
is united with the sky in a body of light.
Unblemished by desire,
his immaculate body of primordial wisdom
subsumes the three realms of samsara
within uncontaminated space.

Blissful Source of Great Exaltation,
Supreme Hero,
you're unchanging Samantabhadra,
aren't you?

You've seen the truth of ultimate reality
and are freed from the limits of conceptuality.
In this life you've dispensed with all worldly doings
and, through your father, extracted the secret quintessence
of the direct oral instructions.
You now tame the misguided with power and strength.
You're captain of Padmasambhava's enlightened activity,
aren't you?

You're empowered with the essence
of Padmasambhava's enlightened mind
and discovered the highest insight.
Dancer of Wisdom's Illusions,
Guide of Beings,
you're a regent of all buddhas

gone before, present now, and still to come,
aren't you?

The comportment of your wisdom body
aligns with the deeds of a buddha.
The roar of your wisdom speech
ignites the lamp of Secret Mantra.
The realization of your wisdom mind
protects everyone as your own children.
You're a wellspring of accomplishment for all,
aren't you?

That someone like you,
flawless and perfect with all sublime qualities,
was found by a lady like me
is absolutely incredible!

From this life throughout all future lifetimes,
may I never be apart from you, Wish-Fulfilling Jewel.
May I dance as a consort who delights you,
so that we completely fulfill
the noble intentions of Padmasambhava and consort.

I request your prayers
for us to benefit ourselves and others automatically
through actualizing the wisdom deities
Hayagriva and Varahi,
such that we'll forever be inseparably united!

Kunzang Dekyong Wangmo [Dewai Dorje] faithfully offered these words
along with prostrations to the Greatly Accomplished Awareness Holder
and Precious Treasure Revealer [Drime Ozer].

Prayer of a Crazy, Carefree Lady

Wish-Fulfilling Jewel, you are a great open and expansive sky,
where all the things of samsara and nirvana
arise as ornaments of space.
Beyond the mind of conceptual ideas and analysis,
your exalted state of wisdom is like the sky.
It's a tethering pole of undistracted presence that's incredible.

All-encompassing, the circumference of the sky
is beyond transition or change.
Your realization of the exalted state
of immutable ultimate reality beyond conceptual construct
is unrestricted, impartial, and genuine.
This, the tethering pole of your undistracted presence, is incredible.

You understand the manifest display
of all phenomena to be illusory.
So, whatever appears for you is the ornamentation of primordial
    wisdom,
and you are free from accepting or avoiding anything.
The focus of your undistracted presence is incredible.

As an inward luminosity, awareness replete with kayas and
    wisdom,
your exalted state never wavers from the ultimate expanse,
but for us, your fortunate followers,
profound Dharma teachings flow out
from the secret treasury of your vast wisdom mind,
an arising of phenomenal existence manifesting in signs and
    scripture.
The focus of your undistracted mindfulness is incredible.

You've actualized primordial purity,
the transcendent state beyond conceptual construct.
This naturally occurring luminosity
is unceasing as your innate nature.
Beyond effort and attachment, your awakened mind
has arrived at the ultimate dharmakaya
beyond the confines of the intellect.

Dharmakaya Hero, supreme in every way,
I prostrate to you, my mind in a state
of utterly pure, great recollection.
For me and those like me, mistaken in dualistic approaches,
to be liberated from the dark gloom of ignorance,
please, dispel the darkness of our minds
with the light of your compassion.
Hold us kindly that we recognize thoughts and perception
as ultimate reality.

May I, one with negative karma, be protected by your love
and not fall to samsara's unfortunate states,
but diligently practice the wholly pure Dharma
throughout my entire life.

May there be no obstacles in fulfilling my wishes,
and may I never part from your side,
Glorious Guide and Lama,
and practice the Dharma!

This was offered by a crazy and carefree lady [Dewai Dorje] who just eats,
sleeps, and defecates.

May virtue prevail!

The Ennobling Deeds of All Buddhas and Their Heirs

Ennobling, the deeds of all buddhas and their heirs
gone before, present now, and still to come
are marvelous and unfathomable.
Glorious Vajra-Wielding Lama—
you embody them all.

Heroic Heruka, sublime in every way,
you received your inheritance from Padmasambhava,
mastered the heart-essence teachings,
and now shine the beacon of Dharma
for those who wander in confusion.

You perfected wisdom deeds to train all as needed,
and revealed Dharma treasures of the profound secret treasury.
Now, through your deep realization of the essence of unsurpassed
    mantra,
you protect the fortunate and set them on the paths that ripen
    and liberate.

You're the supreme embodiment of the five Lingpas
and the one hundred great treasure revealers.
Unrivaled is your kindness,
and faithfully, at your lotus feet,
I bow down
and offer you my body, speech, and mind.

Bless me to never part from you,
both in this life and the next.

The beautiful mandala of your wisdom body
is perfect with all the major and minor marks of a buddha.
It's an utterly delightful form I never tire of seeing.

The mandala of your face smiles wrathfully,
and appearances of confused dualistic perception
are liberated into primordial wisdom.

The penetrating gaze of your eyes
outshines evil forces with splendor
and banishes ignorance and deluded fixation
into the empty awareness of the dharmakaya.

Your free-flowing locks wrap around your crown,
and you hold the quintessential life force
of the three-kaya wisdom dakinis.

The light of your wisdom body fills the buddhas' pure realms,
and lifts the dense gloom of beings' befuddlement.

You've found a powerful wisdom body
ornamented with perfect qualities,
and the roar of your wisdom speech
resounds the teachings of Secret Mantra.

You have the discriminating intelligence
to understand everything exactly as it is.
You unimpededly comprehend how the paths and levels
are traversed by beings according to their individual natures and
    capacities,
as well as the many divisions of totally pure teachings
for both worldly and spiritual approaches.

Master of Speech, Great Being of Love and Knowledge,
All-Knowing Sovereign of Triple Time, and Vajra Holder,

you never waver from the actualization of the three kayas
and are completely beyond conceptual construct.

With your sublime insight,
great primordial wisdom with twofold omniscience,[11]
you don't need to renounce the afflictions.
For you, they're naturally freed within ultimate reality.
The innate and unchanging space of the ultimate expanse,
where confusion and liberation are nondual,
is your primordially liberated dharmakaya wisdom mind.

Simply hearing your name
allows me to sever dualistic fixation.
Witnessing your renunciation with samsara
and perfectly pure Dharma conduct,
I purified my ignorance and twofold obscurations into space[12]
and actualized my true nature, the wisdom of great bliss.

You mastered wind-mind through the practice of union,
directly perceived ultimate reality,
and realized the youthful vase kaya[13]
of a great transference wisdom body.
You're the supreme key that unlocks the essential profound meaning,
an eternal spring of accomplishment
for longevity, merit, glory, wealth, disciples, and vast activities.

I never found someone like you before,
and now that I must separate from what I see,
I'd rather lose my heart, my eyes, and even my life
than leave you.

But my merit is less, and I'm controlled by another.
So, when it's time for me to leave, please, don't stop loving me.
Hold me continually with your compassion, I pray.
I have no other hope or protection than you.

When I, a person with such bad karma,
go elsewhere, I lose all strength of heart.
Dumbstruck and aimless,
I have trouble distinguishing day from night.

Thinking of your compassion and noble qualities,
the one who has been kindest to me,
I'm weeping, moaning, and praying to you intensely.
I have no other protector.
Wherever you, my sole refuge, go,
my mind separates from my body
and goes with you.

Nri is the life-support that gathers longevity, merit, glory, and
    wealth.
The element of mind, the unborn, self-emergent syllable *ah*,
is liberated indivisibly as Dhatvishvari.[14]
It is self-arisen and spontaneously present as Buddha Dakini,
gliding in the singular expanse of dharmadhatu wisdom.

The element of flesh is indivisibly liberated as Buddhalochana.
It is self-arisen and spontaneously present as Vajra Dakini,
gliding in the singular expanse of mirrorlike wisdom.

The element of blood is indivisibly liberated as Mamaki.
It is self-arisen and spontaneously present as Ratna Dakini,
gliding in the singular expanse of evenness wisdom.

The element of heat is indivisibly liberated as Gokarmo.
It is self-arisen and spontaneously present as Pema Dakini,
gliding in the singular expanse of all-discerning wisdom.

The element of breath is indivisibly liberated as Samayatara.
It is self-arisen and spontaneously present as Karma Dakini,
gliding in the singular expanse of all-accomplishing wisdom.

The perfectly pure five afflictions
are liberated, indivisibly, as the five kayas.
Present in and of themselves
in the expanse of the immutable
exalted state of wisdom,
they are a single taste of nonduality,
moving inseparably with method.
Appearance and emptiness are a unity,
liberated within the dharmakaya.

When primordial wisdom mingles indivisibly
with the deathless vajra kaya
and moves in the expanse of method,
the aspect of appearance,
illusory bodies disappear,
dissolving within luminosity.

May I remain no more in samsara,
with its good and bad relations,
and become freed in a pure buddha field
present beyond causes and conditions!

Oh dear! Oh my!
Dakinis of earth, sky, and in-between,
if you have powerful compassion and blessings,
help me by constantly manifesting your formidable troops.
May all adverse outer, inner, and secret obstacles
be averted and severed from the root by your fierce wisdom
    activity!

Swiftly reunite method and wisdom inseparably,
increase their wisdom activities like the sky,
and fill existence, the noble state of peace,
and the three worlds with their fame!

May this come to be.
By the power of dakinis of the three places
may my wishes be spontaneously fulfilled
and all accomplishment granted!

[In the Dog year, on the thirteenth day of the third lunar month, when circumstances stirred up sickness, a lowly woman [Dewai Dorje] in a state of intense sorrow said some nonsense based on whatever came to mind in her state of threefold perception.

May virtue prevail!

I Supplicate Pema Totreng Tsal

Pema Totreng Tsal, who embodies all triumphant buddhas,
Mistress of Space, Dakini Yeshe Tsogyalma,
Kyuchung Lotsawa, Namkhai Nyingpo,
and other root lineage lamas—I supplicate you!

When I think about the display of the natural defects of these
    dark times,
sadness grows in me from deep within.
The earth is full of fake treasure revealers
who lack the singular instructions that combine the key points of
    all nine vehicles[15]
but nevertheless improperly present and extensively spread
    profound teachings.

In the name of giving wise predictions to others,
they fool themselves.
In the name of benefiting beings,
they poison themselves.
Without concern for purity or filth,
their conduct resembles that of dogs and pigs.[16]
Their faith is low, and their minds are tough like horns.
They have no ethical discipline,
and their behavior is twisted by the five poisons.

Criticizing sublime beings of the past,
they claim to be accomplished
but amass all kinds of negativity.
Inappropriately dressed,
they carelessly do whatever they want.
Though they haven't benefited themselves at all,

they manipulate others in the name of helping them.

They haven't diligently accomplished practice for even one month
but run after wealth throughout different regions,
villages, monasteries, and towns everywhere.
Day and night, nonstop, they wander around these
    environments—
how pathetic it is to sell the life essence of Padmasambhava.

I'm not embodied like these treasure revealers!

Throughout all my lifetimes,
may I continue to be protected by the awareness-holding father
    and son,
enjoy the glorious ripening and liberating instructions,
and without needing to progressively traverse
through the key teachings of the nine vehicles,
finally actualize the supreme vehicle, the Great Perfection,
and fully ripen the luminous result of this great approach!

Feeling revulsion at the behavior of those of us named as treasure revealers
in these abysmal times, the one called Sukha [Dewai Dorje] wrote this
aspiration.

May virtue prevail!

A Mother's Prayer for Her Son

Listen up now, heart son!

Like the sky, the view contains nothing upon which to focus.
Don't taint it with intellectual fabrication, dear son.
Rest in its great openness,
completely beyond ordinary mind.

Meditation must be free from attachment
to the natural clarity of mind.
Don't constrict it by reifying subject and object,
but sustain mind within its innate and natural condition.

Conduct is the great self-liberation of whatever arises.
Don't fabricate it by tainting it with hope and fear,
but rest in the expanse that has never known attachment.

Son—don't sully self-occurring awareness,
pure from the beginning,
with the contrivances of restrictive mindfulness.
You don't need development-stage practice
that reifies your own body as the mandala of the wisdom deities.

Son, you won't need to welcome
the ultimate self-arisen Akanishta pure realm
through the practice of transference.

Unimpeded, awareness is inexpressible.
It appears as spontaneously present wisdom,
an unceasing empty lucidity that pervades everything.

Since they have never been produced,
never cease, and don't abide anywhere,
this life and future lifetimes don't truly exist my son!

Within the indivisibility of the relative and ultimate,
the nature of reality dawns as the ornament of awareness,
and the false cave of hope and fear is collapsed.
Son—seize this advice to enjoy illness
and be happy upon death!

Written in the manner of a prayer from a mother [Dewai Dorje] for her son.

A Dog Called a Lion

Listen, sublime hero, most beloved of my heart.
Though I'm a woman deserving compassion,
without a hair's tip worth of positive qualities
of body, speech, or mind,
through the clarity of your enlightened heart's pure perception,
you call me, a dog, a lion.
If others hear this, I will be the basis of ridicule
and feel embarrassed!

Nevertheless, due to our pure prayers and karmic connection
    from past lives,
I met you, an excellent companion aligned with me for life,
and through the intensity of becoming your consort on the path
    of union,
I was able to embrace threefold progress and stability
and thereby completely release the knots of my five chakras[17]
and actualize realization of primordial wisdom's inner meaning.

May method and wisdom become accomplished indivisibly
as the wisdom bodies of awareness
and be together always and inseparably throughout all our lifetimes!

I'm just having fun, my heartmate!
Let me tell you a little bit about this lady's situation.

From my youth, I had great interest in the Dharma,
and at age five, gave rise to the intention to practice.

From the age of seven onward, the dakinis took care of me,
and I received both common and extraordinary teachings.

When I was twelve, I entered the door of mantra
and trained fully in the three aspects of emptiness.[18]
Gradually, I received the pith teachings on the four chakras.[19]

When I was thirteen, I received instructions on the five chakras
based on the unsurpassed inner tantras in a one-to-one
    transmission,
and after my channels, winds, and vital essences matured a little
    bit,
I discovered some of the prophetic inventory for my first
    treasures.

In my dreams and delusionary visions,
the dakinis took me under their care,
and from their many predictions about what was happening
and what was yet to come,
I wandered without any direction
to this place when I was fifteen.

At sixteen, I encountered my destined teachings,
and at nineteen, per the lama's command,
I traversed the lands of Golok,
a place aligned in name and meaning.[20]

Through the convergence of previous karma and temporary
    circumstances,
I became involved in samsara for a long time.
Every now and then I would find treasures and treasure
    companions,
but because of other circumstances and my humility,
these were obscured by obstacles.

From age twenty-nine onward, I did discover my own treasures,
and with the fortune of good companions
and my wish to preserve the Dharma,

I benefited the teachings and beings for a little while.

When I was thirty-three, tragedy occurred.
Alone without my guide and protector,
I wandered and drifted aimlessly
like a lion crisscrossing the plains,
joy, sorrow, and weariness
flowing as an undulating stream.

Nevertheless, the compassion of Padmasambhava and consort,
and the blessings of the sources of refuge
and the great treasure-revealing father and son,
made it possible for me to slightly benefit the teachings of the
    Buddha and beings.

However, lacking my partner, I experienced acute pain and
    illness.
These circumstances caused me to wonder if, in my forty-fifth
    year
my illusory body, just on loan as a gathering place, would
    collapse.
Yet, our past connection and aspirations were such
that I came to you in my forty-fourth year.

Since I'm humble and very much doubted by everyone,
I was nearly overpowered by circumstances that weren't truly real.
Yet, the hundredfold light of your enlightened heart's clear wisdom
enabled me to fulfill my wishes by the strength of its compassion.
Supreme clouds of empty bliss from our immaculate union
brought forth the potency of *gendhe*[21]
by the vital essence of the young moon.
Channels and winds restored,
my body was freed from all illness.
The noble qualities of your kindness are tremendous, my heart
    friend.

I'm not a lady who is intoxicated by the flavor of lust.
Rather, through the skillful methods and timeliness
of an exceptionally qualified consort who has entered the path of
    Secret Mantra,
outer, inner, and other are the display of the five chakras;
purification, maturation, and perfection are the space of the five
    wisdoms;[22]
and supreme joy, extraordinary joy, coemergent joy, and freedom
    from joy
are great primordial wisdom.
Actualizing space and awareness as the youthful vase kaya
without discarding our illusory bodies is the supreme path of
    luminosity,
the swift path of traversal in a single lifetime—how amazing it is!

I've come close to this
through my aspiration to practice in this way.
Since it all comes down to the key points
of interdependent timing and method,
I request your prayers and intention for it to unfold as it should!

The secret words of what I have said above—
once I saw how you call a fox and wolf a lion—
were written without proper order
by the one named Dewai, who is neither nun nor wife
but is a crazy, bad, and carefree mantra practitioner.

She, Kunzang Chonyi Wangmo [Dewai Dorje],
peeled these bad words from the coffers
of the radiant clarity of her infinite mind,
and riding the windhorse of her fingertips,
put them into writing.

May virtue prevail!

CLOUDBANKS OF BLESSINGS

A Prayer to Yeshe Tsogyal from the Secret Treasury of the Reality Dakini

How wondrous!
From the purely appearing buddha field of ultimate reality
comes the increase of experience, Padmasambhava,
and awareness reaching its full extent, Yeshe Tsogyal,
to whom I pray from the innate state beyond ordinary mind.
May we actualize realization of ultimate reality, primordial
freedom,
and become liberated within the youthful vase kaya in rainbow
bodies!

2. POEMS

All of Dewai Dorje's writing is imbued with a poetic quality. The bulk of her shaldam are presented in metered verse, and her prose is rich in imagery and metaphor. She was masterful in drawing on the natural world, with its abundant flora and fauna, to infuse the stories of her own life. She was in relationship with her environment in ways that defy conventional understanding of the limits of human communication. Her phenomena—animate, inanimate, human, animal, and spiritual—were alive with ongoing information, messages, and teachings unique to her sense-making capability. To listen to her poetry is to listen to the birds of Golok's vast green plains, to the endless and timeless blue of its skies, and to the tender and playful heart of a woman whose life was about finding home in a never-ending drama of discovery, loss, and the unknown.

"Advice for Sherap Lhamo" and "Metaphors, Not Words" showcase how Dewai Dorje relied on the natural world as metaphor. Both pieces feature the presence of the cuckoo, a metaphor for Dewai Dorje herself, in relationship with other birds, her students, as a guide and teacher. Each composition includes cryptic references to prophecy in twilight language decipherable only to those destined to understand it. And both offer visual images of the landscapes—green in summertime, vast and open, punctuated by rocky mountains and cliffs, and endless against the horizon— across which she traveled, continually meeting and parting from those closest to her. There, against dazzling blue sky and white clouds, she made meaning out of impermanence and applied the timeless truths of the Great Perfection to her own life.

At the tender age of eleven, Dewai Dorje lost her own mother. She describes this time in her long autobiography,

After [mother's passing], my father cared for me, his own precious child, but missing my mother was utterly unbearable. Unaware of day or night, I thought only of how I could meet her again. I climbed up on the roof, my face searching the sky, and while sitting in tears, from the southwest a white vulture circled with a *whirr* and hovered directly in front of me. I thought, this vulture must be the life force of the dakinis—maybe it knows where my mother has gone. So, I said,

> From the womb of space in the vast sky above,
> you, the life-force bird of the dakinis' utterly pure
> activity,
> please, hear me with your mind at ease.
> Where are you going, and from where have you
> come?
> I'm a motherless orphan.
> It has been one month since my mother departed
> to who knows where,
> and my grief is excruciating.

> You, skillful, white vulture—
> have you seen where my mother went?
> Do you know where she is now?
> I'm a girl without her kind mother,
> lost like a blind person on the plains,
> a wingless bird fallen into a deep crevasse.
> Now as I remember everything,
> I miss my mother so much.

> A beautiful body and senses are her kindness.
> Jewelry and provisions are her kindness.
> Wealth, food, and possessions are her kindness.
> Sound words of advice are her kindness.
> Getting along with everyone is her kindness.
> Knowing the six Dharma words is her kindness.[1]

Meeting sublime lamas is her kindness.
Please, help me meet my supremely kind mother
once again in this life!
Keep this request in your heart,
white life-force bird!

Several selections in chapter 2 explore the theme of the mother. Later in her life, as she devoted herself to the core Buddhist teaching of inseparability after losing her guru and consort Drime Ozer, Dewai Dorje further assuaged her grief at the loss of her mother through connecting with the principles of the ultimate mother through the teachings of the Dharma. Three poetic explorations of this endeavor, "Sky-Mother Samantabhadri," "Remembering Mother," and "Mother of View, Meditation, and Conduct," unfold the theme of motherhood as Dewai Dorje experienced it, both as a daughter and a mother in her own right.

Dewai Dorje had three children, two of whom lived past childbirth. Her daughter Yangchen Dronma was born in 1913 and lived up to adulthood, eventually starting a family of her own with Drime Ozer's son Sonam Deutsen. Dewai Dorje's son Rigdzin Gyurme Dorje passed away in 1924 at age five, during an epidemic that swept the area of Dartsang where he was living with his mother and Drime Ozer. Drime Ozer himself passed away a few days later. These experiences of intense grief that peppered Dewai Dorje's life propelled her spiritual practice. They forced her to find solace through realization of the "ultimate mother," the vast space out of which all the things of the world manifest and into which they finally dissolve. The Buddhist teachings call this great open expanse by many names including the unborn, the great mother, the Perfection of Wisdom, Buddha Samantabhadri, and more. It's often represented metaphorically by the sky.

Mothers and motherhood deeply resonated with Dewai Dorje. As a mother herself, she frequently referred to her closest disciples as her children. She lived her life in dedication to the great mother, the feminine principle that symbolizes the source of all that appears to exist: the empty nature of all phenomena. This empty nature is the reason Dewai Dorje "doesn't believe in samsara." In other words, she didn't believe that the phenomena of samsara are things that ultimately can be established to *truly* exist. Her path was one of severing attachment to everything and most especially to the reification of all thought and sensory perceptions.

In Dzogchen, the empty, unborn nature of phenomena is presented hand in hand with their luminous aspect. Emptiness and luminosity are considered nondual. For the Dzogchen practitioner, this nonduality is what is recognized to be the mind's true nature. Beyond form and all characteristics, the mind nevertheless *knows*. Its empty aspect and its lucidity or clarity are experienced as its essence and nature, which have an inherent capacity that is widespread and compassionate. These three aspects of mind—empty, lucid, and capable—are designated by the dharmakaya, sambhogakaya, and nirmanakaya, respectively, in the Dzogchen teachings of Trekcho that directly introduce awareness, mind's nature, to practitioners. This is frequently referred to as the great "three-kaya nature" in Dewai Dorje's writings.

Trekcho and Togal comprise the twofold approach of the path of Dzogchen. This path is regarded as the most sublime and exalted of all Buddhist approaches according to the Nyingma tradition and is thus taught to be the "pinnacle of all vehicles." It is the approach of atiyoga, whereby practitioners are equipped to take wisdom and not ordinary mind as their personal practice experience, at last. Doing so requires an authentic recognition of wisdom, ascertained through properly differentiating awareness (*rig pa*), mind's nature, from ordinary or conceptual mind. Recognizing awareness through being introduced to it by qualified lineage masters, endowed with the blessings of their own accomplishment, is essential. Such discernment and subsequent establishment of confidence in awareness is the main practice on the path of Trekcho. This approach is posited for practitioners more inclined to be lazy.

The companion path to Trekcho is Togal, posited for practitioners more inclined toward industriousness. Togal practice is both predicated on and enhances the Dzogchen practitioner's recognition of awareness. Through special techniques, the practitioner harnesses the pathways whereby wisdom moves to directly perceive its external manifestations, while knowing these are but reflections of what has been recognized internally. This process unfolds four "visions" of pure phenomena that increase before becoming extinguished back into the expanse of ultimate reality from which they arise. Enlightenment for a Dzogchen practitioner consists of culminating either or both Trekcho or Togal practice to experience their results, which include actualization of the "youthful vase kaya," the deathless domain of primordial wisdom abiding within.

Dewai Dorje's poems, letters, advice, and personal practice instructions are infused with profound insight about Dzogchen practice, evidencing her deep experience on this sublime path. It is paramount of what she practiced and taught. Despite tremendous struggles of basic survival and periods of destitution such that she literally begged, and thus frequently refers to herself as a beggar lady, she was rich with the teachings and inner experience of Dzogchen. And she knew, undoubtedly, that such came about not just through receiving these teachings but through her unwavering faith and devotion to her lama, Drime Ozer. After all, at the core, Dzogchen depends on devotion and receiving its instructions from an authentic lineage master. Her joy in this wealth seeps through her poetry and prose equally with reverence, lightness, and profound sublimity that infuse them with blessings.

Chapter 2 concludes with several examples of a beloved poetic form, the alphabetic acrostic, well known and used by many Tibetan writers. Beginning each line with the letters of the Tibetan alphabet, this form requires both creativity and discipline. Dewai Dorje's playfulness, elegance, and language proficiency are on full display as she uses the alphabet to give advice while having fun with words at the same time. "A Poem for Changchup Dron" lets us imagine a sunny afternoon in an open-sided tent with Dewai Dorje and a few close disciples. She is laughing in easy comfort as she pens, on beautiful handmade paper, pithy advice on living a life according to the Dharma using the alphabet. May the translation of these compositions bring smiles to all contemporary readers as well!

Advice for Sherap Lhamo

Listen up!

On the lonesome plains of green,
linked with prayers from times gone by,
male and female golden geese
and me, a Lhasa cuckoo, bide.

Profound connections, some we have,
and in the cliff abodes,
the white vulture's daring flight
is sharper than a razor blade.

Cuckoo's power being small,
she has no way to bear it all,
and time to time to other lands,
the pain of icy winds does call,
and go she must,
no way to stay.

Mind as pure as silken scarves,
stainless white with thoughts of good,
hold within yourself and then
stay firmly in the mountain wilds,
and don't be swayed by evil friends.
Engage with body, speech, and mind
nothing but the Dharma path.

Cuckoo's vital essence drops,
deep profound instructions—
these are the key points to apply.

When the mighty eastern sun
blunts the sharpest of all blades,
geese and swans the cuckoo helps,
though much wearied by her flight.

Thinking of you, dearest ones,
she'll come but when
we shall not know.
Until that time, for one and all,
you must act just as is right.

When joy departs from these green plains,
the cuckoo has no way to stay.
Oh dear, oh my, how sad 'twill be,
but meet we shall before too long!

A clever vulture of the same type, Sherlha,
encouraged me, an old lady of a bad type,
and I jokingly wrote something.

In the year of the Earth Rabbit (c. 1939), while straying from home,
Dewai Dorje gave some advice to her student Sherap Lhamo.

Metaphors, Not Words

Gathered by previous connections,
students as dear as my heart—listen up.

A blue cuckoo from the east
stirred by karmic destiny,
was led to southern darkness,
propelled by earlier prayers.

With the courage of tigers and lions,
she clears the darkness of these lands.

When the jewel-source for all desires,
sole ornament of the world entire,
dispels all darkness with its light,
garudas, dragons, eagles, and geese
will enjoy their share of wealth,
and hundredfold light for all will shine forth.

Once the green plains show their beautiful faces,
and the sweet roar of the turquoise dragon resounds,
the cuckoo may think about going home.

Yet, celestial sun and moon in the west
make her postpone, time and time again.
When she hasn't any way to do what she must,
and tips of golden horns are seen,
the reasons to go from south to east will be sure.

Until then, as nothing is at all certain,
high above in rocky cliff abodes

flocks of white and brown vultures—
just as earlier promised,
practice each your share of instructions.

When three strengths of body are complete,
soaring in space isn't tiring!

Everything here is metaphor, not literal words.
Wandering lands unknown,
mother cuckoo and her children,
for their flock of dearest birds,
give advice on the true meaning
with the writing of illusion.
How things are throughout all times,
I've offered respectfully, keeping nothing secret.
Those who can analyze this should,
and then the cuckoo's melodious song
will show the way to the springtime sun.
But even if this is investigated,
I don't know what can be understood.

For experts with analytical insight,
this advice has both expedient and definitive truth.
All that has happened, is happening, and will come to be
I've said,
without hiding anything.

Ha, ha!
It's a silly song of crazy advice from an old lady [Dewai Dorje].
Ho, ho!
I wrote down whatever came to mind.
Hey, hey!
I offer it respectfully to my students.

May virtue prevail!

On Severance

How marvelous! Listen up, yogis.
If you wish to sever from the root the one single thing,
the charnel ground of both samsara and nirvana,
it comes right down to your very own mind.

When mind's true nature of nonduality,
wisdom primordial, is known as it is,
beyond severance and all things to sever,
you will be.
Rest there, in that unimpeded state,
on the far side of ordinary mind.

If, in case, you want to sever something,
then sever the mara of pride,
the afflictions of confusion,
into great primordial wisdom beyond all thought.

I sever the mara of the aggregates,
confused perceptions, and the illusory body,
into the state beyond selfishness and attachment.

I sever the godly mara that deceives through total distraction
into the state of the naturally liberated six consciousnesses.[2]
I sever the male demon, the havoc-wreaking Lord of Death
into the unborn, unceasing, and unchanging state of
    transcendence.

Like this, self-knowing awareness is the supreme pith instruction
with which to liberate the four maras into space.[3]

Sustain this original and unchanging state,
and through it, sever the totality of samsara and nirvana!

Something to sever apart from that
doesn't exist in the tradition of a lady like me.
Mine is the tradition of uncontrived, ultimate severance!

When I was oppressed by the sleep of ignorance,
these unnecessary words suddenly arose.
I offer them to fulfill my sacred bond with all.
They are the confused talk of one named Dewai.

I Don't Believe in Samsara

Oh my!
I don't believe in samara.
If I did,
what "nirvana" could there be?

I don't believe in mind itself.
If I did,
what "awareness" could there be?

I don't believe in a view.
If I did,
what primordial emptiness
beyond all conceptual construct could there be?

I don't believe in meditation.
If I did,
what ongoing flow of my innate nature could there be?

I don't believe in conduct.
If I did,
what effortlessness could there be?

I don't believe in the appearances of the ground.
If I did,
what primordially pure original ground could there be?

I don't believe in the appearances of the path.
If I did,
what unity of luminosity and emptiness could there be?

I don't believe in a result.
If I did,
what unimpeded state beyond expression could there be?

I don't believe in relative reality.
If I did,
what unity of appearance and emptiness could there be?

Nothing truly exists.
Everything is empty.
Nothing is nonexistent.
Everything is very clear.

When I just rest
within empty lucidity,
the false cavern of all things of samsara and nirvana implodes,
and everything dawns as the ornamentation of ultimate reality.

Empty awareness free from conceptual elaboration
is a luminous glow beyond clarity or obscuration
that pervades all samsara and nirvana.

I don't expect any result apart from primordial perfection.
I have mingled with the expanse
of great, blissful, self-knowing awareness
and rest within the indivisibility of threefold space.

This is the fanciful writing of a beggar lady,
the unspiritual prattling of a parrot.
If seen by others,
it will be a cause for my embarrassment.

In my spiritual tradition, that of a beggar lady,
all phenomena of samsara and nirvana appear as they are.

How can someone who practices samsara
understand the doings of nirvana?

These words are false, my divine friends!

Written by Dewai Dorje.

Sky-Mother Samantabhadri

Sky-Mother Samantabhadri
inseparable from her little-boy awareness
has no need for worldly sons.

Within the expanse of sky-mother's space-awareness
is the young child of unchanging awareness,
who suckles the milk of immaculate samadhi,
plays in the wide-open sky,
keeps company with five self-existent dakinis,
and gazes at the spectacle of objects that seem to exist.

Having looked out there, everything is clear inside,
and within this state of empty lucidity, the child gazes mindfully.
I've no need for children of the eight worldly concerns.[4]
Beyond birth, death, and living,
this young son of awareness is my companion.

Your seeing is utterly amazing!
Now shut your mouth and practice.
Otherwise, I have nothing to say.

A lazy beggar lady [Dewai Dorje] wrote this.

REMEMBERING MOTHER

Kye ma! Oh dear!

The expanse of Mother Samantabhadri
is empty of phenomenal existence—
all the things of samsara and nirvana.

Mother Luminosity is unimpededly clear and beyond expression,
primordially liberated from objects of dualistic perception.

In this nonreferential expanse, Mother Openness
met the child of unattached awareness
and entered the original state of the primordial ground.

Beyond all limitations, Mother herself
raised her children within spontaneous presence
in the ineffable nature of blissful emptiness
and then dissolved into the sky of great unattached emptiness,
mingling as one taste with the expanse of the dharmakaya.
The unity of the two kayas, emptied of samsara,
became the attainment of the exalted state of Samantabhadra.

Some things I perceived were the circumstances for me, a beggar lady
[Dewai Dorje], to remember my mother. Pitying myself and in tears, I,
one who has nothing but faults, wrote these lies as a way to console myself.

May virtue prevail!

MOTHER OF VIEW, MEDITATION, AND CONDUCT

How wonderful! Supreme heart son—
when you sustain the view of the fundamental nature,
you encounter the mother of indivisibility.

In undistracted, uncontrived, non-meditation,
you encounter the mother of spontaneous presence.

Through conduct like waves on water,
you encounter the mother of nondual arising and liberation.

It's difficult to meet mother through other methods apart from
these.

Mother's heart son—earnestly practice as the father has taught.
This is my heart advice. Please keep it in mind.
Do you understand, mother's heart son?
You're never apart from me.

Arising unceasingly in the unborn sky,
all appearances and possibilities are symbolic images.

Apart from this, don't say crazy things and just sleep!

May virtue prevail!

INDESCRIBABLE AWARENESS

Awareness, primordially pure, is indescribable,
beyond attributes such as color.
Carefully and logically examine it, and then
destroy the basis of "I"!

Ha, ha, ha!

Composed by one named Sukha [Dewai Dorje].

A POEM FOR CHANGCHUP DRON

Ah! Listen up now, faithful Changchup Dron!
Be sure to remember these three words of advice.
Carefully resolve the thoughts of your mind.
Don't you know—believing the "self" exists is exhausting.
Excessive gibberish is pointless—recite the six syllables.
Forge a good heart—act according to the Dharma.
Good tea, beer, and such increase craving and
hook you deceptively, like taste does for fish.
It, the Great Perfection, is the quintessence of the buddhas.
Just try to practice like an ordinary person, and
keep your hundredfold faith from now until awakening.
Look to the lamas with respect.
Mind your intentions, vast and pure, like planet Venus.
Now, practice the sole father and lama's instructions.
Otherwise, don't be arrogant like a tall tower.
Prostrate, circumambulate, and don't be rude.
Quite tiring it is to survive by shepherding and such.
Really practice the sublime Dharma to clear away despair.
Stop anger and nasty words with loved ones.
Tune to everyone like a fox.
Undo craving for clothing and the like.
Very skillfully care for relatives and parents.
Without babbling and blathering on and on,
extract refuge and practice Tara in line with the noble Dharma.
You who tame your horn-like minds will reach the
zenith, but except for a few, most find it hard to do!

Advice like this for the faithful Changchup Dron
by Dewai Dorje, a beggar lady from distant lands,
is not a big deal, but even so,

do know there is something to understand
in these novel words!

Consider this at all times and circumstances!

This beggar lady far from home, like a stray dog,
has no choice but to roam, teaching the Dharma.
From now onward, we won't have the fortune to meet again,
but in the future we'll gather in a buddha field
ever beyond meeting and parting!

Ha, ha, ha!
This is just strange talk from a beggar lady [Dewai Dorje].

An Acrostic for the Khenpo

Dharma Lord, Great Treasure Revealer,
who embodies all triumphant buddhas,
and Protector of the Dharma, Pema Ledrel Tsal—
pray, remain inseparably upon my crown chakra of great bliss
    evermore,
and bless my mind that it ripen and become liberated!

How marvelous! Listen up my dear Dharma brother.

Awareness is primordially pure. It transcends the realm of
    thought and expression.
But its complexion is indeterminate, spontaneously present, and
    intrinsically perfect.
Carefully training in this luminosity through Trekcho and Togal
does bring liberation of self and the three realms in the threefold-
    kaya expanse.
Emptied of useless human babble, awareness is
fashioned in the arising of manifestations of kayas and
    primordial wisdom.
Great enjoyment of the immaculate essence of desirables (tea and
    more)
happens as supreme ornamentation, like the glow of the full
    moon.
It's the path of your luminous buddha nature.
Just rest within this, your ordinary state uncontrived in four ways.[5]
Keep to your seat of unchanging self-awareness right now.
Look upon your guide's face, naturally appearing through
    hundredfold faith and pure like Venus,
met within the state of nonduality.
Noble qualities of the ten paramitas,[6]

once perfected within, are the kingdom of the dharmakaya, like a
multistoried palace wherein,
pouring loosely as free-flowing tassels of long locks and
quite pure, are the sacred places of Tsaritra and more, where the
dakinis
readily will welcome you like their delightful grandson.
Side-by-side with good friends you'll come to the Lotus Light
Palace at the Glorious Mountain.
There you will enter the dakinis' silken path with unobstructed
clarity.
Utterly purified of all confused perceptions of hats, clothing, and
such you will become.
Vesting the miraculous five-colored silken brocade,
with the roar of clashing symbols and offerings of juniper,
extremely noble as a male hero and fully adorned yogi,
you will revel in the five buddha fields, such as Rameshvara and
more.[7]
Zestfully, you will manifest within the devoted perception of
those you must train,
and then you must cultivate the awakened intention to tame the
wild flesh-eaters.
Beautiful and amazing are the enlightened deeds of the heroes,
who
cultivated realization on the spiritual grounds.

Ha, ha! These lies of a crazy beggar lady
were written in a letter symbolically to indicate something novel.
Seal this advice about the certainty of uncertainty in secrecy.

Since I was unable to refuse the profound urging
of the khenpo who is my pure Dharma sibling,
I, Sukha Vajra Tsal [Dewai Dorje],
the lazy one who is always lying,
wrote down these words.
May virtue prevail!

Awareness Defies All Description

Ha, ha!
Awareness, primordially pure, is unspeakable and unthinkable,
    defying all description,
but its coloring, indeterminate, arises as the perfection of its
    qualities, present of themselves.
Carefully sustain this uncontrived natural state of letting-be and
dualistic confusion from self-attachment will be liberated into
    the space of nonduality!

Although relative phenomena are things
apprehended to have real characteristics,
they are pure within the domain of ultimate reality
beyond all conceptual elaboration.
All that appears and arises is the dynamic energy
of great primordial wisdom.
Everything is primordially liberated,
out of reach of the thinking mind,
and equal within the transcendent state of the dharmakaya.

Without delimiting, rejecting, or accepting anything,
seize this everlasting kingdom of wisdom realization
by remaining within its actualization.

A woman like me has no place expressing in this way
the meaning of the great unmistaken nature of ultimate reality,
but to fulfill the wishes of my students,
I said a little bit.

Don't leave this as an example. Strive to practice its meaning.

Dewai Dorje wrote down whatever came to mind.

For Dechen Drolma

Awareness, primordially pure and rootless, is the dharmakaya.
Beyond attributes such as color, it's a luminous state.
Carefully, sustain its continuity by letting it be, uncontrived, and
destroy the root of the self into the great sphere of ultimate
    reality!

For the nun Dechen Drolma,
the one named Sukha [Dewai Dorje] wrote this as a little prayer.

3. PROPHECY

Prophecy involves both clairvoyance and guidance. Dewai Dorje's life, as well as Drime Ozer's, were continuously influenced by prophecies, predictions about what was going to happen and what to do to ensure favorable circumstances. They brought warnings as well about dangers to guard against. This isn't surprising considering the central role prophecy played in the eastern Tibetan culture where Dewai Dorje's life unfolded. In the treasure-revealing communities where she lived and taught, it was a given that spiritual treasures and their discoverers were predetermined long ago, during the time of Padmasambhava and Yeshe Tsogyal. In this context, prophecies were specific directions to ensure that treasure-revealing activity would occur according to the enlightened intentions of these earlier masters due to the appropriate auspicious interdependencies coalescing.

Prophetic interludes are frequent visitors in Dewai Dorje's writings. Not only were prophecies delivered by dakinis, but they were often packaged in dakini language: cryptic syllables with often undecipherable meaning except for those karmically linked to understand. Dewai Dorje did understand them and used similar elements in some of her own writing. The prophecies that colored her life were often delivered by beings beyond the tangible and observable domain of relative reality, such as mother-dakinis who sometimes appeared in bird forms or other manifestations of dakinis in dreams and visions. Dewai Dorje's visionary life unfolded in her dreams and in experiences of altered perception during her waking hours. In both cases, the messages that she received as prophecies were greatly impactful in guiding her decision-making and life choices. The visionary encounters wherein she received prophecies commonly occurred in sacred places she had journeyed, in central and eastern Tibet alike.

The first piece in this chapter, "Dakini Kunsel Wangmo's Prophecy," takes place in the year of the Iron Dog (1910–1911) when Dewai Dorje was nineteen. She signs this piece using the name Pema Dronkar. In her long autobiography, Sera Khandro writes of visiting a mountain called Lhari Go, which was "arranged like a mandala," the year she was eight. While there, she went off to play with many other children and discovered a *purba*, a ritual dagger, with three faces and four arms made of precious substances on top of a huge boulder in the road. She recounts pulling forcefully with both hands but only extracting it four or five inches out of the boulder before the other children arrived. She writes, "'Pema Dronkar stabbed a dagger into the rock,' they said, and everyone roared with laughter." This is the first time in her long autobiography that Dewai Dorje mentions being called by the name Pema Dronkar.

Dewai Dorje received a prophecy from Dakini Kunsel Wangmo during a feast offering ceremony on the twenty-fifth day of the month, the day dedicated to dakini practice for many Vajrayana practitioners. The message predicts Drime Ozer as her destined consort and treasure-revealing partner. For treasure revealers, timing is everything. This union, foretold and encouraged by dakinis many times, is urgent. Dewai Dorje is warned that if it doesn't happen soon, *siddhis*, spiritual attainments achieved through practice or bestowed by wisdom beings such as dakinis, may no longer be accessible. The dakini's message is clear: waste no time in uniting with the spiritual hero Drime Ozer, and positive things will happen as they should. This is sealed as a *samaya*, a sacred commitment by words of honor.

Next, "Prophecy from the Dakinis" lays out another prophecy in a beautiful presentation of dakini language, evocative in imagery and elusive in meaning. This piece too is dated. It takes place in the year of the Water Pig, 1923, which would have been a time of great joy for Dewai Dorje, who had left her domestic life in Benak with Gara Gyalse for good and was reunited with Drime Ozer. However, tragedy was soon to come in 1924 with the deaths of both her son and Drime Ozer.

"The Vulture at Nedro Dorje Dzong" is part of a larger collection titled "Vajra Laughter: Connecting Signs with Meaning" from her "Profound Secret Treasury of the Dakini's Pure Visions." Pure vision (*dag snang*) is a method of transmission common throughout the Nyingma tradition and the nomenclature among the lineages of treasure revealers with whom Dewai Dorje spent most of her life. In dreams, conscious, or semiconscious waking experiences, adepts experience visions of past or present masters or journey to pure realms where they receive teachings and transmissions. Such seeing usually results in the conferral of special insights and sacred instructions that the visionaries then bring into their activity of serving others.

The account begins with a vulture carrying a message from the great mother, most likely Yeshe Tsogyal, and alighting upon a box of *tormas* in Dewai Dorje's room. Tormas are Secret Mantra ritual implements, and they are constructed from a variety of substances. When made from edible ingredients such as roasted barley flour and butter as offerings, they are either taken outside the practice space to be consumed by whatever finds them or are consumed by practitioners as part of feasts. When constructed from wood or earth as symbolic representations of wisdom deities, they are placed on shrines. That Dewai Dorje had a box to hold her tormas indicates her Secret Mantra practice.

What follows next in the vision is words of prophecy from the vulture, communicating both present and future circumstances in secret language. Reference to the "Red One" for example, while possibly indicating the deity Vajravarahi, is best left uninterpreted. Here, as in all prophecies, the meaning is clear to those for whom they are meant.

The place of this encounter, Nedro Dorje Dzong, the Diamond Fortress of Nedro, plays an important role in Dewai Dorje and Drime Ozer's relationship. In her long autobiography, she recounts first visiting the site when Drime Ozer was there in retreat, during a period of discord in her living situation with her partner Gara Gyalse. After quelling obstacles from a malicious local protector by visualizing herself as the mantrin Dorje Dudjom, she meets Drime Ozer during one of his session breaks. She shares her deepest wishes for her own practice and Dharma activities with him. He, in turn, relates his many difficulties in supporting his own family and the challenges these present to his ability to live together with her. During the exchange, he promises to support her with food and clothing if she chooses to stay apart from Gara Gyalse in retreat with her young daughter. The meeting concludes with Dewai Dorje offering Drime Ozer some of her most precious teachings. She writes,

> Then I offered the pith instructions for *Drinking Vajra Water*, the innermost secret quintessence of the mother lineage, without hiding anything and as my most cherished wealth. Specifically, I fully opened up the four empowerments of the ultimate yoga based on the mandala of the *Secret Sky of Unelaborate Great Exaltation* and introduced the coemergent great dharmakaya, together with the hidden bare instructions on the key points for the exalted state of the practice of union and liberation and more. I selected my most valuable wealth, all the oral instructions that I had been holding in my mind, without holding anything back, for my secret consort, Wish-Fulfilling Jewel.

Dewai Dorje's experience of her rich visionary world bequeaths us some of her most precious teachings. May her insights from them further our own seeing.

Dakini Kunsal Wangmo's Prophecy

On the evening of the twenty-fifth day of the seventh month in the
Iron Dog year, Dakini Kunsal Wangmo, while sitting in a row at
the dakinis' feast, said,

Hey, hey!
In the east, bees swarm around fragrant sandalwood.
In the south, the turquoise dragon's roars echo
throughout the three-thousandfold universe.
In the west, the peacock's glow lies low.
The consort is snared in the fangs of a lion from the
     borderlands.

Your hero, the secret consort with whom you are connected
     from before,
an incarnation of Berotsana and Palki Wangchuk
and a reincarnation of Longsel,
was born in the year of the Snake.[1]

Known as Samanta, he wears white. He has long locks,
moles in his five places, and eyes like a deity.
He has attained proficiency with the ten winds
and the highest mastery of the practices of method and
     liberation.

If you can quickly meet him not far from here,
you will be empowered with the very best auspicious
     interdependence
to perfect the activities of the two treasure lineages
and nourish the teachings of the Buddha and beings.

Finally, an age of war and strife will be averted for fifty
    years,
and at age seventy-five, you will journey to the Glorious
    Mountain.
Examine the secret hidden meanings of these signs!

Quickly and swiftly, method and wisdom must unite!
If this is delayed, the dakinis' siddhis might vanish.
If you accomplish what the dakinis ask,
benefit for all will be accomplished.

Samaya. Seal. Seal. Seal. Sign dissolved.

When she was nineteen, Pema Dronkar [Dewai Dorje] wrote this based
upon the direct speech of the dakinis.

May virtue prevail!

May all be auspicious!

Prophecy from the Dakinis

Hey, hey!

When a sky-blue cuckoo from the east
shows its magic skills to north,
and sunlight, golden, from the south
mounts upon the bird-water horse,
you will surely roam in lands unknown.

When roars of tigers and the lions
shake the three worlds to their edge,
southern sun and moon mandalas
must take great care with ways and means.

Demon forces from down east,
rat-faced, they will come to greet
with fiery mouths and bellies joined.
Swiftly if you try, defeat is sure.

We dakinis bound by oath,
quickly, before long must go.
Signs and meanings apropos,
these we've hidden in your heart.

They spoke and then said,

> *para niku mitrata*
> *thana saya ragami*
> *sanga siddhi dharmaka*
> *buddha bhara namami*
> *aksha rasayana shri*

prabhawara nirmaka
tsandra yana petali
rameshari kisatsa!

"These are profound predictions of what is going to happen," they said and then disappeared.

During an empowerment on the evening of the sixteenth day of the sixth month in the Water Pig year (ca. 1923), Dewai Dorje wrote this down at the request of Wish-Fulfilling Jewel [Drime Ozer].

THE VULTURE AT NEDRO DORJE DZONG

In a vision mingling meditative experience with luminosity,
a white vulture, agile as a bird,
alighted upon box of *tormas* at my place.
In a sweet and melodious voice, it said,

> *Hey, hey!* Powerful yogini—listen up.
> From the island of Ngayab,
> we white vultures
> carry for you the clear words
> of the great wisdom mother.

> The mandala of the eastern sun
> dispels the darkness of beings, doesn't it?

> The jewel of the southern seas
> is the life of the Dharma, isn't it?

> The roar of the western tigress
> comes when it shouldn't, doesn't it?

> The magical display of spirits
> shows in the lower east, doesn't it?

> The embrace of snake and dragon
> retrieves your own jewels, doesn't it?

> Obstacles from evil demons
> come from time to time, don't they?

The Red One's iron hook incites
the retinue of students to gather, doesn't it?

The southern victory banner of gold
spreads to the border lands, doesn't it?

Hey, hey!

When rabbit shows its smiling face,
then wander lands unknown.
If no way for that is found,
your magic form will die.

The belly moves of two fanged-snakes,
when striking from the east,
with skill and logic must be known,
and wisdom's arrow is the key.

When blurred by broken promises,
it's sure sad things will come.
Vajra words from mother, these,
are sealed in yogi's heart—*a tam*!

Flapping its wings three times as it spoke, it rose higher and higher
and then disappeared in flight toward the southwest.

This was a confused vision of one called Sukha [Dewai Dorje] at Nedro
Dorje Dzong.

4. PROCLAMATIONS OF
REALIZATION, WONDER,
AND DESPAIR

There are three principal ways of serving one's lama according to the Tibetan Buddhist tradition: through service, through material support, and through practice of the teachings. The last is considered the best. Dewai Dorje's life circumstances were such that she had little opportunity to offer Drime Ozer day-to-day support through material means or other forms of service. She did however dedicate herself completely to practicing the teaching she received from him. And she did, frequently, offer her experiences and realization of these teachings to him in letters, songs, prayers, and more. These testify to her profound internalization not only of fundamental Dharma teachings but also of the subtlest and most exalted states of practice on the path of the Great Perfection.

View, meditation, and conduct guide Buddhist practice. Boasting as many approaches to buddhahood as there are afflictive emotions to derail the same, Buddhism offers its followers a plethora of techniques to refrain from harm, act virtuously, and tame the mind. These span a great range from those involving conceptuality to those that rely on a process of deepening personal experience of nonconceptual wisdom awareness. The latter are special features of the path of the Great Perfection and especially of the practice of Togal found therein. The "four visions" of Togal practice mark the progressive unfolding, externally, of the expression of inner primordial wisdom. The visions are (1) the vision of the direct perception of reality (*chos nyid mngon sum*); (2) the vision of the increase of the experience (*nyams snang gong 'phel*); (3) the vision of the full extent of awareness (*rig pa tshad phebs*); and (4) the vision of exhaustion of attachment into the *dharmata*, or "ultimate reality" (*chos nyid du 'dzin pa zad pa*). The "pure appearances" that are features of the first three visions, while appearing to the advanced practitioner in the outer field of perception, are nothing other than a reflection of indwelling wisdom awareness. Qualified practitioners, realizing this, conduct themselves by their very nature of being in the world in ways that induce these visions to become apparent. Togal practice completely depends on receiving personal instructions from a lineage master.

Dewai Dorje not only had such instructions from "the sole father and realized lama," but she put them to good use as evidenced by her awe-inspiring proclamations of realization that begin this fourth chapter. Among them, "Gaga's Song of Wonderment" takes us into the world of nonhuman spirits that animated Dewai Dorje's life and into her playful spirit. Male, female, and gender-neutral spirits populate internal and external Tibetan landscapes. Sometimes helpful, sometimes harmful, their presence is mostly unquestioned by those affected by belief in them. Since, according to Buddhism, ordinary people attribute a truth to things that cannot be ultimately substantiated, for many ordinary people these spirits "really" exist. Dewai Dorje, a practitioner well trained to see the illusory nature of all things, perceived spirits, gods, demons, and the like in ways that deepened recognition of her own awareness. She knew that ultimately none inherently existed outside of her own mind. Her writing is filled both with stories of encountering such presences and with accounts of seeing beyond their trickeries into the genuine truth of her experience.

In "Gaga's Song of Wonderment," Dewai Dorje suggests that "craziness" is a quality that can be linked to high levels of realization. Transcending the narrow confines of ordinary subject-object dualism with its incessant judgments about right, wrong, good, bad, and the like, an accomplished Great Perfection practitioner becomes carefree, like a child, though by no means unskillful or careless. Such freedom is intoxicating. Indeed, the Tibetan verb "to

be crazy" implicates intoxication as one cause. What is the intoxicating substance? Dewai Dorje brings the image of her young
child Rigdzin Dorje to point out that the real source of exalted
craziness is uncontrived awareness, great primordial wisdom, the
union of Mahamudra. The different terms all point to the same
peak attainment: a personal experience of ultimate reality wherein
emptiness and appearance, or emptiness and wisdom, are inseparable. In using her son, Rigdzin Dorje, as her example, Dewai Dorje
draws upon the childlike qualities of Dzogchen practitioners with
genuine recognition of uncontrived awareness.

Not all Dewai Dorje's songs are happy ones. The magnificence
of her intimate offerings of realization are matched in intensity by
the heartbreaking despair found in other songs that address outer
and inner struggles. "From the Clear, Clear Sky," "Dewai Dorje's
Actual Situation," and "Ananda's Words" exemplify ways that
Dewai Dorje worked with sorrow and grief through writing about
them. Most of her early and middle years in Golok were marked by
crushing physical hardship. When she was nineteen, though filled
with longing to live and practice near her lama, Drime Ozer, she
was blocked from doing so. The feeling of ambivalence bordering
at times on great distaste for continuing to live was something
she wrote about frequently. For her, the choice between staying in
the world in situations that kept her small and enslaved to others
and journeying to the pure land of Padmasambhava, the Glorious
Copper-Colored Mountain, was a serious one.

Dewai Dorje's choice to remain in the world was intentional and
informed by her dakini guides and their prophecies. She stayed as
long as she did only to benefit others and fulfill expectations that
she propagate the treasure lineages of Dudjom Lingpa and Drime
Ozer, along with her own. Otherwise, the overwhelming grief of
losing her son, Gyurme Dorje, and her lama, Drime Ozer, in 1924
could have been a dealbreaker on living. It almost was.

After 1924, Dewai Dorje's life was forever changed. The tragic
deaths threw her into such deep despair that she questioned her
will to live. Several of the songs in this chapter including "Dewai

Dorje's Actual Situation," "Ananda's Words," and "A Big Joke"
reflect the depth of her grief as well as her capacity to use the experience for more thoroughly internalizing and teaching the timeless
truth of impermanence.

In the aftermath of the events of 1924, Dewai Dorje was ostra-
cized by the close circle of Drime Ozer's family and students based
at Dartsang Kalzang Monastery. She had a vulnerable eleven-year-
old daughter but no family to rely upon for support. It was Sotrul
Natsok Rangdrol, one of Drime Ozer's heart disciples, who saved
her from the further misery of being homeless. At his invitation,
she took up residence at Sera Monastery, located in the valley of the
Nyichu River, and was assured at least of basic provisions for living.
From this platform, benefiting from his support, she began to teach
her own as well as Drime Ozer and Dudjom Lingpa's treasures
more extensively. Her evolution as a lama-dakini takes off from
this point in her life, and her most profound direct instructions to
students begin welling forth from her ever-increasing embrace of
the role of teacher.

Dakini and lama Dewai Dorje never assumed a high seat. Chatral Sangye Dorje described her as always seated in a low position,
whether she was teaching or not. Her humility was informed by
her constant self-reflection. Chapter 4 lets us see how she spoke to
herself about herself, based on what she observed. Several pieces
of advice are offered from a personification of her own wisdom as
Sherap Wangmo to herself as Dewai Dorje, including "So-Called
Obstacles," "Uncontrived Practice," and "Counsel from Sherap
Wangmo." Sherap Wangmo, meaning "powerful lady of sublime
insight," is Dewai Dorje herself.

In these beautiful and poetic songs of self-talk, Dewai Dorje
reminds herself of what she already knows, thereby encouraging
and inspiring herself to apply it. Likewise, "An Unborn and Self-
Emergent Little Song," and "In the Bad Lands of Golok" are teachings for herself, while of course applying to all. The former, written
in 1927, her thirty-fifth year, was undoubtedly reflective of a time
when she was still processing the loss of her beloved and adjusting

to her new life based at Sera Monastery, including her increasing role as a teacher.

Unlike intellectuals who ponder their words to find the most erudite forms, Dewai Dorje simply channeled her teachings from the empty space of all phenomena, the unborn from which all creation blossoms. There was nothing in the way to block this unfurling of wisdom as it presented itself in her songs, poems, and compositions. It was also infused with levity and joyfulness, amid external circumstances of great pain. "A Big Joke" is just one of many pieces that testify to Dewai Dorje's capacity to speak the truth of her suffering and desire to depart from the world. This appears side-by-side with her sage determination to fulfill her life's purpose as a treasure-revealing teacher and propagator, in language that conveys what must have been a wonderful laugh to our ears now.

Blessings of the Sole Father

Due to the blessings of the sole father and realized lama,
I've gained confidence through ripening and liberating my mind
and now directly behold my true dharmakaya nature.

I've realized the great spacelike expanse of the view
and rest in its natural state
beyond any point of reference or fabrication.

Like sunlight in a cloudless sky,
luminous is my meditation.
It's not a thing that traps me
by dualistic fixation with a focus.

Exceptional is my conduct,
unfolding the empty luminosities of the four visions,
without concern about getting trapped
in accepting, rejecting, expecting, or fearing them.

Awareness, self-occurring wakefulness
beyond transformation and change,
is actualization of the original buddha, Samantabhadra.

I've embraced this, my true nature,
and no longer hope for a future result
or search for some other attainment.

What has been said above
is just the practice of a humble beggar lady,
offered with faith
just so as not to disregard a request.

May virtue and goodness prevail!

Gaga's Song of Wonderment

For her most beloved, peerless hero,
Sonam Wangmo offers a silly song.

Young child of awareness, Rigdzin Dorje,
you've definitely gone crazy,
but your madness is inimitable.

Blessed by the Demonic King Samantabhadra
from the male spirit classes,
you've become crazy with uncontrived awareness
of all things of samsara and nirvana.

Blessed by the Demoness Samantabhadri
from the female spirit classes,
you've become crazy with the great primordial wisdom
of unobstructed empty lucidity.

Blessed by Gyalsen Vajradhara,[1]
you've gone crazy on the nectar of Mahamudra union.

Blessed by great self-arisen, spontaneously present assemblies of
    spirits
to actualize kayas, wisdom, and enlightened qualities,
you've gone crazy in the expanse
of the youthful vase kaya's inward luminosity.

Although crazy,
you're crazy within the ultimate expanse.
Although deluded,
you're deluded within the ultimate expanse.

Although there's nothing to reference or measure
in the ultimate expanse,
for beings like us, you show how to be crazy.

Lunacy like yours is totally amazing!
What would be wrong if I too
were crazy like you?

This was offered by a carefree wanderer named Gaga [Dewai Dorje].[2]

Song of the Vajra Wisdom Consort

Nirmanakaya Bodhisattva, all-knowing throughout triple time,
whose kindness surpasses Samantabhadra and Padmasambhava,
I've found you, completely endowed with all sublime qualities.
Pray, from today onward throughout all future lifetimes,
may we never be apart!

Effortlessly, I see my impure body, speech, and mind
as dharmakaya buddha fields within infinite purity
and behold my true nature but still,
my eyes of wisdom are weak.
Subtle cognitive obscurations shroud my true essence in
    obscurity.

Wish-Fulfilling Jewel, my supreme consort,
kind in the three most important ways,[3]
your teachings condense the essential meaning in few words,
and your oral instructions, like a golden needle,[4]
are exceptionally precise.
Transmitting the power of their profound encapsulation
of development and completion practice to me, a woman,
with your love and compassion,
opened my eyes of clear wisdom.

Now, phenomenal existence has become a palace of infinite
    purity.
Like waves on water, objects of perception
are liberated within the dharmakaya.
Forms appear as an infinite purity of wisdom deities,
without any reference for their creation or dissolution.
They are empty awareness, freed as the dharmakaya.

Sounds are an infinite purity of self-occurring vajra wisdom
    speech,
the unborn, empty nature of sound,
liberated as the dharmakaya.
Thoughts are a luminous expanse of infinite purity,
the actualization of primordial purity that has always been.
They are liberated as the dharmakaya.

Like space reaching everywhere,
I've merged with phenomena
and become the nature of sky,
manifesting in myriad ways
as primordial and self-originating mandalas
present in and of themselves.
Not even the word impurity remains;
purification and maturity are primordially perfected.

Self-knowing awareness, naturally lucid,
is liberated as the ground of the three kayas.
Mountain-like, it is unchanging and nondual.
Spacelike, it is devoid of entrapment and release.
Oceanlike, it is brilliant and limpid.
Veils of obscurity completely lifted,
this primordial wisdom is luminous
in its very essence,
like sunlight.

Obscuring clouds of ignorance purified into basic space,
I rest in this fundamental nature,
primordially unconfused,
and blossomed within the dharmakaya.

Actualizing awareness abiding as the ground,
a treasury of kayas and wisdom,
in the inward luminosity of the youthful vase kaya,

I've awakened within the ground of the resultant state,
the benefit of self and other complete.

Relative appearances are completely encompassed
by the expanse of ultimate reality itself.
Everything arises equal and free,
totally beyond sessions or breaks of practice,
released within the vast sole sphere of the dharmakaya.
Dewai Dorje has reached the level of original extinction!

Fortunate students—in this way you too must perfect
development and completion practice as well as the swift path.

The vajra wisdom consort [Dewai Dorje] offered this song with faith
to the yogi, the supreme consort endowed with twofold purity.

May virtue prevail!

A Little Song

Ha, ha!
My lama is Orgyen Pema.
My companions are the mother-dakinis.
My sacred Dharma is the Great Perfection.
My joy arises as a little song!

Tare [Dewai Dorje] wrote this.

From the Clear, Clear Sky

Oh my!
From the clear, clear sky
falls a light, light rain,
and I met a kind, kind lama.

When the blue cuckoo sings,
tears of sorrow naturally fall.
Now, thinking how first
my body was conceived,
I feel grateful for my mother.

Turning my back on my fatherland,
I ventured to unknown lands,
where a regent of Orgyen Pema
was residing in a delightful lotus grove.

I wanted to go to him,
intending to practice Secret Mantra
and the Great Perfection,
but, tortured by obstacles and dark spirits,
he departed for a pure realm.

The wretchedness and bad karma
of being a beggar lady,
constantly in my mind,
is upon me.

With utterly pure intentions
and compassion to help others,
I intended to recite mantras daily,

but this body of mine is so lowly,
without a higher rebirth,
what can I really do to help?

Although my lama has gone to a pure land,
the golden drops of his instructions held by heart disciples
live on in lonesome and isolated practice sanctuaries.

Buddhahood can be realized in a single lifetime
when the luminous Great Perfection is practiced.
In my next life, I am sure I will journey
to the feet of the awareness-holding guru
at the Glorious Mountain in Ngayab.

Due to having met an awareness-holding lama, the beggar lady Kalzang
Drolma [Dewai Dorje] sang a worldly song at age eighteen.

May it be virtuous!

HARK, MY HEART SON!

Hark, my heart son—
turn your ears to me.
I'm a dakini from the basic space of wisdom
who holds the lama's blessings in my mind.
I've discovered the siddhis of the wisdom deities
and am supported by the mother-dakinis.

My mind is like space,
baseless and without origin.
The world of appearances and possibilities
arises as symbolic teachings.
Unwritten, they escape from my mouth unceasingly,
and although others don't like them,
there's nothing I can do about it.

My view is without reference points,
center, or limit.
Primordially, it transcends all focal points
of conceptual mind.

My meditation is naturally occurring,
and in essence,
beyond the mind of conceptual ideas.
Unsullied by a focus or manipulation,
it is a natural state of being,
devoid of attachment
to both clarity and emptiness.

My conduct is like an uncoiled snake or the sky.
It is naturally liberating whatever is self-appearing,
without rejecting or accepting anything.

The *ground*, empty and lucid awareness, is like the sky.
Primordially pure, it's wide open and impartial,
and therein appearances of the *path*
are inherently and spontaneously present and perfect.
All phenomena of the world of existence
arise as its ornamentation.
The *result* is the liberation of everything
beyond hope and fear
in the expanse of Samantabhadra,
just like the sky dissolving into space.

A beggar lady [Dewai Dorje] who is faulted in all ways wrote these lies at age twenty-one. But they don't suit anyone, and they made me tired. This is just crazy talk, deceptive words that have nothing to do with the Dharma. *Ha, ha, ha!*

DEWAI DORJE'S ACTUAL SITUATION

Oh dear!
Dearest Dharma friends whom I hold in my heart with great love,
if I tell you about the actual situation of Dewai Dorje,
without hiding or concealing anything,
you all must help me with my sadness.

On the right-hand side of the retreat center at Sera Monastery,
this protectorless girl from Central Tibet
has been exiled alone.
Never have I had a starker time of greater sadness.
My protector departed for the ultimate expanse
of all triumphant buddhas, gone before, present now, and still to
    come,
and not for a moment can I forget about him.

White cranes know when it's their season,
and they go, sweetly singing *tring tring*.
With that, I remember my sublime lama.

From the tops of trees yet to flower,
bevies of chattering birds, big and small,
each sing their own clear and melodious songs.
This too makes me miss my sublime lama.

Nourishing red grass covers all the land,
beautifying the shiny golden earth.
This too makes me miss my sublime lama.

In the springtime sun,
which shines longer than all the bad times of life,

cows lead their calves to play.
This too reminds me of my noble lama.

Common folk sing joyous songs
after racing on the plains of wild horses,
while I'm blown by the winds of my despair.
With this too, I think about my noble lama.

Protector, Buddha of Triple Time, and Wish-Fulfilling Jewel—
I think about the qualities of your peerless wisdom body, speech,
    and mind,
the direct oral instructions you gave,
and the way you cared for me with kindness, love, and more,
and continuously miss you.

Generally, everything is illusory and dreamlike,
but super illusions came from the earlier illusions.
When you, our sublime lama, was physically present,
many students were around.
You offered them whatever they wanted
without a single thought for your own body and life.

Since you've departed for the ultimate expanse,
everyone is just looking after themselves,
trying to get whatever has been offered, large or small.
When I, a girl without any protector, am mentally destroyed,
I remember you, my sublime lama.

I was the consort lovingly protected by you, our sublime lama,
the lucky one among the entire entourage,
and ordinary folk as well as your students treated me well.
Now, I've been banished far away like someone evil.
This too makes me miss you.

Sad and sadder, I'm so very sad.

Down and low without you, my protector,
I'm miserable.
Missing you intensely,
I think about your extraordinary kindness.
Thinking and thinking,
I wish these thoughts would stop!

Listen once again, my dear son—
the meditation of one who practices patience
and me, a patiently suffering girl,
seem similar but that similarity is a mistake.
Through meditation, the true nature of ultimate reality is seen.
Through suffering, depression intensifies.
This too makes me recall my sublime lama.

He was a wandering yogi with no fixed abode,
and I am a homeless exile without any protector.
We seem similar but that likeness is a mistake.
Being unplanned brings accomplishment of benefit for all.
Being homeless brings limitless suffering.
Again, I remember my sublime lama.

He was a carefree mendicant free from ordinary doings.
I am a beggar woman without any protection.
We seem similar but that likeness is a mistake.
For carefree medicants, appearances arise as wisdom ornamentation.
For beggars, appearances are the foundation of confusion.
This makes me miss him, my sublime lama.

He was a realized being who lived in the solitudes of the mountains.
I am someone feeling sorry for myself in solitude.
We seem alike, but that similarity is a mistake.
Accomplished beings increase meditative experience
and realization in mountain retreat.
Though I am in mountain retreat,

I'm just creating suffering.
This too causes me to miss my sublime lama.

He was a patient and awakened person.
I am a humble girl.
We seem alike but that likeness is a mistake.
With patience, the excellent path to awakening is discovered.
My humility makes me reviled by everyone.
This too makes me miss my sublime lama.

Please consider my situation.
Suffering like this is unbearable!
I have no power to go as I wish.
I cannot fulfill the wishes of my Dharma sibling (Natsok
    Rangdrol).
Though I intend to stay, I find no joy in remaining.
I am weak—what can I do?

This song of bewilderment,
a recollection of the father and lama
comes from unbearable suffering deep inside me.
It just erupted from my mouth automatically,
through no power of my own.
I offer it to my beloved Dharma brothers and sisters.

The mendicant Dekyong Wangmo [Dewai Dorje] offered this with devotion to her oath-bound vajra siblings nearby the isolated mountain retreat at Sera Monastery with an auspicious scarf on the twenty-eighth day of the first month of the Wood Ox year.[5]

May virtue prevail!

May all be auspicious!

ANANDA'S WORDS

Kye ma!
Padmasambhava, embodiment of all triumphant buddhas,
and Yeshe Tsogyal—please think of me!
Gaze upon me in my wretchedness with compassion—
I'm alone and have no one to guide me.

The force of earlier karmic connections and Yeshe Tsogyal's
    compassion
brought forth an illusory wisdom form of Longchenpa,
who arose as a buddha of triple time.
He, the Protector of the Dharma,
directly saw the immaculate truth of ultimate reality
and illuminated primordial wisdom itself,
the inner meaning of the unborn.

Manifested from the pure and equal expanse
of the luminous nature of reality
as well as from the heat of compassion,
our lama and protector of beings
excellently appeared as the glorious boon of our merit.

Yet, since the nature of everything is conditional,
now we are apart,
and have no way to ever see or hear him again.
It's utterly devastating!

When the all-illuminating sun peaks from the tip of the eastern
    mountains,
I remember his beautiful face,
caring for me with a loving smile.

When its light rays naturally clear the darkness of beings,
I remember his giving Dharma instructions
with words of loving-kindness.

I think about how, when the cooling nectar of the gods rained
down from space,
I sought out the secret key teachings from his realized and loving
mind,
and then he bequeathed me my inheritance,
our minds mingling as one.

I remember the time when flowers and trees bloomed across the
earth,
and he opened the door to a secret treasury of Dharma
instructions,
containing everything one could ever want,
and then bestowed upon us sublime teachings,
according to our interests and capacities for practice.

Then, when it came time to enjoy the ripe fruits of the harvest,
I recall how he introduced me to my true nature—
luminous and uncontrived self-knowing awareness—
the excellent path of self-existent wakefulness.

When I see the rise of the sacred orbs of sun and moon in the
heavens,
all possible concepts naturally subside
through the powerful force of connecting with nondual
primordial wisdom,
and I recall the highest path of great unified Mahamudra.

When the sparkling lights of myriad stars appear in the universe,
I think about the penetrating knowledge
of all the students and vajra siblings in the retinue.

When the eastern sun moves toward the western mountains,
I remember my soulmate, the purest part of my heart.
I think about the teacher who appears separate but never is.

Kye hu! Kye hu!
Three Supremes and Three Roots, please consider me!
I'm thinking of him.
I'm remembering him.
I'm missing my lama.

Now quickly, let us practice the sublime Dharma before it's too
   late!

Since all that is accumulated eventually is lost,
what use is there for illusory wealth and possessions?
Since all that gathers eventually must part,
what use is there for attendants, students, or power?
Since life ends in death,
what need is there for cherished children?
Since all talk is lies,
why bother quarreling back and forth?

Now all the things of samsara and nirvana
appear to me just like magical illusions.
Everything is impermanent,
the ground of myriad suffering,
so, what's the use of getting exhausted
by tying yourself up in attachment to anything?

I no longer think of friends.
I've no interest in love or trusting intimacy.
I no longer think of food.
I've no interest in nourishing my body.
I no longer think of clothes.

They don't feel warm or soft anymore.
I no longer think of a home,
since my soulmate is gone.

I will wander in mountain solitudes without any fixed abode,
practicing the instructions of my lama
who possesses the realization of the sole father.[6]
I will sustain the natural state of no-mind,
nonconceptuality,
and behold my true dharmakaya nature
within the meditation of non-meditation.

Once I establish my practice in mountain retreat,
firmly committed to the conduct of natural liberation,
I won't fixate upon or fabricate this natural mode of being.
Instead, I will nurture it, the exalted state
of innate and uncontrived self-knowing awareness
and thereby encounter the true nature
of the self-existing ultimate lama.

The glorious self-appearing Copper-Colored Mountain isn't far
     away.
It is completely and thoroughly encompassed
in this great self-occurring, awakened experience,
present in and of itself.

Should a Dharma brother or sister want to meet our lama,
alight upon this—the primordial throne of self-knowing
     awareness!

The Lake-Born Vajra, born from a naturally occurring lotus,
appears for the fortune of karmically connected beings
as fully qualified lamas who guide all connected to them
to the pure realm of Lotus Light,

escorted by dakas and dakinis
manifesting as their own dynamic energy.

Singing beautiful songs and bathing in floral nectar
in that pure realm of Akanishta,
which has no fixed location,
lama and students, as teacher and retinue,
enjoy the glory of the profound and vast instructions of the
Dharma.

Even now, as the intentions of the Lotus Born and consort are
being accomplished,
I'm praying for all who are connected to me to awaken in the
realm of Lotus Light.

These words come from a heartbroken beggar lady named
Ananda,
when she was overcome with grief and had no idea what to do.
With her heart son Shila Vajra [Tsultrim Dorje] beside her,
she wrote them with the wind on her paw and offered them to
him.
May he now, awed by the illusory spectacle of an illusory girl,
realize the unchanging everlasting kingdom!

This was written by Sukha Vajra [Dewai Dorje].

May virtue prevail!

Without Any Wisdom Qualities

Ha, ha!
I don't have any wisdom qualities,
but I write and propagate treasure teachings,
ruining both myself and others with big lies
as an unspiritual teacher.

Motivated by the waste of ink and paper
and by my own laziness,
I will stop now and definitely behave myself.

Fortunate supreme son—I'm only joking!

My body, defiled aggregates that I've appropriated,
simply appears to be inferior,
but I've been protected by the immense kindness of my consort,
Wish-Fulfilling Jewel,
and have actualized the inner meaning
of the swift path of great primordial wisdom.

Manifestations of infinite purity arise as volumes of scripture,
an inexhaustible sky treasury of Dharma teachings
over which I have authority.
The right amount of writing down
everything that is arising
has not yet occurred.

Having relied upon imprints left by releasing the knots
restricting my throat chakra in the central channel,
I don't need to train in tongue flapping,
like paper strung between trees, through the hardships of study.

I've extracted the essence—the primordial wisdom
of the dharmakaya, pure and equal.
So, I've no hope in the result of childish games of dos and don'ts.

Ha, ha!
These are the words of a foolhardy lady, a disembodied dakini.

Hey, hey!
I spoke directly about my situation without hiding or making up
   anything.

Ho, ho!
If learned people with intelligence and twofold knowledge see
   this,
and the status of Demonic Uncle Pride gets inflated,
burn it completely in the expanse of the fire goddess!
I've no need to create attachment and aversion
for myself or others
and can throw away whatever I want.

May virtue prevail!

An Unborn and Self-Emergent
Little Song

I pray, Omniscient Father, Pema Ledrel Tsal,
grant your blessings
that my mind turns toward the Dharma!

Listen up, Dewai Dorje!
If you want to be happy in this life and future lifetimes,
hurry up and practice the totally pure Dharma.

Otherwise, if you want to create suffering for later,
put your efforts into obsessing about samsara.

If you wish to realize spiritual attainments to benefit yourself and
    others,
meditate upon the crucial points of Secret Mantra.

If you intend to follow long and lesser paths,
practice the immature teachings of the provisional meaning.

If you desire buddhahood in a single lifetime,
don't you need confidence in the teachings
of the luminous Great Perfection?

If you want to act within the confines of cyclic existence,
practice the lower path of characteristics.

If you're thinking to receive the blessings of the close lineage,
practice the profound treasures of Padmasambhava.

If you wish to go to the palace of the Glorious Mountain,
recognize everything that arises as wisdom.

If you want to effortlessly benefit others,
transform the phantasmagoria of illusion into a magical dance.

These words are an unborn and self-emerging little song
about the characteristics indicated by the nine vehicles.

It burst into my mind from the beautiful scenery of the open
    plains
in my thirty-fifth year, the year of the Fire Tiger,
as I recalled the certainty of uncertainty.

The words arose without any text.
Inspired by the power of the unceasing winds of speech,
the gullible and confused yogini Dewai Dorje wrote them down.

May they be virtuous!

So-Called Obstacles

Hey, hey!

So-called obstacles don't come as horned animals.
They are sudden thoughts,
which are unrivaled by hundreds of armies.
They are the butchers
that sever the life force of your liberation.
Within the darkness of ignorance,
thoughts accompany you.
Sherap Wangmo, may you repel them!

Written by Sukha [Dewai Dorje].

UNCONTRIVED PRACTICE

Hey, hey!

My lama is the buddha of triple time,
whose blessings are unbroken.

My instruction is luminosity,
which is present in and of itself,
uncreated and unceasing within awareness.

My companions are the mother-dakinis,
who are unremitting in their love.

My little boy is wisdom awareness,
who is beyond meeting and parting.

Whatever arises is the dynamic energy of mind.
Don't evaluate or appropriate it.

Rest in the state beyond thought and expression,
and whatever appears
will be freed right where it is.

How delightful is the practice of being uncontrived!

This is advice from Sherap Wangmo to Dewai Dorje.

May virtue prevail!

Counsel from Sherap Wangmo

Wisdom-Eyed Lady who sees others' faults—
take a look at your own!
They are blooming as poisonous flowers.

Realize that, within the dharmakaya,
all actions of the lama, whatever appear,
are the equal taste of great self-liberation.
See the downside of thinking
in mistaken ways about them,
whereby you just exhaust yourself
and amass the worst kind of negative karma.

Not knowing that wisdom deities are the essence of empty
   lucidity,
you are exhausted from fixating upon other deities as truly
   existent.

Lacking the realization and conduct to hear sounds as mantra,
you are exhausted from endless thinking.

Not realizing thoughts as equal within the dharmakaya,
you are exhausted from thinking highly about yourself.

You have amassed dormant negativity
from your own faults,
which are as big as a mountain,
but exhaust yourself correcting the behavior of others.

How pathetic you are amid your dark unawareness.
It's exhausting to sell the life energy of the mother-dakinis.

Think about this and promise to yourself
to let everything be
with a mindset of impartiality.

These words, a brief blaze of five poisons,
are advice for one named Sukha [Dewai Dorje] from Sherap Wangmo.

Seen from my perspective, it's best to just stay sleeping in silence.

A LITTLE SONG THAT BURST OUT

Oh dear!
Padmasambhava, universal embodiment of all triumphant
  buddhas
throughout triple time and Yeshe Tsogyal—
pray, see me with compassion from your invisible buddha fields of
  purity.

Reflecting upon my wretchedness and vulnerability,
I'd have no regret about ending the life in this, my cherished
  body.

My lama, kinder than all buddhas,
gone before, present now, and still to come,
appears no more.
He is hiding in the Palace of Lotus Light at the Glorious
  Mountain.

My son, the apple of his mother's eye,
was led away by the heartless and cruel Lord of Death.

My lama's students and followers are countless,
like a constellation of stars,
but I, alone, have been exiled to the ends of the earth
without any support.

Never have I suffered greater physical or mental anguish than
  this!
I pray—Sole Father Pema Ledrel,
please, see me from your invisible realm!

This noble human lady that you loved in earlier times
is now wandering around homeless
after you discarded her.

Forget about preserving the profound treasures of the lama and
    sole father!
I am a woman with a bad body from bad karma,
oppressed by suffering.

Wish-Fulfilling Jewel, my lifelong companion and meditation
    partner—
you cared for me as your beloved with a kind and loving heart
and didn't hide any instructions on the most profound meaning.

When I think about your outer, inner, secret qualities and more,
the stress of my grief feels like an executioner.

Who is there in the three-thousandfold universe
with pain greater than mine?

Noble Wish-Fulfilling Jewel,
please, see me with your compassion.

Forget about practicing and praying to the lama.
All I can do is just attend to my grief and physical illness!

Forget about upholding the profound treasures and gathering
    students.
Everyone gossips about me as a woman and avoids me like poison.

Forget about remaining at the lama's residence to practice.
Everyone treats me like a thorn in their eyes,
and like evil, I've been banished
into a defenseless and homeless condition.

Forget about help or consolation from anyone in the retinue.
They are just making things nice for themselves with what they
    want.

I am a wretched girl without any friends or protection,
oppressed by a load of suffering,
lying down utterly disheartened.

In most circumstances, I can take care of my suffering.
Yet, through the force of the winds in my heart
moving in the depth of my mind a little bit,
your mother who is staying at the right side
of the mountain retreat center at Sera Monastery
burst out with this little song for her beloved heart son.
Little guy, I have nothing else to say besides this!

The mother Sukha Vajra [Dewai Dorje] offered this to her sole son, Shila
Vajra [Tsultrim Dorje], without hiding anything about her situation.

A Big Joke

Self-knowing awareness is pure from the outset.
It is the dharmakaya, *the body of ultimate reality.*

Self-arising, it forever expresses itself
as the sambhogakaya, *the body of complete enjoyment.*

Self-liberated and uncontrived, it appears in manifold ways
as the nirmanakaya, *the body of emanation.*

Self-experienced as the teacher,
it is the svabhavikakaya, *the essence body*:
Pema Ledrel, whom I continuously remember with deep faith
and pray—remain always and forever as Lord of the Family.

Kye ma! Kye hu!
How very sad!
Samsara's phenomena are just conditioned things,
and when I think about them,
sadness grows from deep within me.

The purest part of my heart
is hidden away at the Lotus Light Palace,
and my only son, my very heart,
is no longer in the world.
I have been left behind
and am now just a thing to be pitied.

Deep inside, I am seriously considering journeying to a buddha field—
a pure realm beyond fixed location—
but since I vowed to myself

to preserve the profound teachings and benefit everyone,
I guess I should stay on for a few more years.

Our intentions have been perfectly pure,
but a call for you to oversee things back home has come.
Now, no matter what I think,
I just feel exhausted.

At this point, the force of my unfortunate karma from before
is such that I am completely sure
I won't be able to benefit beings at this time.

Now, Shila Vajra [Tsultrim Dorje],
when you and I
must definitely separate
my despair is unbearable,
as though my heart is being torn out.

I am just writing down whatever I think.
Who can substitute for my only son, the nexus of my heart?
With whom can I share my pure visions?

Whatever I think causes my sorrow to grow.
Whatever I do is suffering, by its very nature.
My intentions never go well and just bring weariness.

I am sure about one idea for happiness:
my deep wish to go to the Lotus Light Palace at the Glorious
    Mountain.

Due to the power and excellent aspirations
of the regent of Padmasambhava,
my sole protector Pema Drodul Sangak Lingpa,
and Padmansambhava himself,
my longing to go there becomes greater and greater.

I pray that all who are connected to me,
both positively and negatively,
will take rebirth there, first among my retinue.
Benefiting everyone will be easier in a buddha field.

I am completely joking, my heart son!

Although nothing is certain about conditioned things,
I do strongly wish to stay for a few more years.

If *sagadawa*[7] doesn't bring a summons for me,
we'll never be apart.
Together, may we spread the teachings of the two treasure
    lineages
to the fullest extent!
May the lives of the treasure holders be long!
May the profound treasure teachings reach to the ends of the
    earth,
and may the treasure protectors swiftly enact their wisdom activity!

I offer these words of sorrow-laden advice from a girl of illusion
to you, my supreme son of magical emanation.
Like a painting of billowing cloudbanks,
they are a magical manifestation matrix of lies.

Ha, ha! This is just crazy talk, my heart son!
Hey, hey! These are just words of confusion, my dear Dharma
    friend!
Ho, ho! Beloved son, this is just silly advice!

These words, Dekyong Wangmo's [Dewai Dorje's] crazy counsel,
were virtuously offered just as a joke,
something to laugh about, for Shila Vajra.

May virtue prevail!

ILLUSION'S DYNAMIC DISPLAY

Ha, ha!
I'm not someone whose Dharma
is immature and intellectually fabricated.

I just engage with the arising of whatever arises
and the being of whatever is.
I don't seek out antidotes to accept or reject
the ornamentation of ultimate reality.

What do the profound assertions of philosophical tenets
    achieve?
They don't control the mind
and can be the basis for attachment and aversion to grow.
The one that liberates all is awareness,
the awakened mind.

Primordially liberated and beyond ordinary mind,
it's an uncompounded phenomenon,
the primordial buddha endowed with the seven vajra attributes.

The basis of all phenomena is suchness,
the ultimate essence perfected as self-occurring awareness.
Seize the throne of this great vast and pervasively open
    transcendent state!

I don't have any anxiety about the displays of illusion.
I, Sukha Vajra [Dewai Dorje], a practitioner of illusion,
put into words illusion's dynamic display.
Even if this doesn't accord with others, I am happy.

The magical displays of samsara and nirvana's illusions are
   wonderful!
With the three perceptions of a crazy beggar,[8]
I said this to myself.

May virtue prevail!

BED OF THE OPEN PLAINS

Ha, ha!
I haven't witnessed buddha
by becoming accomplished through practice.

If you don't realize the natural lucidity of your innate nature,
beyond the mind of conceptual ideas,
then just like a mouse sleeping in a hole,
you won't become enlightened.
So, rest spaciously in openness
without needing to keep or discard anything.

If you don't realize the recitation of mantra
as the natural resonance of ultimate reality,
then, just like a mute that can't speak,
you won't become enlightened.
Let be whatever arises
without talking about accepting and rejecting.

If you don't extract the wisdom intent
of the lama's oral instructions,
you won't understand the meaning
of the many profound pith instructions
or see the essence of primordial wisdom
through objects of mere intellectual understanding.

The conduct is to let be whatever arises,
without any division between meditative equipoise and
    post-equipoise

and to remain with the oral instructions for the secret path of
    luminosity,
just as it is.

Development, completion, mantra recitation, sessions, oaths and
    more
are the cause for fixating upon characteristics
and increase discursive thinking.
Having abandoned all thought,
my heartfelt wish is to sleep like a beggar.

The bed of the open plains
is free from all attachment.
It is very comfortable.
The perfect throne is limitless self-cognizance
beyond all fixation.
The automatic self-liberation of whatever arises
is the carefree state.

I, Kunzang Lhundrup Dekyong Wangmo,
sleep in the expanse of primordial liberation,
free from anything to avoid or attain.
I have no hope for a later result—
I am freed right where I am.
How amazing it is in the primordially pure dharmakaya!

This worldly beggar lady sang a song of the experience of sleep.
Listen, hero, my supreme method and heart support,
if I am mistaken and deluded,
I confess within the vastness of the ultimate expanse.

This is advice for Dechen Dewai Dorje herself.
May all beings awaken as buddhas through this discussion of sleep.
May virtue prevail!

In the Bad Lands of Golok

Hey, hey!
Stubborn Dewai Dorje
can't reign in her wild mind.
Left to the troupes of laziness,
her study and reflection faded into the sky.

Silken knots of attachment to things,
she has tied with a tight seal,
and in her black tent of desire,
she is so comfortable on her bed of hatred.

Upon her throne of pride,
dressed in jealousy,
sleeping in the taste of ignorance,
enacting the five poisons in an ordinary way,
Dewai Dorje—this is definitely you.

Enthusiasm for study, contemplation, and meditation
I don't see in you.
Enthusiasm for children, you definitely have.

If you can have fewer needs,
you will certainly become carefree.
If you're caught up
in gathering or avoiding big or small retinues,
it is certain that you will never be carefree.

Mediocre renunciation and faith
you surely have,
but you're the worst

of those who don't practice
the profound quintessential instructions of the lama.

You certainly know about a view as sharp as the sky,
but when you encounter the troops of the five poisons,
you're no different than an ordinary person.
It is true—you're a child on a battlefield.

Not married, not unmarried, far away,
not human, and not animal,
the girl Dechen Dewai Dorje
reveals what seem to be treasures but really aren't.

Boasting about what the great vehicle is
even though it really isn't,
she knows nothing but carelessly talks.

In the bad lands of Golok,
the woman Dewai Dorje,
controlled by the maras of evil thinking,
continuously turns the wheel of negativity.

Quarreling but thinking it's true benefit for beings
is lowly Dewai Dorje.
So as not to do more that is destructive
and cast away negative thoughts and pain,
firm up your mind like a horn.
You must practice the profound quintessence.

When you meet fully qualified friends,
you should serve to please them in the three ways.
When your own perception rises up as an enemy,
you must let negative circumstances become liberated
right where they are.

Your mind is like bag of poison,
so don't teach the Dharma to others.

Taught by nonhuman beings in visions,
you received the key instructions
for the supreme paths of ripening and liberation.
Now practice these, your own fortune,
and don't fall under the power of laziness.

When negative companions irritate you,
don the armor of patience,
and don't quarrel with the entourage.
Sleep in silence.
Stop anger that hurts others
who have no development and completion practice.

With your mind out of tune with the Dharma,
you can't help others.
So, just sleep.

You must understand things in this way
and get your mind under control.
Full of faults, your good qualities all gone,
beggar lady named Dewai, understand—
this is advice for you!

Ha, ha!
Hey, hey!
Ho, ho!
This bad writing by Dewai Dorje
on the face of the final pages of bad paper
are the bad words of your various faults,
written with the charcoal of bad ink.

Bad student Tupten Zangpo—
don't blow the bellows of evil talk.
Sit and be quiet!

Though I have no positive qualities,
I definitely understand my faults.
I haven't seen others like me
with such bad karma.
Refuges of the Triple Gem,
please transform my mind!

When locals said I was stubborn,
I felt happy and composed a bit about my faults.

5. PURE VISIONS

Pure vision as a modality of transmission is widespread and accepted throughout many schools and lineages of Tibetan Buddhism. Fortunate individuals, in clear and luminous visions, meet masters and wisdom beings from the past and present times and receive empowerments, teachings, and advice, which they then pass on to others. Dewai Dorje's pure visions encompass a wide range of experiences. In the treasure traditions of her time and place, pure vision was common and particularly potent as a portal through which treasure revealers acquired important information including prophecies and discovered their destined treasures and other important teachings.[1] Dudjom Lingpa's famed text, *Nang Jang*, or *Buddhahood without Meditation*, is an example of the latter. Dewai Dorje was intimately familiar with it, having recorded Drime Ozer's commentary on it.[2] The text is a compilation of Dudjom Lingpa's visionary encounters with wisdom teachers who transmitted key instructions of Dzogchen practice for him, while clarifying questions on the same. Dewai Dorje's treasures include practices and teachings revealed to her in pure visions, and her shaldam also contain many visionary accounts that are, by their very nature, possible only for those who have refined ordinary perceptions of reality and are thereby attuned to pure wisdom phenomena.

Dewai Dorje writes about the circumstances surrounding the first piece, "A Visionary Experience during the Teaching of *The Precious Treasury of the Dharmadhatu*" in her long autobiography. The importance of this text, Longchenpa's seminal work on the Great Perfection practice of Trekcho, cannot be understated. A spectacularly exalted presentation of the practice's most subtle techniques, it is an indispensable guide for anyone committed to its approach. Dewai Dorje writes,

> During this time, while *The Precious Treasury of the Dharmadhatu* was being taught to Drime Ozer's actual students Desal Gyatso, Drime Namdak, and others, my experience shifted. I became the secret spiritual consort of Drime Ozer when he was Longchenpa, and emanating as a vulture when he was Ledrel, actually generated secret bliss and such. I wrote spiritual songs and more about this actualization of realization and offered them to him. When I told him that I had come to a place of not knowing anything, like a lunatic, and asked him what to do, he said, "It's the attainment of the blessings of the lamas' wisdom mind lineage within your own mind, so there is no need to do anything. Rest in empty awareness, the state beyond thought."

This account is a magnificent example of Dewai Dorje offering her realization to her lama, Drime Ozer, for his interpretation and commentary. It also blurs the line between meditative experiences and visions. Finally, it evidences the power of Longchenpa's teachings for Dewai Dorje and the communities of which she was part. Later in her life, Dewai Dorje herself accepted an invitation to teach some of Longchenpa's quintessential Great Perfection teachings to members of Sanglung Monastery.

Other accounts in the chapter reflect a more classic notion of what a vision would entail. "A Visionary Experience," for example, finds Dewai Dorje witnessing purity in the form of wisdom deities. These include Chemchok Heruka, the wrathful aspect of Samantabhadra (or Mahottara Heruka), usually appearing as the central deity in the mandala of the eight herukas.[3] His consort here, Namshyalma (or Krodhishvari), represents the wrathful aspect of Samantabhadri. Vajradhara, a tantric deity considered to be the sixth buddha and representing the quintessence of the five buddhas and five buddha families, makes an appearance with his consort, who is usually Vajravarahi. The buddhas of the five families also appear in "Knower of Triple Time." They represent different dimensions and characteristics of the same exalted state of realization and are commonly listed as Vairochana, Akshobhya, Amitabha, Ratnasambhava, and Amogasiddhi from the Buddha, Vajra, Lotus, Jewel, and Karma families, respectively.

The five buddhas appear again in "A Visionary Experience during the Wood Bird Year." In this, the longest vision of the chapter, Dewai Dorje receives from Drime Ozer transmission and pith instructions on the ultimate meaning. Through essentializing the vase, secret, wisdom, and word empowerments, he introduces her to wisdom body, speech, mind, and primordial wisdom awareness. The red and white essences, symbolizing the female and male vital energies, show up in the third wisdom empowerment, while the fourth word empowerment involves the direct pointing out of mind's true nature. True to the Great Perfection flavor of all Drime Ozer's teachings, his reminder that the ultimate empowerment is beyond conferral and attainment speaks to the very heart of empowerment transmission: the disciple's recognition of awareness itself.

Dewai Dorje indeed achieved this recognition. "Dewai Dorje's Dream" endorses that. In this exceedingly subtle presentation of how the three kayas manifest from one inner experience of awareness, Dewai Dorje concisely and penetratingly lays out the entire process by which the phenomenal world springs from and dissolves back into this same awareness, which is *rang rig*: "self-knowing" or "aware of itself." This, awareness that "knows itself," is the ultimate lama, realized through the intimacy of personal experience, in both dreams and waking life.

A Visionary Experience during the Teaching of *The Treasury of the Dharmadhatu*

Precious Guide, your great kindness
surpasses all buddhas throughout triple time.
Upon you we are depending, now and forever.
Though your wisdom mind never wavers
from the ultimate expanse,
please, now, lovingly consider us
with the light rays of your compassion.

Wish-Fulfilling Jewel, due to your incredibly kind compassion,
the veils of my cognitive and emotional obscurations lifted
and I now directly see
the great dharmakaya of primordial liberation.

No matter what positive or negative visions and thoughts arise,
I remain there, in my innate nature,
and don't need to refresh a meditative state to liberate them again.

I have seized the natural place of the result,
the nonduality of hope and fear,
and consider myself to be
a happy practitioner of ease.

Otherwise, if that isn't true,
then kingly spirits must have possessed me.

Phenomena, unidentifiable as existing or not, are a wild disarray.
Gross appearances have disappeared,

and everything amounts to just light.
My consciousness is erratic.
I can't recognize if it's this life or the next.
My perception is unfixed, open,
and beyond rational and intellectual processes.
I have eradicated the faults of expecting positive thoughts
and am totally free from striving for anything.
Since negative thoughts have no essence,
my effort is minimal.
I have no way to struggle for either the good or the bad.
The entire basis of hoping for buddhahood and fearing
     ordinariness
has fallen apart.

As soon as I see you, Wish-Fulfilling Jewel,
the actual embodiment of all buddhas past, present, and still to
     come,
my faith and devotion are unshakable.

I am beyond grasping,
and within the equality of the dharmakaya,
you arise as the essence of my awareness,
without appearing separate.

Country, home, retinue, and students are just appearances.
Ultimately, none of them are fixed.
Sometimes they appear, sometimes not.
Deity visualization, mantra recitation, meditative equipoise:
these are just manifestative powers.
I don't view them as ultimate, hoped-for results.

For me now, all phenomenal appearances have become chaotic,
haphazard,
arbitrary,

as though my mind and body have separated.
What's going on?

Whatever appears hardly appears.
Whatever is just barely is.
Whatever isn't just barely isn't.
Whatever arises simply arises.
Whatever is freed is simply freed.
Everything is baseless, without any ground.

It's like everything is just the great three-kaya nature,
and yet, what is this random chaos,
disorderly and insubstantial?
Is it the magical display of kingly spirits or not?

Please, Lama, Wish-Fulfilling Jewel,
Omniscient Sangak Lingpa—
look upon me!
Give me the strength to dispel hindrances and enhance my
    practice,
or explain to me—is this the here or the hereafter?
Or else lead me to the ground of great transference,
beyond dwelling anywhere.

This—my slurred speech, random visions, and haphazard
    perception—
is all so strange!
Is it a dream?
Or the appearances of this life?
Or the bardo?
Whatever it is, Lama, you know.
Wish-Fulfilling Jewel, please, look upon me with
    compassion!

After I said this in a confused state, I saw my lama sitting in an expanse of blue light about to laugh and then was freed from the vision.

When Tulku, Wish-Fulfilling Jewel, was teaching *The Precious Treasury of the Dharmadhatu*, Dewai Dorje wrote down this hallucination.

May virtue prevail!

WE ARE BOUND

Tied up in attachment to the belief
that the defiled and closely held aggregates—
our bodies—truly exist,
we are bound.

When experiencing the sensations of pain from illness,
like a mother birthing a child,
I wish that this defiled body would pass
into the undefiled realm.

Yet, due to the great kindness of my lama
who is endowed with his father's realization,
I have instructions on the dharmakaya for intense pain,
on the sambhogakaya for medium pain,
and on the nirmanakaya for mild pain.

I'm unafraid of the pain of death.
The dying state is the kingdom of the dharmakaya.
If it were otherwise,
there would be no place of buddhahood.

Those gone to bliss throughout triple time, celestial mansions,
    deities:
all these arise as magical manifestations of a single nature.

I wonder if this yogi of illusion
will depart to the sky-expanse of the queen of empty space,
or, to support the heart of my method-hero,
should I stay right here for a few years?

You, dakini from a nonhuman realm—
What healing rituals should I do for my painful illness?
Please, tell me without hiding the signs.

She replied,
"The object is samaya breakers that cause irritation,
and their curses and poisonous behavior are affecting you a bit.
You have been struck by obscurations from the deceased of this
place and those mourning for them.
Burn cleansing incense and make smoke offerings on mountains
and blessed water.
You must repel these objects of irritation through powerful
methods.
To clear away the poisonous vapor of their curses,
don the vajra armor endowed with power and glory.
Within three intermediate times, there is great harm for you.
Examine this intelligently and gradually it will be clear."

She finished speaking. Then she said, "I am Dorje Kundragma, the proprietress of this land." She threw some milk and water at me and said, "Don't you go to the buddha fields yet!"

On the first day of the second month in the year of the Water Pig, in a confused vision, a girl asked, "How are you?" In response, the simple beggar lady called Dipham Tare [Dewai Dorje] replied that she doesn't have any dakini prophecies or freedom, and not only that but she also doesn't have even a single good dream! She then let this vision be for the time being, but Wish-Fulfilling Jewel [Drime Ozer] pressed her, asking, "What visionary experiences have you had?" Since he said it wouldn't be right to hide them from him, I, the one named Sukha [Dewai Dorje], wrote this down.

May virtue prevail!

A Visionary Experience

Omniscient Protector, Refuge throughout Triple Time, and
  Vajra Holder—
though I am just a confused wanderer, under the power of
  delusion,
just like before when I was resting in a state
completely free from the doings of body, speech, and mind,
an experience arose, like that of a child gazing into a temple.

Out of the sky came naturally occurring sounds:
hrih, hung, ah, om.
Their reverberations dissolved into my right ear and instantly,
everything I perceived was like sunlight shining on snow.
Brilliant white light pervaded inner and outer space,
and miragelike orbs of light limitlessly appeared.

As I rested in that state,
at ease in the nature of mind,
a sphere of white light, round as the full moon,
arose before my eyes.
Inside it were hand emblems—vajras, jewels, lotuses, and crossed
  vajras—
surrounding a central crossed vajra and bell,   .
which appeared again and again.
Sounds of mantra dissolved into my left ear three times,
and (instantaneously) my entire perception
was like the gleaming of one hundred thousand suns.
Brilliant red light pervaded inner and outer space,
and orbs of light like a pearl garland appeared.

I remained unmoving from that experience,
at ease in the nature of mind,
and then a red sphere of light arose before my eyes.

In its center, which was just like the heart of the sun,
were the great Chemchok Heruka and consort,
appearing like rainbows in the sky.
They were fully perfect in glorious attire and resting in an
  expanse of fire.

An assembly of wrathful deities filled the great Heruka's heart
  center,
and an assembly of peaceful deities filled the heart center of his
  consort.
All appeared clearly and distinctly, unmingled like the colors of a
  rainbow.

The heart syllables of all the deities, as blue light,
dissolved right between my eyebrows and instantly
my entire perceptual field was like a stainless pure sky.
Radiant blue light permeated outer and inner space,
and five-colored orbs of light appeared beyond measure.

As I remained unmoving from that state,
at ease in the nature of mind,
a deep blue sphere of light appeared.
It was about the size of a half pea,
and in its center was Vajradhara in union with consort,
both perfectly adorned in sambhogakaya attire and vividly clear.

I remained unmoving from that state,
at ease in the nature of mind.
Then Vajradhara instantly transformed into a radiant blue *ah*
in the center of orbs of five-colored light.

Light rays from it dissolved between my eyebrows,
and the entire network of subtle energy centers and channels in
    my body
filled with the syllable *ah*, which spread throughout my entire
    body.

I remained unmoving from that state,
at ease in the nature of mind,
and all the *ahs* in my body melted into light and dissolved into
    space.
Within this skylike state of nonconceptuality,
an *ah* of the ultimate expanse
melted in between my eyebrows as light,
and my body of flesh and blood transformed into a transparent
    body of light.
The *ah* traveled through the central channel
and dissolved into the center of my heart.

Then, in skylike undistracted mindfulness,
thoughts and perceptions were the unceasing nature of ultimate
    reality.
I had no attachment to them.
Mindfulness was a great letting-be,
a state of primordial wisdom,
the actualization of utterly pure mindfulness.

All dualistic thinking was naturally lucid
and liberated as the dharmakaya.
Confusion was there,
but it was confusion within the expanse of Samantabhadra.
Liberation was there,
but it was liberation within the expanse of Samantabhadra.
I relaxed my mind in the expanse of nondual confusion and
    liberation.

Though I'm someone under the power of the five afflictions,[4]
I still wonder, why would such a deluded vision occur?
You with eyes of omniscient wisdom,
please pacify this, my confused perception, into the ultimate
   expanse.

Since I have not even a sesame seed's worth of noble qualities,
I wonder, could this be a magical display of disembodied spirits?
If others realize the implications of this, they'll worry.
My secret consort, I offer you these secret words
and request you to show me the way to still this.

Composed by Dewai Dorje.

KNOWER OF TRIPLE TIME

Knower of Triple Time, Holder of Secret Mantra's Warmth,
All-Seeing and Knowing Sovereign, Omniscient Vajradhara,
My Beloved—your light beams of sublime insight
banished my dark ignorance from its very root.

Originally, awareness is unconfused.
It is the awakened mind,
the source of everything,
the essence of wisdom and kayas,
present in and of themselves.

Naturally lucid, it is primordial wisdom devoid of attachment,
which, when experienced as the qualities of the levels and paths,
comprises the profound instructions to actualize the result
of development- and completion-stage practice.

Subtly attached to visionary experiences, I've objectified them
and transgressed your enlightened mind with its eyes of wisdom.
This I confess within the expanse of the dharmakaya,
the great purity and equality of samsara and nirvana.
I request you—please be patient with me
and bestow the instructions to achieve supreme accomplishment.

As before, at a time when I was uninvolved
in thinking, saying, and doing anything,
avadhuti, the central channel,
appeared unobscured and clear, both inside and out.
Awareness pervaded everywhere
and abided inside it as a blue syllable *hung*.

At the channel's upper end,
the crown chakra of great bliss,
the white vital essence melted into light.
At its lower end, the red vital essence below the navel
was like a flickering tongue of fire, the nature of light,
dissolving into the *hung* in the center of the gathering chakra.[5]

Without moving from that state,
at ease in the nature of mind,
I clearly experienced immaculate great exaltation,
the primordial wisdom of supreme joy.

From the *hung*, rays of red and white light radiated
and filled my entire network of subtle energy centers and
    channels with light.
The white essence of male, method, and the red essence of female,
    wisdom,
completely filled my channels as male and female spiritual heroes.

At the five chakras, dakinis of the five classes
embraced male consorts of their likenesses.
All were surrounded by male and female spiritual heroes
of their respective buddha families.

Additionally, appearing throughout all my channels and pores
were indeterminate seed syllables, light, light rays,
and wisdom forms of the hundredfold classes of peaceful and
    wrathful deities.
The principle three channels were flawless channels of light,
and the syllables *om*, *hung*, and *ah* vividly appeared.
There was no demarcation between inner and outer.
Everything was luminous in and of itself.

Free from grasping that,
I experienced so-called "appearances as deity"

as non-objectifiable thought activity,
like the reflection of stars upon crystalline water.

Everything was beyond intellectual fabrication
and perfect as a self-arisen expanse.
The unborn was whatever appeared
arising as the nature of wisdom deities.

Phenomenal existence was infinite purity, spontaneously
present.
Non-meditation was whatever appeared becoming liberated as
the dharmakaya.

Unchanging, spontaneously present, and perfected as awakened
mind,
everything was unwavering from the ultimate expanse.
Therein, the dynamic energy of self-existing wakefulness
was the arising of an indeterminate magical display of anything
and everything.

Omniscient One of Triple Time—except for someone like you,
ordinary people cannot understand this.
They make distinctions and arbitrary divisions
and get trapped in attachment,
entering the cocoon of dualistic hope and fear.

Therefore, I am telling only you my physical, mental,
and visionary experiences without hiding anything.

All-Knowing One, through your compassion,
I have actualized the primordially perfect result.
I have transcended the duality of hope and fear
and completely understand whatever there is,
as it truly is.

Illusory displays arising from the expanse of the ground
are unblocked and unconfined,
and primordial wisdom, omniscience of triple time,
is unhindered.

You are endowed with the authority over a treasury of
    instructions
to dispel hindrances and enhance practice,
and are kinder than all buddhas gone before, present now and
    still to come.
I request never to part from you for even a single instant.

For my fortunate disciples, with completely pure intentions,
I make an aspiration for auspicious interdependence:
My first wish is that all visionary experiences of body ripen as
    nirmanakaya.
My second wish is that all visionary experiences of perception
become liberated as the sambhogakaya.
My third wish is that all visionary experiences of mind
become liberated as the dharmakaya.
Once the two stages of ripening and liberation are fully
    perfected,
may there be the auspiciousness of the inwardly luminous
    youthful vase kaya.

Except for this much, I will not carelessly expose secrets
and be the basis of confusion for those with lesser capacity to
    understand.

This is sealed in the ultimate expanse,
the secret space of the female consort.

Composed by Dewai Dorje.

A Visionary Experience during the Wood Bird Year[6]

During a visionary experience in a midday practice session in the fortunate year of the Wood Bird, a blue orb of light appeared. In its expanse was a vast and beautiful land full of many kinds of flowers and varieties of birds humming the song of Guru Harinisa.[7] I experienced the entire array with utter joy.

In the center was my lama, Pema Ledrel Tsal, inside a beautiful dome of rainbow light. He was with Dudjom Dorje and many other accomplished lamas that I didn't recognize. Together with the dakinis Dewai Gocha (Saraswati), Raltri Barma (Kalasiddhi), Salche Wangmo (Shelkar Tso), and other male and female spiritual heroes, they had opened the infinite *Gong Du* mandala, the Gathering of Commands, and were making medicinal nectar. I went and took the hand of my Wish-Fulfilling Jewel. I felt extremely sad and just wept. My great hero smiled with tremendous love and said,

> Oh dear—noble and beloved companion,
> be still your heart and relax your mind.
> There is no other metropolis of heroes and dakinis
> apart from our own perception,
> which isn't other than the magical manifestation
> of the singular nature of ultimate reality.
> Noble Lady, be seated in the rows for the feast and rejoice!

He spoke and lovingly gave me a skull cup full of beer. He danced with his body and then appeared as a heruka ornamented with six bone ornaments. Holding a crossed vajra and bell, he gazed directly into space and said,

Hung hrih!
Fortunate child, I empower you
with the unchanging and indestructible vajrakaya
endowed with pure and radiant light aggregates.
May you attain the power of immutable wisdom body!
dharmakaya abhishintsa om

Hung hrih!
Fortunate child, I empower you with the speech
of the natural melodies of inexpressible mantra.
May you be empowered with inexhaustible, secret wisdom
    speech
indivisible from my own.
dharmawaka abhishintsa ah

Hung hrih!
Child of awareness, by empowering you
with the secret wheel of nondual wisdom mind,
primordially pure self-existent dharmakaya,
may you realize the empowerment
free from something conferred and attained,
indivisible from my wisdom mind.
dharmacitta abhishintsa hung
ah ah ah

As soon as he finished, my ordinary thinking suddenly stopped. Earlier karmic propensities awakened and instantaneously I appeared clearly in the wisdom form of Vajravarahi embracing her male consort, an unfathomable awareness body manifesting instantly as the wisdom realization of nondual male and female deities. Her retinue of dakas and dakinis said in a single melodious voice,

ah tam siddhi sukha satvam
How incredible and wonderful!

Heruka, Secret Mantra Master,
Vajradhara with your wisdom kaya—
you are a marvelous and astonishing phenomenon,
the great source of all mandalas,
a most secret treasury for male and female heroes,
and a wellspring of siddhis. I praise you.

Secret Mantra is the unsurpassed and supreme approach,
the most direct path to the secret wisdom mind of all
    victors.
You've attained confidence in its actualization
and discovered an awareness kaya.
Vajradhara, I praise you.

Your wisdom form of union surpasses that of all wisdom
    deities.
You're the lord of all magically manifest mandalas
encircled within the pure space of kayas and wisdom.
I praise you, Victor of Manifest Perfection.

They spoke and then laid out a magnificent feast. Dudjom Heruka
and consort, the principal deities of the mandala, transformed into
light and dissolved into the hero, who promptly danced. He then
transformed into a heruka holding a full skull cup, dressed as a
yogi, and said,

Ah tam!
Vajra wisdom body, encountered through the touch
of male and female union, is indivisible empty-appearance,
perfected as the essence of the vase empowerment.

Vajra wisdom speech, transmitted through the flow
of bodhichitta nectar, is indivisible empty lucidity,
perfected as the essence of the secret empowerment.

Vajra wisdom mind, beheld as the countenance
of red and white essence drops, is indivisible empty bliss,
perfected as the essence of the wisdom empowerment.

The ripening of connate, primordial awareness as vajra
   wisdom,
is indivisible empty awareness,
perfected as the essence of the word empowerment.

The ultimate secret empowerment transcends anything to
   confer or attain.
Bestowing it upon you, noble dakini,
purifies your coarse body into its subtle channels and
   elements,
ripens your coarse speech into its subtle wind elements,
and perfects your coarse mind as the subtle essence drop.
Once you are freed from all habits of ordinary body, speech,
   mind,
concepts, and obscurations, may you attain the ultimate
   empowerment
to manifest the exalted states of Mature, Immortal,
   Mahamudra,
and Spontaneously Accomplished awareness holders!"[8]

He stared at me with his eyes wide open. After meditating like
that for a little while, he said, "This is the conferral of the fourth
empowerment of the ultimate secret, the essence of method and
wisdom. Don't reveal it to others. When the time is right, we'll
come together again. Until then, befriend the consort of unchanging great exaltation as the supreme method to realize that appearances do not truly exist."

Then, Vajra-Karma Dakini Zhiwa Tso led me into the feast from
the eastern door of the mandala and said with a lovely voice,

Wondrous!
In the ultimate dharmakaya buddha field, unborn and
    self-occurring,
where the infinite purity of form appears as mandalas of
    method and wisdom,
enjoy the ambrosia of uncontaminated great exaltation
and request the siddhi of the infinite purity of empty bliss.

Dakas and dakinis, the infinite purity of the vibrant
    display,
after partaking of the nectar of infinitely pure desirables,
request the siddhi of infinitely pure freedom from
    attachment.

The infinite purity of the universe and its contents is the
    arrangement of mandala.
Imbibe the nectar of self-occurring infinite purity
and request the siddhi of the infinite purity of phenomena
    and thought.

Within the joyful sanctuary of self-existent Akanishta,
brothers and sisters, vajra siblings with singular sacred
    commitments,
enjoy the feast offering of nectar
that liberates through the experience of method and
    wisdom,
and request the siddhi of the infinite purity of all that
    appears to exist.

Mingle realization of teacher and disciple, indivisibly as one
    taste,
and request the instructions for accomplishing a
    dharmakaya rainbow body."

After she spoke, everyone sang and danced with their own consorts, reveling in the feast celebration. Then I thought, "They are probably the manifestation of my Wish-Fulfilling Jewel's wisdom body. Could there still be another buddha field?" However, I thought that this one was where I needed to be, so I didn't leave. My hero said,

> Now then Noble Lady, listen.
> Manifestations of buddha fields, heavenly palaces, and
>   wisdom deities
> are the expressive power of suchness, the nature of ultimate
>   reality.
> This is nothing other than self-occurring wakefulness.
> You must understand it.

Then he manifested a display of five deities from his one single wisdom body. In the center was Vajra Heruka and consort. In the east was Buddha Heruka and consort, in the south Ratna Heruka with consort, in the west, Pema Heruka, and in the north Karma Heruka. All were accompanied by their own consorts, heirs, and retinues, present as an elaborate manifestation of myriad, inconceivable wisdom mandalas. I prostrated with intense faith and devotion and said,

> From this life onward throughout all future lives,
> may I never be separate from you, awareness-holding lama.

> May I perfect the supreme path of the two stages
> and come to realize the empty bliss
> at the level of Mahamudra.

> In reliance upon the practice of the union of method and
>   wisdom,
> from now on, though I may be in lower worlds,

may I meet you through the power of these aspirations
as a dakini, consort, companion, and wife
who will bring you delight, my hero.

Once we've found each other again,
may we not be overcome by circumstantial obstacles
but serve the Buddha's teachings and beings to the end of
  our lives
and perfectly accomplish the noble deeds of the victors.

May keys to the secret Treasures, root Dharma holders,
and karmically connected students gather without obstacles
  and adversity
and become realized through the undeceiving strength of
  the two truths.

May all beings with connections to me, both positive and
  not,
from now until attaining enlightenment,
never be separate from you, my awareness-holding lama.

Once we have enjoyed the splendid ocean of profound
  treasures,
please bless us to accomplish a dharmakaya rainbow body.

After I finished my prayer, I said *"Ah, ah, ah!"*
  The wisdom manifestations gathered back into one who said,

Concerning wisdom deities, you, yourself, are the deity.
Everything emanates from a single sphere of wisdom.
My arrangements of wisdom are beyond expression.
Conceptual appearances are perfected as the form of the
  deity.
Sounds resounding are vajra speech of great exaltation.

Thinking is suchness, the nature of ultimate reality.
Consummate within the essence of nondual wisdom mind,
they are not separate, noble child.

He finished speaking and handed me a scroll. Then he said, "This
is the Dharma cycle of the secret dakini. When timing and auspicious interdependence align for its decoding, it will be exceedingly
profound."

Immediately, two dakinis arrived. They took my left and right
hands and said,

Oh dear! Noble Dakini, Divine Princess,
wearied with sadness,
you have come to this buddha field,
and we will help you.

You will have excellent circumstances for perfect happiness
with us, your vajra siblings holding sacred commitments,
and the exalted meaning of these quintessential
instructions.

This buddha field has many more excellent companions for
you:
dakas and dakinis who are freed from obscurations
caused by breaking their sacred commitments.
Our Dharma brothers and sisters are pure in their vows
and aren't sullied by stains of negativity.
This sanctuary's wisdom qualities are unfathomable.
It's a superior place to benefit beings through the Buddha's
teaching,
and it will be good if you remain here.
Benefiting yourself and others will be natural and effortless.

Worldly peoples' thinking is controlled by demons,
and genuine Dharma practitioners are rare as daytime stars.

Neither teachers nor students maintain vows and
    commitments,
and happiness is like mist on mountain passes.
When consideration for helping others is set aside,
both oneself and others are tainted by faults of
    transgression.
These and more sudden misfortunes
constantly sadden and weary the mind—
so please, come now to our buddha field.

My heart was glowing with happiness, but I thought I should stay
next to my hero and not go outside, so I sat for a moment without
saying anything in reply. Then a few Dharma brothers (Natsok
Rangdrol and Shila Vajra) and some others (Tishta Vajra) said in
unison,

Hark! Dakinis of wisdom space, please listen.
You led our sole refuge,
the great treasure-revealing lama to the buddha fields,
and each of us has been implicitly expelled from his heart.
Without a protector, we've been cast aside
with no place to request Dharma teachings,
and now you are inviting the dakini to your buddha field.
What are we to do?
From whom are we to receive the sublime and profound
    Dharma?
Who will preserve the profound treasures?
In whom shall we place hope for protection?
It isn't right that she goes to the buddha field!
Please, we request all dakinis to ask her to stay.

The two dakinis replied,

Listen vajra brothers!
Samaya has brought you together

here and now in this pure land,
and your previous aspirations will bring you joy.

Now, as you have requested,
here are one or two, three, and four magical letters
that will help, for it's time to be in this buddha field.
The command of the dakinis is not transgressed!

They dissolved into my great hero's right and left hands, and then
progressively the entire assembly dissolved back into his wisdom
body. I remained for a moment with two dakini companions and
the hero himself. I prostrated and said,

Oh, how miserable!
Great Compassionate Guide of Beings,
please hold me, wretched and unprotected,
with your love.

Why should I return to the world?
I've no refuge, hope, protector, friends, or family.
Auspicious timing and circumstances get lost to demonic
    forces,
and except for my intimates, everyone reviles me
and denigrates the students with pure vows.

Forget about benefiting beings with the two treasures,
I've become the source of everyone's wrong views.
I lack the ability to uphold, protect, and spread the treasures.

You, my lord, the purest part of my heart,
have departed for the buddha fields.
Whatever is someone like me, a deplorable thing, to do?
I've no one from whom to request profound oral teachings.
With whom can I share my practice and innermost
    thoughts?

Unbearable, my suffering is killing me.
Now, no matter what, may I not have to go back!
It is difficult for someone like me to help worldly people.
Evil disrupts the few fortuitous connections to reveal
    profound treasures.
Companions and Dharma holders are involved only in
    other things.
Even if I were to meet the right companions through
    auspicious interdependence,
forget about meeting someone like you, my dear hero.

Understanding the descent and drawing up of essence drops
    is difficult.
Disregard the awareness body of method and wisdom in
    union,
and seeds of children, karmic debts, are continuously sown.

Forget about accomplishing
the goal of the profound and swift path!
Attachment to mere physique just brings rebirth in samsara.

Ignore the results of purification, maturation, and perfection,
and day and night, desire will be continuous.

Neglect the essence of indivisible empty appearances
and in just a few months or years everyone will come to ruin.
When I reflect this way, I realize how difficult it is
for someone like me to help others.

By the powerful force of the Lotus Guru's aspirations,
at age fifteen, I turned my back on my own home
and carried you, my hero, as Lord of the Family.

You cared for me since I was twenty-eight,
and I perfected the two stages of the supreme path.

In particular, I actually awakened the inner meaning of
　　wisdom
and opened many doors to profound treasures.

Although I made persistent wishes to vastly benefit others
by spreading the teachings of the two treasures,
I'm overwhelmed by evil forces
from perverted aspirations and untimeliness.

The more and more I think now,
the more my sorrow grows.
I can't benefit others and am just extending samsara.
I can't even think about a partner.
One like you is extremely rare.

Hero, quickly protect me
and don't let your earlier love fade away.
Pray have compassion for Dekyong Wangmo!
I request your permission—
please may I not return to the world!

I took his hand and sobbed uncontrollably. With deep love and
kindness, he replied,

Oh! Beloved and noble partner,
don't weary yourself in sorrow.
The dharmakaya is beyond coming and going.
How could our meeting and parting ever exist?
Sustain luminosity, the expanse of awareness and space,
and I will appear as the vast sky of the ultimate expanse.
Now I am abiding in space as its manifestation.

After he finished, the principal deity and the threefold retinue
transformed into a sphere of light and dissolved into the center of
my heart.

Samaya.

Ha, ha!
The ordinary and worldly Dekyong Wangmo,
the lowliest of all of his students,
wrote these confused words
within a continual state of delusion that persisted day and night,
and even though they have no purpose,
Shila Vajra encouraged me with great desire
and vajra insistence (based on our vajra bonds).

I'm just a beggar woman
putting confused perceptions into words,
but I have great students with faith in me,
and so, I offered Shila Vajra and other disciples
a little something meaningful to understand.

May virtue prevail!

Dewai Dorje's Dream

The aspect of lucidity that doesn't waver from the dharmakaya of the inward luminosity contains the mere potential to arise as sambhogakaya. From it comes half-nirmanakaya sambhogakayas, and from there, the capacity of compassion arises as nirmanakayas.[9] These appear as teachers who train beings in any and every way needed. Until there are no more sentient beings to be tamed, such teachers will unceasingly appear.

Phenomenal appearances such as those of the self, bodies, and aggregates are all ornamental appearances. They are manifestations of primordial wisdom. They are its unobstructed expressive power. All these arise, but they arise from within awareness. They appear but appear as the essence of awareness. They become liberated but are liberated in the state of awareness. Awareness that knows itself is the teacher of personal experience. It is taught that there is no lama apart from self-knowing awareness.

This was Dewai Dorje's dream.

6. Pith Instructions

This chapter showcases Dewai Dorje's elucidation of exceedingly subtle teachings on Dzogchen's view, meditation, conduct, and result. Individual pieces explicate the consummate intent of this approach, which is no easy task. Ultimately, the meaning of Dzogchen is beyond the reach of all thought and expression. Relatively, words and their meaning remain inadequate tools to lead disciples to the personal experience of direct realization. However, Dewai Dorje's mastery of the meaning of Dzogchen permeates her words, which blaze with her realization and surely penetrated the hearts and minds of those closest to her.

Among them, no one was closer to her than her student and scribe, Tsultrim Dorje (Shila Vajra). He appears in Dewai Dorje's long autobiography following a long and heartfelt meeting with Drime Ozer at Nedro Dorje Dzong. On this occasion, Dewai Dorje offered Drime Ozer some of her most precious and profound teachings such as *Drinking Vajra Water* from the *Quintessential Secret Mother Tantra*. She conferred empowerment based on the mandala of the *Secret Sky of Unelaborate Great Exaltation* and "an introduction to the state of the great connate dharmakaya." Along with these transmissions, she bestowed "the hidden naked instructions containing the pith points for the wisdom intent of the practices of union and liberation and more." Auspicious indications followed this exchange, and shortly thereafter, Dewai dreamt of Drime Ozer looking upset, along with other portents of obstacles. The following morning, feeling uneasy, she brought teachings from the dakinis on ceremonies to dispel obstacles along with auspicious substances and met Tsultrim Dorje, who brought them to Drime Ozer. This marks the first time we meet Tsultrim Dorje, the one who was destined to serve both treasure revealers as a conduit for their most profound teachings and connection.

Tsultrim Dorje was much more than just an ordinary monk and scribe. He was a student of Dudjom Lingpa, Drime Ozer's prophesized scribe and a heart son of both Drime Ozer and Dewai Dorje. He both requested and wrote down many of her teachings. She addressed much of her personal writing to him. In the acute grief following Drime Ozer's and her son's passing, Tsultrim Dorje was faithfully by her side through the travails that followed. A true vajra brother, Tsultrim Dorje was filled with true devotion that induced Dewai Dorje to share her most precious Dzogchen realization. His kindness defies description.

This realization is on full display in these selections of pith instructions. Classic Dzogchen teachings such as "the four without the three" (*bzhi cha gsum bral*) are presented in "View, Meditation, Conduct, and Result." Given to introduce students to the nature of mind, this pointing out involves removing past, present, and future (the three) to reveal the timeless and infinite expanse of awareness itself (the fourth). Sometimes referred to as the time of the dharmata, or ultimate reality, it is the time beyond all time, beyond becoming, abiding, and ceasing. Arriving in the experience of this beyond, and dwelling there, is the great import of the Dzogchen path.

The same selection also includes the practice of threefold sky, whereby mind is melded with the outer expanse of sky, an alchemy that triggers and enhances recognition of awareness. Such profound pointing-out instructions, succinctly delivered with Dewai Dorje's characteristic eloquence, leave no doubt about her comprehensive mastery of these techniques and testify to her skill in imparting them to others. Bringing her students to the nonreferential openness and clarity that lie at the heart of Dzogchen practice required Dewai Dorje to be there herself. That was her true home, her only place of real solace, and of course, her ultimate lama. Being in the world was bearable only due to that home.

"Dakini Gyepe Dorje's Offering" further invites us into this wakeful, spacious state of awareness. The use of this name may come from a dream in Dewai Dorje's thirty-fifth year. In it she met two dakinis and Drime Ozer, who invited her to visit the Glorious Copper-Colored Mountain. There, she encountered the Lake-Born Vajra, surrounded by King Trisong Deutsen and twenty-five disciples and a great gathering of others. She conversed at length with Yeshe Tsogyal and Dakini Dorje Tso. They told Dewai Dorje that her work in the world was not complete, counseled her not to weaken her commitment to benefit beings, and promised to help her fulfill the dakinis' prophecies. Dewai Dorje begged for more advice from them and likened her suffering in the world to the suffering of the lowest of all the hell realms, the Avici Hell. Dakini Dorje Tso counseled her,

> Noble Lady, if you can benefit even a single sentient being, the wishes of the guru and consort are realized. If you decode one single chapter of profound Dharma teaching, even if it doesn't even benefit one other person, the wishes of the guru and consort are fulfilled. If you strive only to benefit beings with complete integrity of your vows and commitments, even if misguided beings slander you, the wishes of the guru and consort are fulfilled.

They then offered an extensive feast, and Yeshe Tsogyal entrusted Dewai Dorje with the fifty-eight parts of the Extremely Secret Heart Essence of the Dakinis cycle of teachings on golden paper, as a whispered transmission. She gave her symbolic empowerment and the secret name, Dakini Gyepe Dorje.

The bulk of the jewel instructions in chapter 6 are directions to the same place, the clear and empty nature of mind: rigpa, awareness itself. It is there and only there that joy and sorrow can be experienced as the same taste, the taste of illusion. "Rest in the Expanse of Nonduality" gives us the secret weapon to do this: the practice of *chod*, "severance." This is a method to cut the belief that things exist as they appear, enabling practitioners to transcend duality and arrive thereafter in the inconceivable experience of all things as equal and pure. The resonant vibration of the powerful seed syllable *phet*, weaving through the practice's rich melodies, dissolves all reference points of self, other, good, bad, right, wrong, happy, and sad. Instantaneously, it rips away the flimsy façade of true existence and blasts the chod practitioner directly into unimpeded openness.

Dewai Dorje relied upon this practice for some of the most intense emotional and physical pain of her life. She held it with the Dzogchen view, as she did with all of her practice and teachings. This view is the "pith" of all her instructions. Chapter 7 lets us feel even more personally how it was the throbbing life force of her correspondences with her community.

SECRET CONSORTS

A "secret consort" doesn't refer to a partner who is hidden due to not being able to keep the vows of individual liberation. A sublime *consort* who directly reveals all the noble qualities of the wisdom of the great *secret* inner meaning is a secret consort. "Wish-fulfilling jewels" (*yid bzhin nor bu*) are just material substances of the world, no matter how good they are, and only bring temporary satisfaction of desires. Since the result of ultimate perfect buddhahood is very difficult to realize, that's not what the meaning is here.

The sublime and unsurpassed source, the secret wisdom minds of all buddhas throughout triple time, is referred to as a *wish* (*yid*). Because the buddhas' wisdom minds are free from the eight conceptual limitations, endowed with the three gateways to liberation, and naturally endowed with all noble qualities of kayas and wisdoms, they *fulfill* (*bzhin*).[1] Furthermore, they un*mistakenly* (*nor*) reveal the utterly perfect, profound approach through myriad spiritual techniques. These are marvelous, enlightened activities of compassion and manifold skillful means that can be easily engaged. They protect disciples as *children* (*bu*) to be tamed and establish them on the grounds of liberation through the totally pure path. Therefore, I have named the one whose name is difficult to say except when there is a purpose in doing so, my secret consort, Yizhin Norbu, Wish-Fulfilling Jewel.[2]

Kunzang Dekyong Wangmo [Dewai Dorje] wrote down some crazy talk for Shila Vajra.

May virtue prevail!

PRIMORDIALLY PURE

Primordially pure, awareness is unimpeded
and unbound by alteration or attachment.
Sustain this state of unattached empty cognizance—
awareness, self-existent wakefulness
beyond the mind of conceptual ideas—
a primordially liberated realization
as your uncontrived innate nature,
and you will seize the everlasting kingdom of the dharmakaya.

Written by Sukha Vajra [Dewai Dorje].

VIEW, MEDITATION, CONDUCT, AND RESULT

Homage to the guru!

Here is just a general explanation for internalizing practice. Remain in the experience of knowing, just as it is, the exalted state of the great primordially empty and baseless nature of all phenomenal existence, everything of samsara and nirvana. Then, don't space out externally, internally, or remain in a state of complacent indifference. Don't pursue thoughts that have already gone, but rest in the experience of its brilliance, lucid to itself. Don't invite future thoughts. Rest in the pristine clarity of this great primordial wisdom. Finally, don't get swept away by present thinking, but rest vividly in this, a luminous expanse, free from attachment to anything that arises. Remaining wide awake in great uncontrived and unimpeded awareness, "the fourth without the three," is called awareness endowed with four special features.[3] It's the unique approach of the Dzogchen tradition.

In sum, there are three essentials for a practitioner's path. First, don't modify or correct anything in the state of meditation. Second, don't repress or establish anything in post-meditation, and third, be free from anything to attain as the result.

The view is the realization that samsara and nirvana are without basis or origin. Meditation is the recognition that everything encompassed by the noble qualities of the path, including the wisdoms and kayas of the result, is the primordial wisdom of the inherently lucid dharmakaya. Conduct is to effortlessly and naturally see that the infinite appearances of the experiences of both existence and peace have never been anything other than the manifestation of the ground's expressive power. Self-knowing awareness, groundless and free from any origin, is the actualization of the space of the great three-kaya equality, just as it is.

Outer space is empty sky. Inner space is empty mind. Secret space is empty awareness. The perfection in the ground within the great inseparability of this threefold space is called the result.

There are many ways that the key points of view and meditation are taught. However, ultimately, the basis of your lama's pith instructions is to recognize that the groundless and rootless nature of your own mind is the great nature that pervades all of samsara and nirvana. Don't manipulate, accept, or reject anything that you perceive. Just drop into this unfabricated, natural state of mind. When you do, after some time you will attain stability in awareness and actualize the space of the three-kaya equality. Then it's sure you will be heading toward the result.

Sukha Vajra [Dewai Dorje] wrote this to fulfill the wishes of all worthy practitioners.

May it be virtuous!

Dakini Gyepe Dorje's Offering

How wonderful!

The accomplished master is the Great Omniscient One.
The exalted state of Samantabhadra
is the fundamental nature of the Great Perfection.
It's an unborn, unimpeded, and skylike experience
where appearances that don't truly exist
arise and become liberated of their own accord.

This state is free from grasping to the universe
and all it contains as objects of purity,
since the nature of ultimate reality
isn't an object brought about
through a practice of meditation.

Relative appearances based on dualistic perception
are empty by nature, utterly beyond the reach
of all conceptual limitation.
Appearances and their empty nature are indivisible.
They're the unity of method and wisdom.

To enjoy this elixir of primordial wisdom—
blissful emptiness, freedom from joy—
you must render awareness
beyond birth and destruction
evident in your own experience.

Primordial wisdom has always expressed itself
in unceasing manifest displays of dynamic energy.
These myriad appearances arise as its ornamentation.

What point is there in demarcating or ranking these?
Buddhahood has never been achieved through conditioned
   phenomena!

Within the unconditioned state
of open and all-encompassing relaxation,
practice the yoga of ultimate luminosity.

What has been said by Dakini Gyepe Dorje [Dewai Dorje],
the consort connected through pure karma and prayers from earlier
   times,
is offered just as crazy advice and lies.

May virtue prevail!

THE MUSINGS OF A THOUGHTLESS
OLD LADY

Once you render unconfused and innate wisdom evident, you must rest at ease in that state without altering awareness. Even though thoughts may arise as you abide there, they are clear and transparent in themselves and dissolve like waves back into the ocean. Even though you may experience various perceptions, they naturally become liberated if there's no attachment to them. Even though consciousness may appear in thought formations, these neither help nor harm awareness, just like slicing water with a sword. Mere perceptions themselves are never beyond the domain of the empty space of ultimate reality. They are like rain mixed with water, indivisible and mutually nonexclusive.

To say it simply, the appearances of thoughts and perceptions are similar to camphor dust that is blown by the wind. Awareness remains unchanging within the experience of ultimate reality. It is like the circumference of the sky that stretches infinitely. Awareness has nothing to do with the efforts and activities of ordinary mind. I have never found the needed innate state of natural mind to be a so-called awareness that is embodied like a guest. Nor have I found such a guest arriving on top of a "meditation" that is like an open cushion. Though I have searched many days for awareness, I haven't found it in the post-meditation experience either, by keeping watch on it like a thief that might vanish. Now, I've totally let go of trying to see awareness intellectually! Everything I perceive has become just like reflections in a mirror or paintings of butter lamps.

Ha, ha, ha!

Once I overheard some practitioners in discussion, and though I too have acted as a sentry in analyzing my own mind, I have never come to the end of thoughts! So, I, Dewai Dorje, wrote down a few lies.

May virtue prevail!

MEDITATION AND POST-MEDITATION

Why look for a practice that alternates between meditation and post-meditation? From now on, you don't need anything other than the essential path of great placement within the uncontrived state of recognizing awareness. If, on the other hand, you want to define meditation and post-meditation, then meditation is like the sky. It has no directionality. It lacks the slightest mental chaff about birth, cessation, bondage, liberation, existence, nonexistence, going, coming, samsara, nirvana, and so forth. Open and pervasive, the state of meditation is devoid of all conceptual elaboration. It is the infinite great purity and equality of the dharmakaya.

Post-meditation is like alchemy that transforms iron into gold. You must apply the key points for directly encountering awareness, the oral instructions that teach how the six consciousnesses become liberated by themselves. Then, everything that appears just arises and becomes liberated in and of itself as your own true nature of awareness.

If you say that you've recognized awareness but need to intellectually analyze your meditation and post-meditation, this means that you still consider realization within the meditation state to be buddha and thoughts within the post-meditation state to be confusion. It means you're still attached to antidotes and bound up in shackles of hope and fear. It's like saying you have eyes but can't see anything.

If that is the case, just as you would need treatment to clear away an eye disease, you need a method to actualize, just as it is, the exalted state of the Great Perfection, the nature of ultimate reality. The method is the pith instructions for differentiating mind and awareness. Once you have completely understood them, the iron grip of a mind attached to its meditation is loosened, and you are free within the great primordial liberation of non-meditation beyond mind. I wonder whether that even comes close to the realization of the great treasure revealers, the father and son.

Otherwise, if you each examine your practice, you might realize that you are, in fact, holding the *alaya*, the all-ground consciousness, and the clear radiance of the intellect to be mind's ultimate essence. Awareness during meditation that looks for mind's clarity with the mental consciousness—as well as conceit about awareness in post-meditation through perpetuating positive or negative concepts with the subtle mental consciousness—are like confusing costume jewelry for the real thing. You are deceiving yourselves. The mara of pride is the meditation, and the long-handed mara is the meditator.[4] When you fall under the power of both, you will definitely have reached the abyss of a major misunderstanding.

Therefore, without clinging to the mind of dualistic confusion, fully internalize your lama's direct instructions and decide on one thing. Hold that as your ground. Nurture the self-liberation of its expressiveness. Settle in the actualization of that state, and then, as you know, presently and afterward, there will be no need to meditate on an object. If you decide upon that with certainty, it appears to me that this is the real meaning of the practice of Trekcho. I have no idea about making the mind agitated and contrived!

Ha, ha, ha!

From a meditation of infinite confusion, Dewai Dorje composed some lies in post-meditation.

Sitting and Moping Around

Homage to Kunkyong Lingpa,
the wisdom mind incarnation of the Lotus Guru from Orgyen,
who embodies all triumphant buddhas.

Free and advantageous,
a precious human rebirth mustn't be wasted.
Once you've attained it,
rely upon a spiritual guide
and infuse body, speech, and mind with the sacred Dharma.

Practice the teachings of the Buddha,
aligned in word and meaning.

Since I met an actual buddha of this Golden Age,
I don't want to squander my precious human body
and am sitting around.

Families are impermanent,
like visitors in a temporary market.
Not wanting frivolous talk or disputes,
I am moping around.

My moping around
is because I'm not tied by knots of stinginess
to the tethering poles of samsara:
wealth, material things, and such.
Such entanglements are just illusions of dualistic perception.

I have relied upon a fully qualified holy being,
and meditated alone in isolated retreat in the mountains,

to sever the basis of such engagements:
attachment to the self.
My moping around is just that.

Beings of the six classes are, by nature, our own parents,
and though I'm uncertain
who has been my actual mother,
to repay their kindness,
I am sitting around in the isolated mountains.

Aggregates are impermanent, like bubbles in water.
Results of the good and evil we do ripen on us.
Since I don't know what to engage or avoid,
I am moping around in mountain solitudes.

By taking refuge in the lama,
whatever we desire
becomes the path to liberation.
With intense longing, faith, and devotion,
and relying on solitude,
I am just doing what my lama told me to do.
I have tamed my own mind,
which was as hard as a horn,
and now I am just sitting around.

The qualities of isolated mountain retreat
are beyond words,
but if I were to say a little bit about them,
they seem to be as follows.

Through isolated mountain retreat,
you can reverse attachment to samsara
and sow the seed of liberation.

You can see the buddhas' wisdom qualities
and increase your faith in the Dharma.

Your kindness and compassion can well forth,
and anger and negativity lessen.

In isolated mountain retreat,
you will have no attachment to friends
or aggression toward enemies.

You increase your recitations of refuge,
are protected by the lamas,
and can imbibe their ambrosial instructions.

In isolated mountain retreat,
you can behold the fundamental nature
of your true mode of being
and directly experience self-existing wakefulness.

You can seize the seat of awareness
and realize the view of emptiness.

In isolated mountain retreat,
things occur naturally and without interruption,
but you don't accept, reject, expect, or fear anything.

You will realize the result, the four kayas,
and alone, conduct yourself completely conscientiously,
spontaneously benefiting yourself and others.

This is just a brief overview
of the special qualities of isolated mountain retreat.

My sitting and moping around
is aligning my life with the Dharma.

I have many virtuous spiritual friends,
but I am doing what my supreme lama,
the inseparable regent of the victorious buddhas,
endowed with threefold kindness,
told me to do, both for myself and others.

Chowang told my student Tupzang, "Be happy and don't mope around doing nothing!" As a reply, the beggar lady named Dewai who has no freedom, practices samsara, and has nothing but faults like an animal, wrote this, just as something new.

May it be virtuous!

Rest in the Expanse of Nonduality

Heart Emanation of the Lake-Born Vajra from Orgyen,
Annihilator of Evil, Hero, and Heruka,
Awareness holder Vimarasmi—I bow before you.
Bless me to mix my mind with the Dharma.

How wonderful! Listen up, fortunate noble son.

Awareness, primordially pure and utterly open, is the
    dharmakaya.
Beyond characteristics such as color, it is present in and of itself.
Carefully, sustain it within uncontrived luminosity,
destroy, forcefully, the evil spirit of "I" and self-attachment,
and without getting too happy or sad,
remain in the expanse of nonduality.

When your prized illusory aggregates,
an imputed body based on confusion, pains unbearably,
don't vacillate between hoping for benefit and fearing harm.
Cut through it with the profound melodies of the swift path of
    pacification,[5]
and take ahold of your inheritance:
the teachings on the self-liberation of whatever appears.

When delusional perceptions of duality rise up as demons,
and chaotic appearances of external dangers swirl like the wind,
reverse these unpleasant sights and sounds by severing their
    cause—anger—with *phet*,
the great penetrating knowledge of selflessness.
Grab ahold of your inheritance:
the exalted state of unimpeded nonexistence.

Rest and let everything that arises be as it is,
without altering anything.

Behold the natural face of the four kayas,
the purity and equality of all phenomenal existence,
and you will arrive at the everlasting kingdom,
the youthful vase kaya of inward luminosity.

These words are lies from a simple and frivolous lady,
offered as a joke before the sword of awareness [Ledrel Tsal].

SELF-OCCURRING AWARENESS IS
GREAT PRIMORDIAL PURITY

How wondrous! Listen up, noble monk.

Self-occurring awareness is great primordial purity.
Beyond the mind of intellectual ideas,
it is inconceivable and inexpressible.
In truth, it's our sublime buddha nature.

All things of samsara and nirvana
are the very nature of this awareness.
It is a way of being
that is uncontrived and fresh.
Its view neither divides nor excludes samsara or nirvana.
Rest in this state of nonreferential openness.

Its meditation must be free from grasping and focal points.
Rest in this state of innate, ongoing luminosity.

Its conduct must be like waves and water,
self-arising and self-liberating,
beyond rejecting or accepting.

The result must be unchangeable self-knowing awareness.
Rest in this state of unimpeded openness.

Composed by one named Sukha [Dewai Dorje].

A Fantastic Show

How wonderful! Fortunate ones, listen.
Self-occurring awareness, pure from the beginning,
transcends being an object of deluded conceptual construct.
Since gods and demons aren't other than mind's magical
     creations,
don't entertain hope or fear about them, noble child.

Your own body, a vivid arrangement of wisdom deities,
has always lacked truly existent characteristics of "I" and "self."
Within the fresh state where there is no attachment and fixation,
all phenomena of samsara and nirvana arise
as manifestations of its dynamic energy.
Their natural state is indescribable,
beyond birth and death.

Don't be attached to the self, noble child.
Grab ahold of the instructions for enjoying illness and being
     happy upon death,
and rest within the dharmakaya for the greatest pains.
Sustain the essence of the sambhogakaya for the medium pains,
and engage the nirmanakaya for the smallest pains.
Recognize illness to be the indivisibility of the three kayas!

The supreme deity, self-occurring awareness,
is complete with the medicinal aspects of the five wisdoms.
When you don't grasp the demonic illness of the five poisons,
they arise as the ornaments
of all appearances, possibilities, samsara, and nirvana.
Don't reject or accept the magical manifestations
of all phenomena, noble child.

Rest within the indivisibility of appearance and emptiness.
In accord with the trainings for taming outwardly,
be a captain who leads through faith.
Inwardly, love all beings as per the excellent path of bodhisattvas.
Secretly, be a practitioner who realizes the equal taste of samsara
    and nirvana
as pure from the beginning.
The show is fantastic!
Don't worry, there must some purport to a parrot's advice offered
    by me,
a carefree liar,
but if others see this,
they'll feel anxious.

Sukha Vajra [Dewai Dorje] wrote this.

May it be virtuous!

UTTER DELIGHTS

Listen up, dear son of triumphant buddhas!
Don't forget about your earlier promise
to go into isolated mountain retreat as you committed.
Not needing activities of the eight worldly concerns
is utterly delightful.

Self-occurring awareness is beyond arising, ceasing, and abiding.
Rest within this great primordial wisdom,
beyond the mind of conceptual ideas.
Realizing samsara and nirvana to be the dharmakaya
is utterly delightful.

You don't need lots of profound Dharma teachings.
Practice the quintessence of the Father's deep wisdom mind.
Attaining the siddhis that are your inheritance
is utterly delightful.

The full ripening effects of taking offerings is heavy,
so avoid them like poison.
Go off far away and practice in the isolated mountains.
Accomplishing the benefit of oneself and others
is utterly delightful.

You don't need agreeable friends
who can be the basis for accumulating negativity.
Alone, meditate on the secret path of luminosity
in isolated mountain retreat.
Having no need for jealousy based on duality
is utterly delightful.

You don't need all kinds of nonsensical talk.
Strive constantly to accomplish practice of the three root wisdom
   deities.
Receiving the supreme and common siddhis
is utterly delightful.

Don't constantly roam from country to town to monastery to
   village.
Stay put and keep your thoughts to yourself.
Apply yourself to the key points
of practicing the wisdom channels, winds, and vital essences.
Bringing wind-mind into the central channel
is utterly delightful.

Practice the profound and sacred Dharma to be happy now and
   in the future.
It is possible for you to take the jewel of benefiting everyone
in your own hands
by practicing these key points.

These words come from a carefree and simple wandering beggar
who hasn't even a hair's tip worth of positive qualities,
but nevertheless, I wrote down whatever advice
came to mind, with the best intentions.
Remember this and there'll be great benefit.
Otherwise, if we don't have the chance to meet again,
we made the interdependence for us to gather as teacher and
   retinue
on the isle of the Glorious Mountain of Lotus Light in our next
   life.

This was composed by one named Sukha [Dewai Dorje].

A Chattering Parrot's Advice

I pray to my peerless master, awareness holder Kunkyong Lingpa,
ultimately indivisible from the father, Padmasambhava,
all-knowing throughout triple time—
please, enable my mind to ripen and become free.

Amazing! Listen, heart son.
The excellent support of a human body
is even greater than a wish-fulfilling jewel.
Don't squander it but depend upon fully qualified lamas.
When meeting them, my son, don't survey their faults.
If you do, faults, by nature, cause more discursive thinking.
Instead, with pure perception,
mingle your mind with the lama's wisdom mind
through the four empowerments.

When studying, contemplating, and meditating on the path,
be conscientious in stilling your body, speech, and mind,
and be free from selfishness, pride, and greed.
Align yourself with these crucial points and practice in stages.

When keeping company with vajra siblings,
cast away competitiveness, jealousy,
and activities of the eight worldly concerns.
Anger is the cause of breaking samaya, my son.
With humility, you get along with everyone.

When practicing in lonesome mountain retreat,
don't rove like a dog through lands, towns, monasteries, and
    villages.
Stay where you are and bring the mind's perceptions inward.

While diligently training in meditative concentration,
don't be concerned with this life's activities of the eight worldly
concerns, child.
If you do, you will run externally after fame and respect.
Sustain yourself with humble food and clothing as an ascetic.

When meditating on Dzogchen, the secret path of luminosity,
don't make the noises of village rituals to subdue demons.
There are many hindrances to meditation when the mind isn't free.
It is extremely important to set boundaries
and employ the key instructions for body, speech, and mind.

When the noble qualities of experience and realization unfold in
your mind,
don't explain them to unfit vessels, those with broken samaya, my
son.
If you do, you risk contaminating these qualities,
which are signs of the path.
Without getting distracted,
rest in the state of non-distraction and non-meditation.

In brief, at all times and circumstances,
stay humbly in retreat, far away in the solitudes of the mountains.
Meditate upon the oral instructions of the lama as the basis for
your practice.
You don't need the activities of the eight worldly concerns,
which just cause delusion.
The best companion is your own self-occurring wisdom.
Leave far behind negative companions caught up in samsara's
duality.
Don't search for clothing.
Rather, light the lamp of the mystic fire.

You don't need illusory material things.
They are just mirages.

Train in wind yoga,[6] the supreme undefiled essence,
and cast away attachment to contaminated defiled food.

Your own pure perception is to possess the most beautiful place.
Village monasteries are the cause of worldly quarrels and
disputes.
Needing nothing, take your seat alone in the solitudes of the
mountains
with the seven exalted jewels as your wealth and possessions.

Rely on four things for this and future lifetimes.
Never assume an ordinary way of being with the support of your
body, son.
Rest, and never separate from seeing your ordinary body
appearing as the wisdom deity,
the sound of your voice resounding as mantra,
and your thoughts arising as the vast expanse of the dharmakaya.
Try to practice this instruction, heart son.

The unborn empty space of ground
can't be understood through expressing it with words.
For example, it is like the clarity of a mirror.
The unborn dharmakaya has no obscurations
within its inner and outer clarity,
just as the heart of the sun does not obscure
the radiance of its own light, child.
Thoughts, like swords slicing water,
ultimately don't benefit or harm, child.

Unimpeded awareness is unobstructed
and pure from the outset, heart child.
The view of no-view is the highest view,
unconfined and nonreferential.
The meditation of no-meditation is the best meditation,
the innate state of effortless meditation.

The conduct of no-conduct is the best conduct,
the conduct of natural liberation beyond accepting and rejecting.

Unimpeded and pure from the beginning,
the ground is the dharmakaya.
The path is the unceasing sambhogakaya.
Their capacity as compassion manifests as nirmanakayas,
which benefit beings.
The result is ascension upon the throne of self-awareness.

Listen up, fortunate child.
The profound instructions that your sole father and lama directly
    taught you
are special teachings, which are the essence of the swift path,
the highest approach of the secret Great Perfection
wherein Trekcho and Togal are practiced indivisibly.
If you practice these progressively,
you will behold your true dharmakaya nature,
your own unborn awareness.

Unimpeded primordial purity is the dharmakaya.
Inconceivable and inexpressible,
it is beyond the mind of conceptual ideas.

Empty and clear, it is unobstructed,
occurring in and of itself.

Completely open and pervasive without center or periphery,
it is unconfined space devoid of reference points.

Groundless and rootless, it is and has always been
utterly pure and naturally free,
beyond any attachment to clarity or emptiness.

It is innate and spontaneously manifesting
as a great boundless and wide-open expanse.

Practice this, the sacred yoga of the intrinsic perfection of the
    three kayas,
and then, upon the first luminosity of death,
when the child hops upon its mother's lap,
you will seize the throne of awareness.[7]

That is where we Dharma siblings shall meet,
within this inseparability of threefold space.

Apart from this, it is sure that this beggar lady
who wanders in samsara,
doesn't have any advice or oral instructions.

Because you insisted, the one named Sukha Vajra wrote some
    words
like a chattering parrot, so as not to disappoint you.
Keep these in your vajra heart and you might get a bit of
    understanding.
Later we'll gather as teacher and retinue in a pure realm.

This parroted advice was written by the unspiritual beggar lady named
Sukha [Dewai Dorje] to increase excellent virtue.

May it be virtuous!

A Response to a Student Who Maintains Samaya on the Topic of Trekcho

You must decide with certainty that all the infinite appearances of myriad phenomena are the magical display of great primordial wisdom awareness. Then, since they rise up as ground awareness, it won't matter whether or not you're able to uproot their seeds. Externally, don't analyze objects of perception, the things that are "out there." Inwardly, don't withdraw into the expanse of the alaya, the all-ground. In between these two, don't contrive empty awareness, the nature of mind, by intellectual ideas. Let go completely without evaluating anything that appears or arises. No matter what you perceive, nothing is outside the sphere of the dharmadhatu, the ultimate expanse.

You don't need wisdom deity practice. It's just intellectual fabrication. You don't need mantra accumulation. It's just discursive thinking. You don't need to have meditated by focusing the mind. This splinters ultimate reality through dualistic fixation.

Since self-occurring wakefulness transcends objects to reject or antidote, relax body, speech, and mind naturally right as they are in the uncontrived state. Since all appearances are the primordial wisdom of nirmanakaya, there is no need to accept or reject anything. The unimpeded gateways of luminosity are such that there is a readiness for anything and everything to appear. Since those appearances are the primordial wisdom of the sambhogakaya, there's no need to suppress or establish anything. Since self-knowing awareness from the very beginning is unconditioned empty space, the wisdom of the dharmakaya beyond thought and expression, there isn't any need to strive effortfully toward a result of getting something.

In sum, rest in the deep confidence born of the direct certainty that samsara and nirvana are the equality of the three kayas. Don't patch ultimate reality by engaging with conditions that stir up the winds through the practices of spreading, dissolving, drawing, gathering them, and so forth.[8]

Everything arises from the generative potential of primordial wisdom. Until relative phenomena come to an end within ultimate reality, superficial appearances—which are the appropriation of mere perception, mere cognizance—definitely will arise unceasingly. You must realize that everything appearing is your own perception. Then, settle down into the natural state, leaving things just as they are, without any need to add or remove anything. This is because everything is the ornamentation of awareness, the dynamic energy of primordial wisdom manifesting as phenomenal appearances.

Advice for a Sublime Monk

Listen up, my fortunate Dharma friend!

Awareness is primordially pure, unimpeded, and free from
  conceptual construct.
Beyond characteristics such as color, it's a sphere of luminosity.
Carefully sustain the continuity of this unfabricated natural
  state, and
dualistic perceptions of "self" will be liberated within the space
  of evenness.

Don't get drawn into thinking about outer objects
and searching for the mind with the mind.

Don't withdraw inwardly
and continue the proliferation of thoughts.

Don't get swept away in hope and fear,
but sustain self-knowing awareness
as an uncontrived state of natural letting-be.

The exalted state of the "four without three" is exactly that.[9]

If you haven't realized the ultimate state of nonduality
beyond the mind of conceptual ideas,
you won't become enlightened
through childish teachings made by intellect.

Though I have low intelligence
and don't even understand the meaning of *ah*,[10]
I am just offering whatever comes to mind as a reminder of
  practice.

May this be medicine that nourishes practice,
when excellently seen by those with eyes of vast intelligence!

The carefree and frivolous Sukha Vajra [Dewai Dorje],
her fingers encouraged by the wind,
virtuously wrote these words for the sublime monk.

May virtue prevail!

FOUR QUALITIES OF THE UNCONTRIVED STATE

Our Guide of Beings who embodies all triumphant buddhas,
Protector of the Dharma, Pema Ledrel Tsal,
manifesting inseparably as the jewel upon my chakra of great
    bliss—
bless me to integrate the Dharma with my mind.

Self-occurring awareness has always been completely pure
and free from any basis.

Primordially liberated from subject-object duality,
it is the great equal sphere of samsara and nirvana,
where acceptance and rejection have never been known
and confusion and liberation are cleansed within the ground.

It is the awakened mind—
awareness that is uncontrived no matter what appears.

It is experienced as *utter clarity* once all unawareness and
    ignorance are cleansed,
alert wakefulness through uncontrived resting in the natural
    state,
open spaciousness beyond fixation on the mind's clear and empty
    nature,
and *vivid brightness* through purifying the apprehending mind
    and its objects.

If you practice the uncontrived state endowed with these four
    qualities,
you will witness the true nature of Buddha Samantabhadra.

Then, once you actualize the result of self-occurring primordial
   wisdom,
you will become liberated in the youthful vase kaya in this very
   lifetime.

These words, requested by the monk,
come from the unspiritual beggar lady Dewai Dorje,
who doesn't have any spiritual advice
but just wrote down whatever came to mind.

May virtue prevail!

The Undeluded Meaning of the Great Fundamental Nature

How splendid!
Awareness is primordially pure, transcending word, thought, and
   all expression,
but its hue is indeterminate and perfected as its spontaneously
   present qualities.
Carefully sustain this state of uncontrived naturalness and
deluded fixation on the self will be liberated within the space of
   nonduality.

Although phenomena are apprehended
with the characteristics of relative truth,
they are pure within ultimate reality,
the state free from all conceptual limitation.

Whatever appears and arises
is the dynamic energy of great primordial wisdom
and is equal as the transcendent state of the dharmakaya,
primordially liberated and beyond ordinary mind.

Since there is no division, exclusion, rejection, or acceptance
   there,
seize this, the everlasting kingdom, by abiding within its
   actualization.

In such a way, the undeluded meaning of the great fundamental
   nature
does not exist through expression from a woman like me,

but, to fulfill the wishes of my students,
I said a little bit about it.

Don't hold this as an example but practice the key points.

Dewai Dorje wrote down whatever came to mind.

May it be virtuous!

7. PERSONAL ADVICE AND LETTERS

Imagine. It is July on the vast plains of eastern Tibet. Summertime is bursting out after a long cold winter. Everything blooms that can. Green fields are carpeted with white, red, purple, and yellow flowers, exuberantly saluting the sun. Midday winds are warm. Far off on the infinite horizon, distant roars of thunder dragons from billowing clouds punctuate happy birdsong melodies. A small cluster of yak-hair tents with carpets warming in the sun and open air, like black pebbles floating on a grass sea, hold the teacher Dewai Dorje and her disciples. Nomadic, free, and vibrant with Dharma blessings, they camp for a spell on their pilgrimage. Devotedly, a disciple gazes at Dewai Dorje, her long majestic braids flowing and her short bangs moving gently in the breeze. The disciple asks, "What is the nature of awareness?" Dewai Dorje is resting, spacious and open, at ease in the nature of mind, and from that state her response wells forth on its own.

Welcome to Chapter 7. By far the longest chapter, it may also be the crown jewel of this book. This is because it's here that we are blessed with an even more intimate journey into Dewai Dorje's Great Perfection realization transmitted through her relationships, in the one-on-one flavor of the shaldam tradition. These selections of custom-tailored spiritual guidance, based on firsthand knowledge of another, paint a picture of her social landscape. As the vehicle for some of her most tender, moving, and penetrating teachings, personal instruction lies at the core of her brilliant teaching style. A teacher of humble monks and nuns, scholars, cave-dwelling yogis, laypeople, and royalty, Dewai Dorje had a core group of students, but as her influence and renown grew, many included themselves among her followers.

These disciples, both in her close entourage and more distant ones, are named in the selections contained in chapter 7. Some may have met her just once or twice, while others were likely by her side continually. Select information about some, when available, has been included in notes. What is abundantly clear is that Dewai Dorje's later life was richly infused with the deep, loving, and uniquely meaningful connection that defines true guru-disciple relationship. Her students sustained her as she did them. This mutuality enhanced their individual and collective realization. Devotion, the elixir and life force of the Great Perfection's alchemical transmission, permeates each selection here. Inhale it, as you feast on these essential instructions.

"Threefold Space," a teaching already seen in chapter 6, opens the way. Dewai Dorje elucidates this teaching in greater detail in her commentary, "Necklace to Delight the Fortunate," composed from notes she took on Drime Ozer's teachings of his father Dudjom Lingpa's seminal text, *Buddhahood without Meditation*, commonly known as *Nang Jang*.[1] The import and impact of *Nang Jang* on her own practice and experience of Dzogchen was colossal. A series of visionary encounters with realized beings, *Nang Jang* reveals the extraordinarily intimate and direct way Dudjom Lingpa received and internalized the highest teachings about ultimate reality. In one of the encounters, the awareness holder Dudul Dorje introduces Dudjom Lingpa to the nature of space, a pith instruction itself, through the teaching of threefold space.

In her commentary to *Nang Jang*, Dewai Dorje elaborates upon the threefold presentation of external, internal, and secret nonconceptual space and further clarifies the import of this pointing-out instruction. In the Dzogchen tradition, space represents the ultimate nature of reality, described as possessing seven vajra qualities. These are that it is invincible, indestructible, real, incorruptible, unmoving, unchanging, and completely unable to be obstructed.[2] In the same text, Dewai Dorje also summarizes the four promises (a "vajra's four promises") mentioned in the first piece. They are presented as four impossibilities: the impossibility of ordinary beings to understand the ultimate nature of reality, the impossibility of fortunate beings to not gain confidence in it once correctly understood through experience, the impossibility of not being liberated through it, and the impossibility of not finding complete enlightenment thereby.[3]

The subsequent selections in the chapter weave, through verse and prose, the same tapestry of Dzogchen teaching. These are all essential upadesha instructions: skillful methods for introducing students to the unconditioned nature of mind itself. This is the sublime and unbroken legacy of pointing-out instructions, enabling adepts to make a clear distinction between ordinary mind (*sems*) and awareness (*rig pa*). It is composed of the warp and weft of Dewai Dorje's loom, upon which she interlaced multicolored yarn to help each and every one of her students understand the crucial key point of awareness. Indeed, introduction to mind's nature is essential, but the main purpose is to induce genuine recognition of it in the disciple. This recognition forms the basis for all subsequent Great Perfection practices and associated clarifying instructions.

For example, the clarifying practice instruction for Lama Tupten Gyatso gifts us in awesome conciseness a laser-sharp differentiation between ordinary mind and awareness. The examples used to understand the difference between ordinary mind and awareness are water and mercury falling on dry earth, respectively.[4] Her use of such instructions attests to her saturation with the tradition as well as to her skillfulness in employing its methods on an individualized basis.

"Advice for Chorap," another exquisite pointing-out instruction, explains the four kayas and five wisdoms specifically from a Dzogchen perspective. What this shows is how self-knowing awareness is the basis for all. While the entirety of awareness's extremely refined and variegated wisdom expressivity is ultimately indivisible and nondual from it, the expressivity presences itself with subtle nuance. This explanation of the five wisdoms—dharmadhatu, mirrorlike, evenness, discriminating, and all-accomplishing—is thus an exceptionally advanced introduction to the way mind's nature experiences itself.[5] What Dewai Dorje is introducing can best be understood by those with some measure of familiarity with Dzogchen meditation. Otherwise, it's inaccessible. In the colophon, Dewai Dorje tells us she was aiming for an easily understandable presentation.

The chapter continues with selections of personalized advice, almost all laying out the ground, path, view, meditation, conduct, and result of the Great Perfection. Indeed, her explanation of the foundational meditation techniques of *shamatha*, peaceful abiding, and *vipashyana*, deep insight, is wholly through a Dzogchen lens. Likewise, she explains within this context how the entire framework of sessions of meditation and post-meditation melts into one unending flow of awareness continuity. It would not be an exaggeration to say, as Dewai Dorje does in her marvelous instructions for the daughter of Miwang Sakyong, that what we are reading herein is equal to her "heart, eyes, and life itself."

The vast and comprehensive letter for the monastic community of Sanglung Yang is notable for its encompassment of foundational teachings, as well as quotations from important lineage masters. The entire path, from the basics of Mahayana practice to the highest Dzogchen teachings, is included. It begins with aspirational and practical bodhichitta, the foundation of the Mahayana, likened to the intention to visit somewhere and the actual setting out on the journey.[6] The intention is awakening to be of service to all who wander, and the setting out is training, purifying, and bringing into sublime perfection body, speech, and mind.

Another core teaching, "the four aims," comes from the tradition of the great Kadampa masters following in the footsteps of Atisha. These self-commitments of uncompromising determination to become awakened are first to decide upon a life of Dharma, second to entrust Dharma practice to a life of poverty, third to accept eventual death as the destination of a life of poverty, and fourth to embrace dying alone in a cave. Dewai Dorje's own life choices reflect this pungent flavor. She taught from her lived experience, the wretched and blissful both.

Many important lineage holders make appearances in the letter. Naropa, Marpa, and Milarepa, the great Kagyu fathers, enter as exemplars of what unwavering devotion looks like and makes possible. The secret sauce of the Vajrayana, and especially of Dzogchen, is therein revealed: mind ripens and becomes liberated through combining realized teachers, devout students, and exceptional instructions in the recipe for the blessed transmission of wisdom realization. Nothing short of unwavering faith in the guru will do at this level of practice, which makes it a risky endeavor. Yet for the resolved, there is no other choice. To emphasize the determination needed, Dewai Dorje quotes Machik Lapdron, the eleventh-century female master credited with introducing the practice of chod to Tibet. Finally, she also draws upon the eighteenth-century visionary master Jigme Lingpa in reminding the community—and us as well—that temporary experiences and intellectual understanding are not the heart of the matter. Realization must be unchanging.

The letter offers more insight into the depth of Dzogchen practice with its reference to *rushan* (differentiating) practices, considered to be preliminary for those wishing to progress through this approach. As part of the Dzogchen preliminaries, practitioners purify their three doors by engaging in analytical investigations of the mind along with specific trainings for body and speech to prepare for the actual practices: the direct encounter of the nature of mind through Trekcho, and the direct witnessing of the appearances of wisdom through Togal. The thorough scope of the content in the letter, including these highest teachings, reflects the sophistication of this practice community and Dewai Dorje's close connection with them.

Several accounts of Dewai Dorje's involvement with the monastery and community of Sanglung appear in her long autobiography.[7] This was an important center of her Dharma activity, a place where she conferred the empowerments and reading transmissions of Longchenpa's *Four Branches of the Heart Essence* (*Nyingtik Yapzhi*). She recounts in her long autobiography that she agreed to do this for not more than one hundred and twenty-five monks and lay practitioners who had received pointing-out instructions. While she was giving the empowerments, she had a vision of Drime Ozer, who appeared before her as Omniscient Longchenpa and blessed her. Afterward, she completely understood the meaning of the empowerments effortlessly, just as if they were her own treasures. On this occasion she also gave the ripening empowerments, liberating instructions, and outer trainings from Dudjom Lingpa's and Drime Ozer's treasures of *Nang Jang*, as well as instructions from the *Quintessential Great Perfection* (*Dzogchen Yangtik*). She reports making a Dharma connection with thousands of male and female lay devotees through bestowing an empowerment for the Great Compassionate Tamer of Beings (Avalokiteshvara).

At least two more trips to the community are mentioned in Dewai Dorje's long autobiography. Both feature her offering the instructions for *Nang Jang* as well as other seminal Dzogchen works. She also bestowed upon this community the empowerments and oral instructions for all her own treasures and others. In her autobiography, she recounts that after receiving specific Dzogchen teachings, the practitioners followed the guidelines for staying in strict retreat for three months and twenty days.

This humble lady resting at ease on a warm carpet of wildflowers on a sunny summer afternoon in eastern Tibet was a highly realized spiritual teacher. She sat on thrones and stones. She taught her students one at a time, and she taught hundreds at once. She conferred and taught the heart instructions of the most revered Dzogchen Nyingma master, the Omniscient Longchenpa. She gave advice that was deep, penetrating, pithy, and delightfully playful. She poured her heart into every single piece in the following pages. Rejoice in the scent of her dakini wisdom wafting through these words!

Threefold Space

Phenomenal existence—
worlds that seemingly appear,
as well as all they contain—
is outer space.

The empty nature of this is inner space,
and the nondual essence of these two,
appearance and emptiness,
is called the secret space of nonconceptuality.

Ultimately, despite labeling space as space,
the essence of space can't be established as anything.
It is beyond all beliefs about existence or nonexistence.

Equal in not existing, not nonexisting,
and neither existing nor nonexisting,
space is characterized as being invincible, indestructible,
real, incorruptible, unmoving, unchanging,
and completely unable to be obstructed.[8]

Pervading everywhere, it is unchanging ultimate truth
endowed with seven vajra qualities
together with four commitments.
It is a profound and direct teaching.

Ultimately, the nondual space
of nonexistent outer appearances
and nonexistent inner mind
is subsumed within the three kayas
of self-occurring awareness.

Once you understand how the fundamental nature of that really
  is,
you won't need any other instruction about threefold space.

Rest within that state, which is totally free from complexity
and endowed with the three gateways to liberation,
quietly and undistractedly, without correcting or modifying
  anything.
Through that, you will realize the everlasting kingdom of the
  dharmakaya in this very life.

Lhaje Kunzang Chopel requested this teaching with a silken scarf, and the
one named Dewai composed it.

AN INTRODUCTION FOR SHERLHA

Self-knowing awareness is luminous and unconditioned.
Its primordially pure essence is the dharmakaya.
Its unobstructed natural expression is the sambhogakaya,
and its unconfined compassionate capacity is the nirmanakaya.
The three kayas, equal and indivisible,
are perfected as the essence of self-occurring awareness.

Don't look for so-called meditation elsewhere,
and don't fabricate this, the essence of self-knowing awareness.
Just rest wide awake within it, a continuous great state
of brilliant, clear, and vivid lucidity.

Once you've actualized your true nature this way,
it is sure you will arrive at the everlasting kingdom of the original
    ground.

These words were written by the one named Sukha [Dewai Dorje] for the
nun Sherlha.
May virtue prevail!

A Clarification of Practice Instructions on the Difference between Ordinary Mind and Awareness for Lama Tupten Gyatso[9]

The "wisdom that knows the nature as it is" knows how all the things of samsara and nirvana just as they are, the entirety of phenomenal existence, are one taste within the singular great nature of ultimate reality. It also knows how they are equal in being both nonexistent and pure. It abides as the empty, lucid, and unconditioned essence of awareness. This, however, isn't a kind of stupefied bewilderment that doesn't understand anything. It is awareness, which is neither affected by sense objects nor fixated upon them. It cuts through sense objects and isn't swept away by them while seeing the multiplicity of all things. Since awareness is self-existent wakefulness, it naturally occurs as an unobstructed consciousness that knows and cognizes everything but doesn't engage with objects. Awareness is like mercury falling on dry earth.

Ordinary mind is that which sees samsara and nirvana to be autonomous and truly existing. It's the ground-ignorance that reifies appearances. From it come thoughts, secondary mental events, which arise and cease. They mingle with sense objects and are affected by them. Thoughts fixate upon sense objects and fall under their influence. The thoughts of ordinary mind are like drops of water falling on dry earth.

In sum, awareness is a great state of being free from all conceptual construction and endowed with the three gateways to liberation. It pervades all of samsara and nirvana. Ordinary mind is ignorance at the time of the ground. Its energy is thinking. Its expression is seeing the universe and all it contains to be truly existent. It arises and ceases.

ADVICE FOR CHORAP

A Concise Introduction to Awareness, the Four Kayas,
and the Five Wisdoms[10]

Mind's essence is empty, lucid, and unconditioned. Within the recognition of that very state, there is resting in relaxed presence and movement of thought proliferation. That which directly knows the clear and empty essence of thought movement is called awareness. In actuality, resting, movement, and awareness are not separate. The empty and uncontrived essence of your own true nature is right there.

Mind's unborn essence is the dharmakaya. Its nature is unconfined, naturally clear, and aware. This is the sambhogakaya. The nirmanakaya doesn't fixate upon objects appearing as form, sound, smell, taste, and so on and remains naturally liberated. When self-knowing awareness manifests as the ground of samsara and nirvana in their entirety, it is called the svabhavikakaya. Once you determine the true nature of the four kayas, you will see that the universe and all it contains, including the aggregates and elements of your own body and more, are beyond defining characteristics.

Dharmadhatu wisdom knows how the pure space of suchness, the true nature of reality, is one taste. As emptiness is not an empty vacuity, mirrorlike wisdom is the readiness for anything to arise, like a clean and clear mirror. Since the purity and quality of samsara and nirvana are perfected within the ground's own nature, there is evenness wisdom. The unobstructed flow of the dynamic energy of awareness is discriminating wisdom. Since all phenomena of samsara and nirvana have never been created by doing, all-accomplishing wisdom is self-occurring resting without achieving through effort.

In sum, the empty essence of self-knowing awareness is the dharmakaya. Its clear and cognizant nature is the sambhogakaya, and the nirmanakaya is its compassionate capacity, naturally liberated. The inseparability of these three is the svabhavikakaya. Dharmadhatu wisdom is the empty essence of the ground. Mirrorlike wisdom is free from the stains of habits. Evenness wisdom is the perfection of phenomenal existence in the ground. Discriminating wisdom recognizes samsara and nirvana to be self-appearances, and all-accomplishing wisdom transcends effort and rational mind.

Sukha Vajra wrote this for easy comprehension according to Chorap's wish.

CLEARING LAMA JIGPAL'S DOUBTS

Mind is beyond birth, ceasing, and abiding. It is primordially empty and without intrinsic identity. That is its unborn nature. Yet, its empty essence is not a complete nothingness but unceasingly arises in myriad expressions. From the outset, it is an unconditioned, great, primordially liberated state that is free from abiding anywhere.

To clear Lama Jigpal's doubts, the one named Dewai wrote some falsities that came to mind.

May virtue prevail!

Advice for Sangye Tashi

Ultimate Teacher of Self-Knowing Awareness,
Sole Everlasting Refuge,
and Protector of the Dharma, Pema Ledrel—
bless my mind and reside as the Lord of the Family until I awaken.

How amazing!
Listen, fortunate, devout, and diligent ones.
To practice the sublime Dharma from your heart,
meditate with sorrowful disillusionment upon samsara,
and cultivate the wish to awaken for others.
Guard your vows and sacred commitments like the eyes in your
    forehead,
and don't be lazy in word and deed but strive to act virtuously.

Once you realize that the view of emptiness, as taught by the
    lama,
is the great emptiness of samsara and nirvana,
you will attain unwavering confidence in self-knowing awareness.
Therein, as it is said, "samsara and nirvana appear as your own
    perception."

Sustain the continuity of that view without fabricating your
    mind at all.
Mindfully rest in its continuity,
simply without losing the clarity and radiance,
and don't intentionally meditate or get distracted.

Within this state of undistracted non-meditation that defies
    description,
having eliminated drowsiness, dullness, and heaviness,

relax into the expanse of awareness without attachment to
    anything that arises.
That is called naturally lucid meditation without attachment.

Once you correctly realize mind's true nature as it is,
you will experience all that appears within that state
to be the dynamic energy of awareness.
Don't accept, reject, stop, or encourage any of it.

Uncontrived, naturally occurring conduct unfolds
when you understand the crucial key points
for the self-arising, self-appearing, and self-liberating
of all that appears.

The buddha of the original ground
is the actualization of self-knowing awareness,
the pure space of the three-kaya equality.
Apart from that, a result to attain has never existed—
not in the past, not now,
and nor will one ever exist in the future.

I have elucidated here a brief explanation
of view, meditation, and conduct
to make them easy to understand.
Ultimately, view, meditation, conduct, and result
are not separate from each other.

What you must do is sustain your own innate wisdom
without distraction or attachment.
Uncontrived self-knowing awareness
is the great state that transcends rational mind,
and the way you will behold the true nature of Samantabhadra
in this very life.

The faithful Sangye Tashi earnestly insisted upon advice he said was needed, and so the unspiritual and duplicitous liar Kunzang Wangmo [Dewai Dorje] composed this.

By its merit may all beings become liberated within the original ground!

May virtue prevail!

Awareness, the Awakened Mind, Is Completely Pure from the Beginning

Awareness, the awakened mind,
is completely pure from the beginning.
Beyond all conceptual construct,
it is emptiness endowed with three gateways to liberation.
Free from ever gathering or parting from spontaneously present
    kayas and wisdom,
it now manifests as ever-excellent Pema Ledrel upon my crown.

The exceedingly profound, secret, and luminous Great Perfection,
the secret path where all oral instructions culminate,
can be condensed with three key points,
which are special features of the ground.

Not arising from ordinary mind,
self-knowing awareness is pure from the outset.
Never depending on the confused mind of dualism,
it is a vast expanse,
primordially liberated from the limitations
of mind and its thinking.
Cleansed of the veils of ignorance,
it expands as the experience of primordial wisdom.

These pith instructions, which haven't come from scripture,
transfer blessings and realization through deep faith
that sees the lineage lama to be an actual buddha.
They are key points, which don't rely on words and metaphors,
for seeing the true nature of awareness
beyond all attachment and naturally free.

230 — A DAKINI'S COUNSEL

[For Samantabhadra,] the primordially perfect result has never
   arisen from a cause.
It was never accomplished
through separate accumulations of merit and wisdom.
The beginningless expression of the vast expanse of the
   dharmakaya,
it is awareness abiding as the ground,
a treasury of infinite noble qualities, kayas, and wisdom.

[Samantabhadra's] meditation that has never known confusion
is the dharmakaya.
Its great actualization is the result,
primordial perfection.

This explanation of the special features of Samantabhadra's exalted state
was composed by the confused wanderer Dechen Dewai Dorje,
in the guise of words that resemble realization,
for the sublime Tulku Chime Namgyal.

It was offered with devotion by Kunzang Chonyi Wangmo [Dewai
   Dorje]
from the secret and isolated retreat place called Dakinis' Fortress.

Since my tradition is only the perspective of a yak horn,
I don't hold a very good or beautiful view,
but to some extent this is a summary
of awareness's mode of being.
Whether it is or isn't, please, be patient with me.
May there be virtue in offering it genuinely without expectations!

ADVICE FOR RIGZANG

Ha, ha!
My meditation isn't a great corpse-like practice
manufactured through the conceit
of thinking I am a great meditator,
while being trapped by attachment to my meditation.

Rather, in my thinking, simple old lady that I am,
an agitated mind is invited by thinking.
Let thoughts be,
and they subside by themselves
right where they are.
Such is the nature of realization.

In the skylike expanse of the ground,
primordial wisdom, awareness's dynamic energy,
seems to come and go,
and yet in this space of purity and equality,
nothing needs to be excluded through conceptual distinctions.
Whatever arises becomes naturally liberated.

Self-knowing awareness
as other than Samantabhadra has never existed.
Sustain it, a natural state of primordial ease,
without any fabrication
and stay close to self-existent wakefulness.
That itself is the dharmakaya
beyond the mind of conceptual ideas.
Then you will behold effortless wisdom
right where you are.

I have meditated by contrivance and fabrication,
but it is like trying to grab a rainbow in the sky.
That approach to realizing inexpressible primordial wisdom
is very difficult.

Just rest in the natural state,
letting it be as it is,
and then, once you see the self-subsiding nature of the
    dharmakaya,
you will definitely arrive at the everlasting kingdom
where all is equally liberated within originally pure space,
in this very life.

An old lady like me doesn't know anything about contrived
    meditation.
Just practice this.
It might be the direct path.

These words are meant for Rigzang's experience.
They are hot with the poisonous moxibustion arrow of
    self-liberation,
written by a foul-mouthed old lady named Kunzang,
in language that just approximates the true nature of reality.
I offer them to my disciple—
practice this and you just might understand something.
Though this is only a reminder,
I have no instructions or advice that surpass it.

Written by Sukha Vajra [Dewai Dorje].

Response to Gotsa Khenchen

I think there isn't anything greater than the luminous Great Perfection. It is the essence of all Dharma teachings given directly by the Buddha and of all treasure teachings. You must establish it by the view, sustain it with meditation, and resolve it through conduct. Then, clearly distinguishing the essence of awareness abiding in the state beyond speech, thought, and expression, you will be without any attachment to experiences of clarity or emptiness. Once you clearly differentiate its expressive power from conceptual proliferation, there'll be nothing to identify, no matter what arises. Once you clearly distinguish the method of resting through the key points, you will attain confidence in the space of three-kaya equality, a state without focal points and attachment. Then you will enjoy the noble qualities of the four visions, the path appearances of kayas and wisdom presencing themselves. That itself appears to be enough.

Dewai Dorje wrote this from discussion with the great Khenpo Gotsa.

A Letter of Advice for Khenpo Norbu Wangyal

Though I have drawn external boundary lines for strict retreat,
my mind is carried away by afflictions,
and I am an expert in the confused perceptions of inner retreat.

My awareness is immature,
and I languish in meditation that is neither here nor there,
dozing off in laziness,
unable to see anything that needs to be done.

Outer appearances are dreamlike and illusory,
and I can't find anything to meditate upon.

Worldly thoughts inside me
are just awareness rising up as the ground,
and secretly, my awareness is the perfection
of the pure and equal nature of samsara and nirvana.

Now, I am spaciously relaxed in the expanse of ultimate reality,
and having dropped all attachment to concepts about meditation
    and meditating,
the lucidity of my awareness encounters wisdom through my six
    senses.

Everything I perceive is naturally and primordially liberated,
free from the confines of arising and liberating.
Uncontrived awareness always has been the natural state of utter
    purity.
I have no doubt that it is realized through effortlessness.

These words, the tradition of an unspiritual and frivolous
    woman,
are offered to a foremost and committed disciple.
Following in the footsteps of the mother,
you also have this natural treasury.

When you rest at ease
in the self-occurring wisdom awareness of the three-kaya expanse,
you won't be far away from Buddha Samantabhadra.

The subtle wisdom of your innate mind
is the exalted state of Samantabhadra.
When you don't mistake it as an object of knowledge,
you will directly behold this three-kaya wisdom that abides
    within
and become liberated inseparably from Noble Padmasambhava,
your own self-knowing awareness.
Then, you will inhale fresh breath as a Dharma sovereign over the
    three realms.
This is sure.

Sukha Vajra Tsal offered this from the mountain hermitage at Sera Monastery on a good day with a crescent moon.

Written Instructions for the Daughter
of Miwang Sakyong, Dechen Tso

You must create as much virtue as you can through word and deed, with a totally pure intention to render meaningful the fortunate support of your physical form endowed with its many advantages. In particular, don't think that the ground is just the empty aspect of how your mind truly abides. You must resolve that the entire universe and all it contains, such as the body's aggregates, elements, and so on, are primordially empty and by nature do not truly exist. Then, through the wisdom that realizes the selflessness of all phenomena, you will gain certainty that samsara and enlightenment are one taste in the singular expanse of the pure space of the ground. To determine the way all noble qualities of kayas and wisdom are spontaneously present and abide as primordial great perfection, it is essential to rely on the lama's oral instructions and gain certainty in your own view and meditation.

Don't stop with just an intellectual understanding of these important points. Internalize them through experiencing the way awareness abides as the ground and how it is practiced as the path. It is very important to be steadfast in practice. After a while, you will realize ultimate reality itself, and then all thought movement will be like writing on water. It will naturally become liberated. Like the flow of a great river, your experience of the unborn will effortlessly unfold. Once you recognize samsara and nirvana to be your own projections, you will actualize awareness, the nonconceptual wisdom that is the pure space of three-kaya equality. This is the unsurpassed special feature of the view according to the oral instructions of our Dzogchen tradition.

If you understand this clearly, even if we both were to meet in person, I wouldn't have anything greater to share with you. These oral instructions are equal to my heart, my eyes, and my life itself. By realizing them, you can become a buddha in the morning if you meditate at dawn. If you meditate at dusk, you can become a buddha in the night. They reveal the three realms alighting as the wisdom of primordial purity, so I request you to keep them close in heart and mind. Because we are one Dharma lineage, please don't share them even tangentially to those who haven't received any instructions on this path. Since it is difficult to understand what they mean through analytical meditations of rational mind, please understand this point.

Kunzang Dekyong Wangmo offered this with respect from her blessed and isolated retreat sanctuary.

May virtue prevail!

Dzogchen View, Meditation, Conduct, and Result

The originally pure essence is the dharmakaya.
Its unobstructed nature is the sambhogakaya,
and its pervasive compassionate capacity is the nirmanakaya.
I bow before the lama, the indivisibility of the three kayas.

Here I will refresh a few key points about view, meditation, conduct, and result. The greatness of Secret Mantra is such that for those with genuine faith and devotion, it makes no difference whether the lama is near, far, living or not. If you pray single-pointedly, the blessings of the wisdom mind lineage will definitely transfer into your own mind.

Well then, what about the luminous Great Perfection, supreme among all spiritual approaches? It's self-occurring wisdom, awareness that knows itself, beyond word, thought, and description. Don't meditate on it as something that exists. That's just an idea. Don't meditate on it as something that doesn't exist. That too is just an idea. Don't try to suppress or establish awareness as something that does or doesn't exist. Just let mind be, as it is, in its natural state, and relax there. There is no need to cultivate the so-called wisdom of nonduality as something else. It is mind naturally abiding in its own essence.

There are many explanations about view, but the view of Dzogchen is to realize mind to be baseless and without any origin. There are many types of resting meditation, but in Dzogchen, meditation refers to confidence attained through recognizing samsara and nirvana to be self-appearing and realizing their great equally pure and empty nature. Conduct is explained in myriad ways. However here, you must determine that buddha is none other than self-knowing awareness and that demons are none other than thinking itself. Then, you will encounter everything as primordial wisdom and will experience all perception as awareness. There will no longer be anything to accept or reject. You will be like a lion reaching a snowy mountain summit: samsara will appear as the ornamentation of wisdom.

There are many ways of attaining the result, but in the Dzogchen tradition, the result—the actualization of self-knowing awareness through the strength of the great wisdom mind lineage of sublime gurus—is taught to be groundless and without origin. It is the great uncontrived state beyond conceptual mind. It's the manifestation of the purity and equality of samsara and nirvana. Understand that apart from this, there is no other result to be attained.

In sum, at all times and in all situations, don't try to correct mind with positive thinking or change it from negative thinking. Remain without distraction in self-cognizing awareness, beyond all thoughts and ideas, and realize appearances are the nirmanakaya. Then, once you see how they manifest as the sambhogakaya, and their baselessness as the wisdom of the dharmakaya, you will realize that these have always been beyond meeting and parting.

Sukha Vajra wrote this from Takseng Nado at the request of the faithful Miwang Tragyal.

May virtue prevail!

A Clarification of Distinctions between Shamatha and Vipashyana and Meditation and Post-Meditation

Homage to the expanse of glorious Samantabhadra!
Pure from the outset, the essence is the dharmakaya.
Its nature as kayas and primordial wisdom is the sambhogakaya,
and its compassionate capacity, all-pervading and naturally
  luminous,
is the nirmanakaya.
Homage to Ledrel Tsal, embodiment of three-kaya equality.
Please, until I awaken, remain as the Lord of the Family,
and bless my mind that it be ripened and freed.

Here I will present a little explanation for distinguishing shamatha
and vipashyana and meditation and post-meditation.

At first, no matter what approach you practice, you must steer
clear of all unwholesome behavior by restraining the actions of
your body, speech, and mind. Once you've completely purified your
mind through nurturing kindness, compassion, and the intention
of bodhichitta, you must turn away from samsara. Practice as the
sublime lineage lamas have instructed by retreating to an isolated
and uninhabited sanctuary where you are alone. Sit on a comfortable seat, ensure that your aim is not to meditate yourself into a
stupefied state through a blank view, and then practice Guru Yoga
throughout four sessions.[11] Receive the four empowerments and
then mingle your mind with the wisdom mind of the lama.

At this time, don't think that the lama is something other than
mind's empty essence. That itself is the enlightened mind of the
lama. The primordial wisdom of mind's lucid nature is the enlightened qualities of the lama. The arising of mind's unobstructed

expressiveness is the lama's compassionate capacity. Knowing that, mingle your body, speech, and mind indivisibly with the lama's wisdom body, speech, and mind, and rest in meditation through the easefulness of unrestricted awareness. When you do that, the exalted state of primordial liberation beyond mind becomes evident. This is the fundamental nature of the original ground, totally free of conceptual elaboration and endowed with the three gateways to liberation. It is called awareness.

Let it be as it is, without repressing, encouraging, or modifying it intellectually in any way whatsoever. When you do that, all gross and subtle thoughts settle down right where they are. There is an absence of thought movement and an aspect that abides as mind's vivid and pristine openness, self-knowing and naturally lucid. That is called shamatha. Once that abiding aspect recognizes itself, there is a nonconceptual clear and aware knowing. The actualization of that is called vipashyana. Within this self-evident experience, everything that arises and appears is embraced with naturally present mindfulness, and you abide without wavering. That is called meditation. Therein, you don't need to seal anything that appears as empty. In recognizing itself, awareness of the self-subsiding nature of everything that appears is called post-meditation.

In brief, what is termed "the transcendent state of the true dharmata in the womb" is the actualization of self-knowing awareness. Apart from that, there is no need to engage anything else as the excellent so-called exalted state of buddhahood. When you practice the great nondual primordial wisdom that has been directly introduced to you, without changing it by repressing or encouraging anything, realization of the unity of shamatha and vipashyana will dawn from within. Then you will know how to take everything that occurs as the spiritual path. As a practitioner of mind in the retreat hut of the body, afflictions will be purified right where they are, and you will abide in isolated retreat.

Sustaining the continuity of the authentic natural state brings your life and practice to their ultimate culmination. No matter what comes up, there is no rejecting, accepting, repressing, or encouraging positive or negative thoughts. You will be like a child gazing into a temple or a mute eating molasses, having resolved that nothing truly exists and never wavering from the great state beyond all conceptual elaboration. This is the achievement of stability within empty awareness free from grasping mind. It is an expanse of great luminosity. It is to recognize all phenomenal existence to be the wisdom mandala of the guru, to know everything that appears to be the manifestation of primordial wisdom, and to become enlightened within the great state of nonconceptual primordial liberation.

The faithful noble monk named Bodhi requested this for a long time, and so as not to disappoint him, Dewai Dorje wrote this from isolated retreat at a secret monastery.

May virtue prevail!

A Letter of Advice for Dechen Tso, the Daughter of Miwang Sakyong

As I shared earlier with you, since we know that joy and sorrow are always uncertain in all the activities of samsara, it is very important to train the mind to take negative circumstances as supports on the path. Through the power of the lama's direct instructions and your own diligent practice on the swift path of the secret of mind, you must internalize the fundamental nature of reality through understanding, experience, and realization. At a certain point, since realization does not come about through mere intellectual understanding, there will only be certainty through having attained confidence in awareness, self-existing wakefulness. From then on, if you can sustain your true nature without forgetting it in any kind of positive or negative circumstances, an exceptional realization will dawn in your mind. This is the special feature of the path.

Understanding means keeping the precise meaning of the lama's oral instructions present in mind. Experience means concertedly mixing the meaning of that understanding with your mind. Realization is the actualization of awareness, unreachable by thought and word. Unmingled with intellectual analysis, realization is beyond attachment, fixation, and any focus on experience. When its dynamic energy is perfected, it is resolved within the pure space of the three-kaya equality. That is called attaining confidence. It is your own personal experience of the genuine state of non-meditation. Until you arrive there, rely upon the method of "short glimpses many times repeated," and don't deviate from the practice. The pure essence of this little heart advice is sealed with *ah tam*.

Offered by Dewai Dorje.

ADVICE FOR JIGCHO TSANCHANG

Homage to the lama!

Fortunate persons who aspire to practice the path of the luminous Great Perfection must first properly train the mind by contemplations that reverse attachment to samsara. Specifically, inspire yourselves with the loving and compassionate motivation of bodhichitta. Then, in an isolated retreat location, upon a comfortable seat, pray to the vajra-holding master and to all the lineage lamas with intense faith and devotion, and recite words of the practice of Guru Yoga while reflecting on its meaning. Take the four empowerments and then rest in the state of meditative equipoise, seeing the nonconceptual wisdom of the lama's awakened mind as indivisible from your own body, speech, and mind.

You must recognize that all appearances of form are the sacred mandala of the lama's wisdom body. All sounds are the wheel of the lama's wisdom speech. All thoughts are the sacred mandala of the lama's wisdom mind. Once you fully understand the great placement in the state of that recognition, the dynamic energy of discerning wisdom blazes forth. It is then essential to take everything that appears as the path within the unimpeded expansiveness of awareness, without correcting, rejecting, or clinging to anything.

During your session breaks, imagine your body, speech, and mind to be indivisible from the lama's wisdom body, speech, and mind. In all activities—eating, sleeping, moving around, or sitting—maintain present awareness, an undiminished, self-knowing, natural lucidity. Don't get trapped by holding on to ideas about being a meditator and having a view. Just rest in the actualization of mind's natural state, and you will arrive at self-occurring wisdom awareness, undifferentiated as the wisdom of the empty essence, luminous nature, and all-pervasive compassionate capacity. I am sure that you then will take hold of the original dharmakaya kingdom in this very lifetime. Relying upon the blessings of the lineage lama is the method to actualize self-occurring wisdom.

The faithful man Jigcho Tsanchang insisted on this again and again, and so as not to disappoint him, the crazy and unspiritual lady who always lies, the one named Sukha Vajra [Dewai Dorje], wrote it.

May virtue prevail!

ADVICE FOR NOBLE SEMPA

Homage to the lama!

All who wish to traverse the path to omniscience in a single lifetime through relying upon the swift path of the luminous vajra vehicle must perfectly internalize all the common and extraordinary teachings that have flowed from the mouths of the sublime lineage lamas. Conscientiousness and restraint are needed in all activities of body, speech, and mind. With thought and deed, practice according to the lama's instructions. Uphold the sacred commitments, vows, and so forth just exactly as they should be maintained without secrecy or deception. Especially, don't blather the meaning of all the direct oral instructions everywhere while proclaiming the view of emptiness.

Understanding comes from proper study of how the fundamental nature of reality is present as the ground of Dzogchen, how it abides as the path, and of the meaning of all the teachings. Don't ever part from that understanding. Mixing this understanding definitively with your mind through practice is called experience. Experience should accord with the oral instructions of the lamas. Don't make up your own ideas about existence. Don't mentally construct nonexistence, and don't fall into a fuzzy neutral experience of emptiness. Instead, resolve that empty awareness is inexpressible and inconceivable luminosity within uncompounded pure space, a primordially liberated great state where the three kayas are equal in nature. To behold empty awareness without any attachment is called realization.

Arriving at the ultimate stable and unchanging nature within realization is the discovery of confidence that whatever arises—all that is perceived—has never been anything other than manifestations of the dynamic energy of wisdom awareness. There, within the immediacy of awareness, the entirety of positive, negative, and neutral thoughts about all that is perceived become like water dissolving into water. They liberate in and of themselves. That is the actualization of awareness. This is the realization of the key instruction concerning the profound transcendent state of primordial liberation, which is completely beyond ordinary mind.

Determine the view through these instructions on understanding, experience, and realization. Sustain it with meditation and resolve it through conduct. Thereby, luminosity will become uninterrupted throughout day and night, and you will manifest the natural state of the original ground of Samantabhadra and become liberated.

If you don't understand how this occurs but instead feel confident based on mere intellectual understanding, you will be mistaken about the empty experience of mind. Following after objects of perception, you might believe that the genuine transcendent state of Dzogchen, the fundamental nature of reality, is wisdom manufactured by intellectual analysis or thought subsumed by fixated mindfulness. When your perception is free from that kind of fixated attention, you might subscribe to a view that sees awareness as a state of neutral nonconceptuality. If you don't understand the key teaching on the way thinking becomes liberated in and of itself, you will remain at the threshold of still differentiating between perceptions and mind. This is like the way naturally free-flowing water gets constricted within ice. Therefore, it is crucial to sever misunderstandings about your practice.

Although, according to the way it is taught, the unique approach of Dzogchen is free from faults, pitfalls, and errors, due to the different minds of individual beings, various paths appear to them. In actuality, when you behold the true nature of awareness that knows itself, "meditation" is not something to seek intentionally. It's also not an indifferent state of non-meditation. Meditation is great nondual effortless wisdom, a pervasive, boundless, and infinite state free beyond all conceptual elaboration. Post-meditation means simply not losing this skylike view, free from center and edge, not leaving the continuity of the oceanlike transparent clarity of meditation, and not becoming careless with conduct. It's to mingle luminosity ceaselessly throughout the day and night and rest in the pervasive openness of awareness.

Sustain awareness without modifying it. Relax as thoughts self-liberate, like writing on water. Then your experience of the unborn will be uninterrupted like the flow of a great river. After you practice this way for a while, at a certain point you will arrive at stability within awareness where ground and result are a unity. Then you will manifest your true dharmakaya nature, Samantabhadra, and I am sure you will become liberated within the inner radiance of the youthful vase kaya.

My student, the faithful and noble Buddhist nun Sempa said she needed something like this. She insisted upon it, and so as not to disappoint him I, one named Dewai, composed it.

May virtue prevail!

ADVICE FOR NOBLE VAJRA

When You Meet a Fully Qualified Sublime Lama
through Pure Aspirations Made in
Earlier Times...

Pray one-pointedly with intense faith, devotion, and confidence, thinking, "You know my mind!" Particularly, train your mind in four daily sessions by visualizing taking the four empowerments within the practice of Guru Yoga. Afterward, mingle your mind with the lama's wisdom mind, and then, without modifying or changing mind's natural state, sustain the state of luminosity that is utterly beyond intellect. In doing so, all chasms, pitfalls, backsliding, and mistakes become liberated. How are they liberated? Mistakes are gone once you realize that mind has always been groundless, rootless, and beyond the eight extremes of conceptual elaboration. It is great primordial emptiness, free from all ideas of the intellect. This approach is unlike that of the lower vehicles, which are not free from intellectual endeavors to negate existence and establish nonexistence.

Once you see the ultimate essence of emptiness just as it is, you will understand the crucial point that awareness is a great openness that has from the very beginning always been utterly pure. Then there will be no need to stick on a seal of emptiness and no place for backsliding. After you see the true essence of the natural state of awareness, you will understand its experience as unobstructed, lucid, unconfused, and nonconceptual like the sky, so there will be no place for pitfalls. Therefore, after encountering the nature of mind just as it is, let it be naturally without correcting or sullying it by anything positive or negative. Then you will swiftly discover the meaning of great nondual wisdom, right where you are.

Simply not to ignore the request of the novice, noble Vajra, Sukha Vajra [Dewai Dorje] wrote some lies from her state of eating, sleeping, and defecating.

ADVICE FOR CHANGWA LHA

Pray, Sublime Dharma Master Pema Ledrel,
holder of the actual wisdom body
of buddhas gone before, present now, and still to come,
hold me with your compassion
and reside as the ornament upon my crown chakra of great bliss.

How incredible! Fortunate child, listen.
Through the power of excellent karma from previous lives,
now you have taken rebirth in a human body, the support for
     freedom.
Hurry, practice the essential, sublime Dharma.

This life is just temporary, a dream.
As there isn't time to remain here long,
all that is meaningful gets lost when you have too many ideas,
so quickly find a way to cut the snares of attachment.

Excessive social obligations increase the five poisons,
both for yourself and others,
and people are never completely satisfied.
From within, don't lose track of your own goals.

Making pilgrimage without pure vision
and yogis subsumed by afflictions
are the laughingstock of all.
Hurry, find a way to tame your own attachment and aversion.

Degenerate times show in intentions and behavior of folks.
When offered love, they return hate.

Aims involving the eight worldly concerns are tough to
accomplish.
Hurry, find a way to realize the utterly pure Dharma.

Even if you trust worldly phenomena,
they have no essence.
Like bamboo, they're empty at the core.
Lost in torpor, human life comes to an end.
So, try now to anchor your practice in isolated retreat,
and don't make long-term plans.

Without cutting through attachment to the belief that the self
truly exists,
it is impossible to realize buddhahood's everlasting happiness.
You must, therefore, properly internalize the true mode
of self-occurring awareness's natural state.

Its ground is from the outset utterly pure
and beyond conceptual construct.
It is endowed with the three doors to liberation.
The basic space of the perfect equality of the three kayas:
that itself is self-occurring awareness.
Rest in realization of this natural state as it is.
That is the key point of the view.

Unobstructed and empty, awareness's bare nature
is an expanse of great self-liberation transcending attachment.
It appears in and of itself
and is luminous beyond all limitations.
The key point of meditation
is to realize the crucial teaching
on awareness's self-arising and self-liberation,
free from acceptance, rejection, and all effort.

Self-knowing awareness, the immaculate dharmakaya,
transcends being an object to establish or refute.
Don't modify it through intellectual analysis.
This luminosity is undifferentiated throughout meditation and
post-meditation.
It must be resolved without distraction and confusion
within the one taste of the all-encompassing space of the ultimate
expanse.
That is the key point of conduct.

Accordingly, this translucent space on the swift path of great
transference
endowed with these three key points
is a secret greater than all others.
The method to actualize it in this lifetime
is to rely on the gateways, objective spheres, winds, and awareness,
grounded in the three unwavering states.[12]

When you single-pointedly strike the key points
and are free from intellectual analysis, you will directly see
the luminous appearances of ultimate reality
through the secret path of the four lamps with eyes of wisdom.

Realization, the experience of the luminous appearances
of the outer universe and its inner contents, will increase,
and you will achieve stability in genuine shamatha.

Then, when the universe and its contents
transfer into five-colored light, bindus, and space,
habits of dualistic mind will vanish into space.[13]

Full encompassment of awareness as the space of the three kayas
is realization through the three doors reaching their full extent.
External and internal phenomena will ripen as great luminosity,

and phenomenal existence will be perfected
as buddha fields and wisdom kayas.

You will be endowed with miraculous powers,
such as the five clairvoyances and more,[14]
achieve mastery over both birth and dying,[15]
and attain the ultimate result of buddhahood.

Subsequently, once the increase of reality is complete,
you will excellently cross over to the ground of phenomenal
    exhaustion
and discover the manifest meaning of indwelling fearless
    confidence, fourfold.[16]

You will attain stability in wisdom's self-manifestation,
seize the everlasting kingdom of the dharmakaya beyond
    ordinary mind,
cleanse cognitive obscurations and associated habits into space,
and mature the purest wisdom kaya of great transference.

Like waking from a dream, all impure phenomena based on
    confusion
will be liberated in the original ground of inner basic space,
and you will attain perfectly pure and perfect buddhahood.

Through understanding these key points exactly as they should
    be,
you will attain the twofold result in this very life.

Don't keep your understanding of these essential words
rotting on the pages of the text.
Even if my explanation doesn't suit the learned,
strive to find a way to internalize it.

I don't know how to compose a beautiful book.
This is advice in harmony with the Dharma.
Understand it to be oral instructions from lineage lamas,
gathered here as singular key points of ultimate meaning.
Don't let them fade. Internalize them.

For a very long time, my faithful and vow-holding student Changwa Lha repeatedly insisted that he needed this and offered a magnetizing-colored (red) mala. So as not to ignore this earnest request, the lowly vagabond Dekyong Wangmo [Dewai Dorje] put some falsehoods that welled forth from the ocean of her mind into writing.

May virtue prevail!

A CLEAR MIRROR THAT SUMMARIZES
THE ESSENTIAL MEANING:
A LETTER FOR THE MONASTIC COMMUNITY
OF SANGLUNG YANG MONASTERY

How wondrous!
Our guide who embodies all noble buddha families,
Samantabhadra appearing as a holy friend,
Protector of the Dharma, Pema Ledrel Tsal—
please, remain as Lord of the Family until I awaken
and bless me to mix my mind with the Dharma.

Here is a written letter to substitute for my speaking. Though I
don't know how to give elaborate and eloquent explanations using
beautiful language, as an old lady pointing her finger at one crucial
point of foolish advice, I offer you here some murky explanation to
clarify your practice.

Like I told you earlier regarding practicing the instructions on
mind's nature: when contemplating the four thoughts that reverse
attachment to samsara, it's crucial to give up activities of the eight
worldly concerns and establish your practice in isolated mountain
retreat.[17] Since qualities of experience and realization depend upon
strong determination, make it your foundation. On top of that,
continuously and thoroughly examine your mind in all aspects
to ensure that every thought, word, and deed is directed toward
the totally pure path. This is essential. If your mind is opposed
to Dharma, but you act as though you have a high view and deep
practice, you will be like a tree with a rotten core. Forget about
benefiting others. You won't make even a tiny bit of progress helping yourself!

First, properly purify your mind through both aspirational and practical bodhichitta and then train in regarding others as more important than yourself. Thereby establish bodhichitta as the foundation. Next, serve the perfectly pure teachings of the Dharma and please the lama in three ways, keeping pure perception, devotion, and stable faith. You must properly bring the noble qualities of your lama's wisdom mind into your own, just like pressing a clay mold. For this you need diligence and patience to withstand hardships.

Otherwise, if you lack the strength of mind to be respectful, faithful, and diligent, even if your lama is an actual emanation of the Buddha, it will be exceedingly difficult for blessings to penetrate you. It's like the impossibility of sprouting a seed from a rock or holding liquid in a leaky pot. Reflect on why it's difficult to practice the pure Dharma when the mind is tainted with doubts and wrong views. Finally, align your three doors, body, speech, and mind, as one with the faith that sees the lama as an actual buddha. This is extremely important.

Past accomplished masters such as Naropa, Marpa, and Milarepa had steady faith and devotion toward their lamas and always viewed them as actual buddhas in all aspects. They practiced the pure Dharma with tremendous fortitude and diligence and received all the noble qualities of their lamas' wisdom minds, like vases filled to the brim. It is very important that we too plant ourselves in isolated mountain retreat, avoid distraction and laziness, and maintain devotion to our lamas and pure view toward our vajra siblings. Diligently practicing the Dharma, we must believe that we can and will attain perfect buddhahood in this very lifetime. We must firmly commit to this in our minds, hold it in our hearts, and turn our backs on samsara.

Buddha, as well, renounced his Shakya kingdom. He went from his home into homelessness to accomplish perfect buddhahood. The Master and Second Buddha (Padmasambhava) also renounced the kingdom of Zahor, just like spittle, and enacted fearless wisdom activities in the eight charnel grounds and other places. At last, he realized manifest perfect buddhahood in the rainbow body of a youthful vase kaya. Many other awareness holders who gradually progressed on the path turned their backs on their homelands. They benefited themselves and others by focusing on the four aims according to the tradition of past masters. They accepted other lands for their homes, disregarded hardships, and set aside concerns for their own bodies and lives. How can anyone accomplish the sublime wisdom of Dharma simultaneously with samsaric goals?

Therefore, establish as your foundation the ability to practice alone in isolation after renouncing samsara. Concentrate on singularly aligning your body, speech, and mind with the pith instructions of the sublime lineage lamas. Pray to your lama intensely, thinking, "You know my mind!" It is very important to meditate properly on the meaning of the preliminaries: the rushan [or, differentiating] practices for body, speech, and mind; analysis of mind's coming, abiding, and going; and its form, shape, color, and so on. It is just as [Machik] Lapdron's oral teachings say:

If they make you postpone Dharma,
even parents or friends can become obstacles.
Leave the iron shackles of relatives and retinue far behind,
establish yourself in isolated mountain retreat,
and embrace a lifestyle of non-doing to meditate upon
    emptiness
once you've severed the root of mind.

First, by the profound view of the ground, you must gain certainty about all phenomena of samsara and nirvana, the world of appearances and possibilities. When you do, you will fully understand the meaning of their great primordially empty, rootless nature. Then, by meditating on the path without confusing the crucial instructions about how to practice, you will actualize the primordial wisdom of nondual empty luminosity. Abide within this self-existent wakefulness, without losing it to mental projections. Don't withdraw the mind inwardly. Just rest naturally, without fabricating it conceptually in any way whatsoever. That is direct placement. It is my practice: mind's nature taking itself as the path.

Just as I earlier taught you regarding self-occurring awareness or the meditation of abiding within the natural state, don't sully it in any way with mental fabrication. Once you have trained with great faith, diligence, and courage in the space of three-kaya equality just as it is, don't leave it in the domain of mere intellectual understanding. Earnestly strive in practice until the genuine meaning has definitively entered your mind. Lapdron says,

> Don't subsume self-knowing awareness,
> the essence of the spontaneously present three kayas,
> within the confines of fabrications that affirm or negate it.
> Let it be as it is, and you will witness its meaning beyond
>   thought
> and seize the everlasting kingdom of great nondual primal
>   wisdom.

It is just like that.

Conduct supports view and meditation as follows. In terms of external conduct, don't be heedless, crazily running around doing village rites and so forth. Be mindful, vigilant, and conscientious, and remain peaceful and subdued. Don't transgress the firm ethical discipline of the vows of individual liberation. In terms of inner conduct, don't act as though you don't understand the fully ripened causal results of the ten unvirtuous actions. Ground yourself in the meaning of aspirational and practical bodhichitta. Even if you can't serve all sentient beings at the highest level like a powerful and compassionate king, conduct yourself with the motivation of bodhichitta and don't contradict the bodhisattva trainings.[18]

The samayas connected to Secret Mantra empowerment number six for the teacher, four for vajra siblings, three for mantra, four for mudra, and the ten secrets.[19] To sum up, in particular, guard the samayas of the lama's wisdom body, speech, and mind like the eyes in your forehead, even at the cost of your life. These are the root mantra samayas. Hold them without a single breakage, transgression, or tear and then energetically meditate on the meaning of profound luminosity.

Secret conduct is to not behave like an ordinary person when negative circumstances suddenly appear. Rather, like a fully perfect and mature garuda, secret conduct is to be free from being affected by the afflictions.[20] For a practitioner at this level, whatever appears is only the nature of interconnected causes and conditions and ultimately isn't real. Everything is just like an illusion or dream. All phenomenal appearances appear as the natural expressiveness of the ground, manifestations of primordial wisdom, and the ornamentation of awareness. You must gain confidence in liberation within that recognition. Don't reject, accept, fear, or anticipate thought movement in any way whatsoever and know whatever is perceived, all appearances, to be manifestations of ultimate reality itself. Then, the attainment of confidence in the self-arising and self-liberating of thoughts as the great purity and equality of all appearances and possibilities is no different from the conduct that supports view and meditation.

The Great Orgyen said,

> Though my view is higher than the sky,
> my attention to karma, the law of cause and result,
> is finer than flour.

The oral teachings tell us,

> View, meditation, and conduct
> are supports for the yogic path.
> Undifferentiated in the ultimate expanse,
> they are resolved in the transcendent state of direct
> liberation.

That's exactly how it is.

Don't leave the stages of the profound path's view, meditation, and conduct as ideas that you have just heard about or sort of understand. You also don't need to ask others to clarify your own misunderstandings. You must come to certainty in your own mind. If you don't, but instead just leave the genuine meaning of ultimate reality as an intellectual concept, you will depreciate cause and result and risk mistaking the true path. The most important thing is to internalize, decisively, the view and meditation of the unmistaken meaning of the fundamental nature of reality, at all times and in every situation. The Buddha said,

> Like smelting, shaping, and polishing gold,
> thoroughly examine my words.[21]

To sum up, never let your conscious awareness become inattentive or scattered. Hold it with the iron hook of mindfulness. Don't separate from natural mindfulness in all aspects of outer conduct, inner thinking, and secret practice. If you do, then even if I were to teach you the secret pith instructions for the approach of the luminous Great Perfection, they will remain just intellectual ideas. If you were to leave them there, you would easily rack up the worst kind of karma for yourself and others both. Therefore, strive with mindfulness, vigilance, and conscientiousness and persevere determinedly until you integrate the essential points to be understood within your own mind. Rigdzin Jigme Lingpa said,

> Spiritual experiences, like mist, fade away.
> Intellectual understanding, like a patch, falls apart.

The ultimate import of everything is self-occurring awareness beyond arising, ceasing, and abiding. When you don't stray from it under the power of dualistic confusion, it is an uncompounded luminous emptiness that can't be established as anything at all, the essence of the fundamental nature of reality. That is the dharmakaya. Its unobstructed nature, a great consummation spontaneously and primordially endowed with all unsought noble

wisdom qualities of existence and quiescence both, is the sambhogakaya. Its clear compassionate capacity, a great pervasiveness that
is self-liberated and without fixation, is the nirmanakaya.

The essence of this three-kaya equality is self-knowing pristine
awareness. Unchanging, it possesses the three gateways to liberation and transcends the eight conceptual limitations.[22] Determine
it by the view. Sustain it through meditation. Resolve it with conduct. The result is to hold firmly to your true nature. These are the
pith instructions on the key points. The oral teachings say,

> Unchangeable and indestructible, the expanse of awareness
> is beyond joining or separating from kayas and primordial
>   wisdom.
> Nonconceptual, the ultimate expanse of luminosity,
> a natural sphere of self-liberation, is the result.

It is just like that.

> Accordingly, this foolish advice clarifying pith instructions,
> for fortunate and karmically connected disciples,
> is offered by the simple vagabond woman, Sukha Vajra,
> with heartful and pure intentions,
> in the form of a letter substituting for speech.

> With the exception of a few lucky and like-minded ones,
> seal this in secrecy from ordinary people faint of heart.
> Without letting its essential meaning fade,
> practice single-pointedly with strong determination,
> and this way you will arrive on the profound path of the
>   heart-essence teachings.
> Effortlessly and spontaneously benefiting yourself and
>   others,
> you will ascend upon Samantabhadra's victory seat, self-
>   knowing awareness,
> in this very life.

These special features of our profound path are the only
    teachings I possess.
I have nothing else.
I'm illuminating them for your benefit, fortunate students.
This path brings liberation without needing to strive for
    eons
and ensures perfect buddhahood in a single instant.

On the second day of the first month, the simple and carefree lady Sukha Vajra composed this explanation for fortunate ones at the monastic community of Sanglung Yang Monastery in Amdo from the pleasure grove of the isolated retreat center of Sera Monastery and offered it virtuously with a sky-blue brocade and white silk scarf.

May virtue prevail!

ADVICE FOR JIGME

How wondrous!
Homage to the wisdom form of all buddhas throughout triple
    time,
Our Guide of Beings, Dudul Wangchuk Ling,
indivisible from Rigdzin Kunkyong Ling.[23]
May I and others turn our minds toward the Dharma.

Having now attained excellent supports
of free and well-favored human rebirths, so hard to find,
we must properly practice the Dharma to realize their essence.
Impermanent and illusory by nature are the phenomena of
    samsara.
To relinquish ties of attachment to them, alone we must practice
    the Dharma,
keeping in mind uncertainty about the time of death.

Buddha taught karma, the law of cause and result, to be infallible.
Since effects of positive and negative actions are sure to ripen on
    you,
don't confuse what to avoid and engage
and precisely examine even the smallest actions.

Samsara's impurity, like a muddy swamp,
is full of unbearable suffering bringing disaster to all.
Reflect on this, and then alone
in isolated retreat in the mountains,
come to certainty about it.

Then, pray to the lama and Triple Gem
and connect body, speech, and mind with the path of virtue.

Strive to gather merit and wisdom, purify obscurations,
and free and protect the lives of beings.

If you don't benefit yourself when you're free,
no one can help on the journey to the next life.
Family and relatives cannot accompany you;
amassed wealth and even your cherished body must be left
  behind.

When consciousness roams the fearsome precipices of the bardo,
the best guides and protectors are our lamas, rare and supreme.
So, persistently pray to them with faith and pure perception,
and to benefit everyone, carve the *mani* mantra.

Negative friends, like lairs of poisonous snakes,
bring the downfall of oneself and others through negative
  influence.
So, remain completely alone in isolated retreat in the mountains,
without anyone else.

By the view, hold your mind with the iron hook of mindfulness.
Through meditation, gain confidence in actions and their results,
by carefully discerning what and what not to do.
For conduct, love all beings throughout the six realms
just like they were your very own children.

Stabilize the basis, the cultivation of bodhichitta as the ground.
Accomplish the exalted Dharma to benefit beings as the path,
and bring yourself and others to the pure land of liberation as the
  result!

A samsara-wanderer, the beggar lady named Tare [Dewai Dorje] wrote this
to fulfill the request of the sublime and faithful Jigme.

May virtue prevail!

AWARENESS IS THE FUNDAMENTAL NATURE OF ULTIMATE REALITY

How marvelous!

Effortless and self-occurring
awareness is the fundamental nature of reality.
Let it be as it naturally is,
unrestrained by the iron fetters of contriving mind's grasping
and sustained within the boundlessness of all-encompassing
    space.
Then you won't be far from Buddha Samantabhadra.

In response to the request of the young monk, Taye Gyatso,
I, a simple, mixed-up, and nonconceptual yogi,
Dechen Dewai Dorje, wrote some crazy advice.

Advice for Chotreng

Refuge and Protector of the Dharma, Ledrel Tsal,
remain as crown jewel forever,
and bless my body, speech, and mind.
Virtuous lady, listen.

Have you understood that samsaric phenomena have no essence?
Through the power of prayers and merit from the past,
you have attained now the freedoms and advantages
of a precious human rebirth.

Don't squander them in meaninglessness.
Stay alone in isolated retreat in the mountains,
and continuously, with faith and devotion,
strive to be virtuous in thought, word, and deed.

The luminous Great Perfection is not something distant or other
than self-occurring primordial awareness,
which itself is the primordial Buddha Samantabhadra.

Without getting dispersed in external projections,
withdrawing the mind internally
or falling under the sway of conditions in between,
don't alter, change, or be distracted from awareness.

Rest without any attachment,
and you will see your true nature—
self-knowing awareness.

Since your illusory body is frail,
it is hard for you to journey to places far,

and now that I, due to negative companions,
need to go away for the time being,
it will be difficult for us to meet in person again,
but I am praying that in our next lives,
we will meet in the buddha fields.

The things of samsara and nirvana don't truly exist.
You must regard them all as magical illusions.
There's nothing permanent or stable,
but don't feel pain or sadness—
I am never apart from you.
When, with intense faith and devotion,
you pray to me again and again,
this magically appearing girl of illusion
will protect you with her skill and compassion.

To fulfill the insistent and repeated requests
of the virtuous woman filled with faith named Chotreng,
the carefree Dekyong Chonyi Wangmo [Dewai Dorje],
who holds the name of Treasure Revealer,
wrote down whatever came to mind.

WORDS FOR KAR CHONYI

At all times, you must try to practice the key points
of the highest instructions,
the quintessential profound teachings
you heard directly from the lama,
whose kindness is not repayable.
And then seize, right now,
the everlasting kingdom of the dharmakaya.

Awareness, pure from the beginning, is like a stainless crystal
beaming myriad colors, spontaneously present, as its natural
complexion.
Carefully sustain it by letting it be in its own way, uncontrived,
and
demonic ego-fixation will be liberated within great primordial
wisdom.
Even grasping at objects will disappear, and you will behold your
true nature of Samantabhadra!

As a simple expression of awe, the vagabond named Sukha offered these
words to Kar Chonyi.

For the Heart Son

How marvelous!

The emanation of the wisdom mind of Padmasambhava,
who actually is all buddhas gone before, present now, and
    still to come,
is Dudul Wangchuk Ling.
I pray to you—please, bless my mind.

Listen to what is primordial, sublime heart companion,
the basis for my practice is like this:
The sole supreme lama is the Lotus Born,
whose blessings are unceasing, heart son.

The sole supreme teachings
are the naked instructions of Dzogchen.
Don't search for buddhahood elsewhere, heart son.

The sole supreme companions
are the assembly of dakas and dakinis.
Their love is unflagging, heart son.

Apart from the spontaneously present pure land
of your own pure perception,
no other pure land has ever existed, heart son.

Your own body has always been the mandala of wisdom deities.
Don't hope for some other development-stage practice,
    heart son.

The innate and primordial purity of your own mind,
free from any basis,
has never been restrained by duality, heart son.

Through the great blessings of the lama's oral instructions
and some of your own faith and devotion,
wishing for the sake of happiness in this and future lives—
supreme child, please keep all this in mind,
and please, don't worry, my heart son.

This is the false writing of a beggar lady [Dewai Dorje].

Pure from the Beginning, Awareness Is Unimpeded

How wonderful!
Pure from the beginning, awareness is unimpeded.
When you don't correct or manipulate it intellectually
but remain within its empty lucidity,
the natural features of the dharmakaya will appear.

Within the state of mindfulness, a natural letting-be,
self-knowing awareness, pervades everywhere
and is beyond expression.
Free from the eight limitations of conceptual elaboration,
it is completely encompassed
within the indivisibility of threefold space,
and its natural glow
is that of unceasing luminosity.
Rest in this uncontrived state of undistracted non-meditation
completely beyond any attachment.

The sublime lama himself said he needed some advice and requested this with an offering scarf. Dewai Dorje simply couldn't refuse and offered these words.

ADVICE FOR JIGME KONCHOK

How marvelous! Listen, my divine noble friend.
I pray to you from the depth of my heart.

Families are impermanent, like travelers in a marketplace.
They're there at dawn but certainly gone by dusk.
I, myself, am impermanent,
like a tigress in the jungle scared by hunters surrounding her.
Oneself and others are impermanent, like magical illusions.
As I reflect on all this, I know I must singularly align my being
with the sublime Dharma for whatever life remains for me.

Don't despair over the deceptive illusions of duality,
but practice as the lamas instructed.
Don't be distracted,
but make effort to practice the sacred Dharma.
This is the lama to focus upon in both this and the next life.

Continually visualize the lama upon your crown.
Pray to her, and all outer and inner obstacles
will be dispelled and your wishes fulfilled.

Since it is never sure when the Lord of Death and his spirits will
come,
even if we welcome them at dawn, there is no benefit.
Strive to maintain the essence: the natural seat of your own
awareness.

Don't kill distinctions between cause and result by a lofty view,
but relax at ease within nonreferential openness.

Without thinking only about the faults of other kinds of
    meditation,
nurture non-distraction as it naturally is without attachment.

Without getting confused,
adopt behavior like that of dogs and pigs
and just rest in the natural liberation of whatever appears,
without pushing away or pursuing anything.[24]

The ground is awareness.
It is unimpeded and inexpressible.
In the dormancy of the alaya, it is space,
unobscured and beyond all conceptual construct.

Don't constrain the innate, unfabricated nature of what appears
    as the path
by fetters of restrictive mindfulness within empty luminosity.

The result is primordially awakened, self-knowing awareness.
Don't try to accomplish buddha as something else.
It is just your own awareness,
an expanse of primordial liberation,
unimpeded and pure from the beginning
and nothing other than that!

The dharmakaya is unborn, inconceivable, and inexpressible.
Its unobstructed power manifests unceasingly and spontaneously
    as the sambhogakaya,
while its compassionate capacity as the nirmanakaya pervades
    everything.
The indivisible three kayas are perfect as the ground of self-
    knowing awareness.

Behold the natural face of the dharmakaya, unrestrained and
  transparent,
and strive to become liberated as the naturally occurring
  sovereign, Samantabhadra.

The carefree wanderer named Tare [Dewai Dorje] offered this to the great
and sublime Jigme Konchok.

INSTRUCTIONS FOR SANGAK

Hey there, Sangak!

Practice these instructions
for the direct path of luminosity without distraction.
Awareness is primordially pure
and without any basis.
Beyond the mind of conceptual ideas,
it is a luminous state
wherein Samantabhadra's true nature
is very close.
You will behold it in this naturally occurring expanse—
uncontrived, fresh, and all-encompassing,
the nature of mind,
self-occurring awareness.
Within this state of unattached non-distraction,
rest continuously in equipoise,
and you will capture the kingdom of Samantabhadra.

These words from Dewai Dorje
are advice from a good heart.
Keep their meaning in mind and practice!

Later, at the Glorious Mountain of Ngayab,
I'm praying that we'll meet again.

Written by Sukha Vajra [Dewai Dorje].

WORDS FOR THE NUN CHOTRENG

Listen up, you faithful nun!
Meditate on the luminous Great Perfection as taught by your
lama.
Self-occurring awareness is beyond the contrivance of conceptual
mind.
Sustain it within the state of unattached yet undistracted
non-meditation,
and you will behold the true face of Samantabhadra
as your own self-occurring awareness.
In this experience of innate luminosity, you will meet me.
I am never separate from you, dear Chotreng.

Written by Dewai Dorje.

AN OFFERING TO SHILA VAJRA

I have seen the view within the expanse of my own mind
and therein am free from the duality of view and object.

My meditation rests upon the lama's oral instructions,
and now I effortlessly mingle with my innate nature.

My conduct transcends objects to accept or reject,
and now, samsara and nirvana arise
as ornaments of awareness.

I have arrived at the result,
ascended the throne of my own awareness,
and found confidence in being liberated
from anything to abandon or attain.

My intention now is to remain in this happy state
in this life and those that follow.

In this skylike view beyond focal points,
if you look at something, there is fixation.

In luminous meditation that transcends ordinary mind,
if you meditate upon something, there is duality.

If there's someone who engages in conduct
that is beyond accepting and rejecting,
there is hope and fear.

If you consider the pure expanse of three-kaya equality a result to
    attain,
there is dualistic perception.

Dewai Dorje offered this to Shila Vajra in playful wonder.

ADVICE FOR TSOGYAM AND PEWANG

Ledrel Tsal, Refuge and Protector of the Dharma,
is the primordial and ornamental manifestation of great bliss.

Listen up, my two dear friends!

Gullible and lowly, I am simple and not very bright.
I am confused about how to act virtuously
and avoid negative behavior.

Though I can't discern what to avoid and what to engage,
perceptions of my six collections appear as ornaments.[25]

I have strayed from fixation on concepts,
and my six senses primordially arise as wisdom deities.

All that I experience, sense, touch, hear, and see
has become the great ambrosial wisdom of empty bliss.
At ease within the expanse of the natural arising and liberation
of my own perceptions,
I have no understanding of what it means to fall into the lowest
    hells.

I am strong through having attained the four kinds of confidence
in the state of the primordial purity and equality
of all the things that appear to exist,
and so sensory desirables and other objects don't obscure me.

I have seen the truth of ultimate reality,
and now whatever I perceive appears as the ornamentation of
    wisdom.

Dualistic perceptions based on acceptance, rejection, hope, and
　　fear are gone.
Once you see the true nature of nondual primordial wisdom,
hell is Vajrasattva's pure land.
Why couldn't this lowly one get there?

Since, simpleton that I am,
I couldn't understand the excellent speech
that came from my two friends,
I am offering the unfabricated conduct of my being,
as I am.

In response to errors about desirable objects,
Dewai Dorje put this forth in wonder
for her two Dharma friends Tsogyam and Pewang.

May virtue prevail!

A PLAYFUL RESPONSE

Dharmadhatu wisdom is lofty and spacious.
What can the eyes of an old dog see?

Mirrorlike wisdom's pure brilliant clarity
is difficult to see when abiding in the dark forest of ignorance.

Since the wisdom of equality is a great encompassing vast
    expanse,
it is impossible for it to fit in the old mind of someone like me.

Discerning wisdom is unobstructed skill.
What can the mind of an impetuous child overcome?

All-accomplishing wisdom is swift and goes everywhere.
A legless person like me has no chance to catch it.

If there were some positive qualities
in enacting the behavior of the five poisons as they are,
what would sentient beings wandering throughout the three
    realms
be confused about?
The experiences of suffering in the lower realms as a result
would be meaningless.

I have no need for lots of words that contradict the ultimate.
Buddha taught relative cause and result to be infallible.
What sense is there in a result that has no cause?
I haven't seen mind burned
by something other than the five poisons.

With their eyes of wisdom, my two friends
see the enactment of the five poisons as they are
to be Dharma practice.
This accords with what previous masters have taught to their
sharpest disciples
and aligns with the pith instructions that reveal how the five
poisons
can arise as supports, without needing to reject or transform
them.

Although I think instructions such as these are marvelous,
they don't fit into my understanding and always remain
disconnected.
It is like pointing out the stars to a dog.

Someone like me isn't even able to understand the lower vehicles.
However, since you requested me to say something,
my tradition does align with the key points of these instructions.
Although they can't be comprehended by small-minded
individuals,
Dewai Dorje still gives expedient and definitive advice.

This was offered as a playful response to both my Dharma friends Tsultrim
Dorje and Tsogyam.

Advice for Two Dharma Friends

I pray to Ledrel, Protector of the Wheel of Refuge—
please bless me and manifest upon my chakra of great bliss
without ever leaving.

Now listen, my two dear Dharma friends.

I, the humble and carefree Dekyong Wangmo,
will share all of the secret key points for practice
without hiding, concealing, or faking anything.

I met a wish-fulfilling partner,
and he taught me all the many instructions I needed.
However, since an understanding of their meaning
didn't land due to my weak intelligence and small mind,
I naturally behave according to my negative karma,
afflictions, and five poisons.

The darkness of my ignorance is especially thick
since for me the luminous aspect of the ultimate expanse is less.
I myself have not arrived at clarity
and am like a human carried away by cannibals.
My anger comes swiftly like a thick mist,
and its contamination obscures the luminosity of mirrorlike
     wisdom.

Like a chicken, the power of my wings is weak,
and the time for liberation from samsara has not arrived.
The ocean of my pride is deep,
and the luminosity of the wisdom of equality is shadowed.

Like all the female dogs around the village,
I have no time to equalize the rampant actions of negative karma.
I have hot flashes of desire that weaken the arrow
of penetrating knowledge's luminosity.

Like a blind bird, I find it difficult to traverse the path,
and I haven't found liberation from samsara.
The dark winds of my jealousy are turbulent
and suppress the luminosity of all-accomplishing wisdom.

Like a rotten hollow tree trunk,
I have no time to be able to benefit others.
Now no matter what I say, I just deceive with the five poisons.
I wander through the three realms as a child of cause and result.

How could such a lowly lady like this
behold Tsogyal and Varahi?

You two—ponder this again and again.
If you take someone with a negative form like me as a support for
    refuge,
learned and intelligent people will worry and make you the talk
    of the town.
When I reflect in this way,
I think you should leave this humble lady behind!

Dewai Dorje wrote this for her Dharma friends, noble Tsogyam and
    Tsultrim Dorje,
by the light of a butter lamp,
without hiding the fact that she has no wisdom qualities
and her practice is simply the enactment of the five poisons.

A Response to Tupzang

Hey, hey! Listen now, my dear student Tupten Zangpo.
Though you think that I should be more relaxed in what I do
    physically and verbally,
I have observed the way Tulku, Wish-Fulfilling Jewel, lives his
    life
and know I mustn't be indifferent about my actions and behavior.

Wish-Fulfilling Jewel's wisdom body
is primordially accomplished as the kaya of the deity.
He doesn't need the constant fixation of so-called strict deity
    retreat.
In the perception of his students,
he appears in a magical wisdom kaya.

He is beyond maintaining silence to realize the resonance of
    sound as mantra,
so inhalation and exhalation of breath is the wheel of recitation
    for him.
He doesn't need to rely on silence to hold the measure of his
    realization,
to train beings as needed,
and to bestow a deluge of ripening and liberating Dharma
    teaching.

Within the great luminous expanse of his changeless and secret
    wisdom mind,
all things of samsara and nirvana are spontaneously perfected as a
    great equality.
Limitless is his primordial wisdom
that sees the nature as it is and the multiple ways it manifests.

Efforts to develop clarity, purity, stability, and more—
he doesn't need these elaborations.

Compared to a buddha endowed with such realization and conduct,
I am like someone boasting to a bejeweled lion.
If my exalted state were equal to his,
I would do whatever I wanted!
That, however, is not the case.
So, I must be careful with everything I do.

No matter what is done in samsara,
where causes fully ripen into results,
difficulties arise.
Therefore, one must examine with discernment and insight
one's own experience and realization.

As for myself, I still place hope in effortful development-stage
practice
and establish its foundation through the key points of clarity,
purity, and stability
according to the teachings on yidam deity practice.

My recitation of the quintessence doesn't mix worldly talk with
silence.
Performing austerities connected to the vows of individual
liberation and more
is my practice of patience.
Making effort to be unmistaken about actual realization, just as
it is,
is my practice of enthusiastic joy.

My practice of discipline is my commitment
to align appearances, sounds, and thoughts as one,
and manifesting the object, agent, and result of purification
is my practice of wisdom.

Transformation of my ordinary body, speech, and mind as the
   three mandalas
is my practice of concentration.

Gathering the accumulations through the result of imagined and
   material offerings
is my practice of generosity.

In reflecting upon all this,
I see that since I still have hope
in searching for some other result,
even if I were to gather the qualities of merely a fraction
of the Great Kind One's wisdom body
in the basis of my own, forget about being equals!
When I think about the qualities within even one of his pores,
I am unable to match him in thought, word, or deed.

Based on the way things look externally,
I have become the basis for everyone's wrong views,
due to the effect of my inferior body.

Based on my inner experience,
concerted training in my commitments
to overcome my gross afflictions is weak.

Secretly, since my wisdom is less,
I haven't been able to extract the essence
of development- and completion-stage practice.

Since I practice deity and mantra
by fabricating them with my body, speech, and mind,
my understanding may just be a focus on eternalism.
Such thinking is the reason I should engage in recitation and
   meditation continuously.

I don't have any positive qualities.
I am an ignorant sentient being.
I am stifled by defilement from a womb birth
and the ripening of my illusory body's habitual patterns.

Rivaling a buddha whose deeds and behavior
display realization of the three mandalas
is like a fox trying to match up to a tiger with great prowess.

Therefore, properly examine your own mind,
and act in harmony with the Dharma
in all you do, say, and think.
Then you will find the way to free yourself
from an attitude of indifference.
Don't confuse yourself by proclaiming that
deeds and behavior equal to the buddhas
come from being briefly unrestrained
in what you do, say, and think.

Learn about the life stories of the triumphant buddhas from
    times past;
buddhahood was never accomplished
through even a short period of indifference.
When you bring forth virtuous activity
in what you do and say,
and meditate with concentration,
I am sure you will come to understand
the instructions for attaining buddhahood in one lifetime.

Tsuldor said to me, "Tupzang said that your retreat is very strict and Tulku
Rinpoche doesn't need to be as confined as you." In response, I, Dewai
Dorje, thoroughly examined my own mind and wrote this reply.

May virtue prevail!

FAMILY ADVICE

Father, Vajradhara, Ledrel Tsal,
don't sleep, your wisdom mind in the peaceful expanse,
but gaze upon us, your students and followers, with compassion.

Due to my lesser merit,
I lack the fortune of being in your actual presence, Father,
but since compassion has neither near nor far,
you are forever residing upon my crown chakra of great bliss.

Thinking more and more just increases my sadness,
but revealing the faults of these degenerate times
through lots of talk from me, an old lady, isn't needed.

However, for my family, connected to me by blood and karma,
I will offer three pieces of heartfelt and sound advice.
Fasten your attention to the gateways of your ears,
and listen to the words of your mother.

Long ago in India, the glorious king of kings
practiced whatever the Mother taught and as a result
became a disciple of Tilopa and realized the supreme siddhi.

Thus, by virtue of the infallibility of action and result,
you too are attuned with the Dharma.
So, here are three words of advice from your mother.
Always and everywhere, you must be mindful, vigilant, and
    conscientious.

The vows of individual liberation, of bodhisattvas,
and of Secret Mantra are a unified path.

There's nothing there that you need to accept or reject.
So, transform your iron trunk of unchanging mindfulness
by adding precious bodhichitta,
just like alchemizing iron into gold
and hold the teachings on mindfulness, vigilance,
and conscientiousness as the most exalted.

Upon the excellent face of the mirror of unchanging
    mindfulness,
the efforts of insight are like a skillful cleaner.
When you properly clean conscientiousness with bodhichitta,
it isn't difficult to discover the purest and highest path.
Therefore, you must be mindful, vigilant, and conscientious always.

Ha, ha!
Tsuldor's mindfulness is like a little bird on a treetop—
sometimes it's there, and sometimes it's not.
Don't be like that.
Be mindful, vigilant, and conscientious.

Tupzang's mindfulness is like water gone to the feet of fodder
    husks—
he uses it in samsara but rarely toward the sublime Dharma.
Don't be like that.
Be mindful, vigilant, and conscientious.

Chodron's mindfulness is like wind howling through a yak's
    horn—
sometimes it's wild,
and it isn't stable for long.
Don't be like that.
Be mindful, vigilant, and conscientious.

Khidron's mindfulness is like a fish in water—
present deep below but not coming to the surface

and becoming conscious.
Don't be like that.
Be mindful, vigilant, and conscientious.

Atsak's mindfulness is like a mole underground.
It arises in the mind but doesn't reach consciousness.
Don't be like that.
Be mindful, vigilant, and conscientious.

Dewai Dorje is like a thorny tree,
saying nasty things to everyone, near and far.
It is truly incredible that a mother and family like this get together!

Keep the meaning of these points in your minds at all times
    mindfully.
I, your mother, have no practice besides this.
Even if your realization is high,
please practice in this way.

Mindfulness doesn't harm realization—why would it?
Utterly pure mindfulness is a spacious skylike expanse
where varieties of thought and perception arise
as the wheel of ultimate reality itself.
Totally pure mindfulness nourishes meditative concentration,
so be mindful, vigilant, and conscientious always.

On fire with five poisons,
a daft old lady with pure heartfelt intentions
jotted down a list for her family
at the retreat hermitage of Sera Monastery
out of laziness.
May its spread bring virtue!

Keep this in mind and practice it!
Saying "Yah, yah! I get it! I get it!" is like boiled lung.[26]

It's obviously meaningless and pointless.
Therefore, make sure to integrate the essential meaning within
your mind.

May the beloved family of the true Mother
enjoy never parting during this life, future lifetimes, and the
bardo
but remain indivisible from the sole Father, Ledrel Tsal.

Sukha Vajra [Dewai Dorje] wrote this confused advice for her family.

Advice for the Incarnation of the Dharma King Namnying[27]

Embodiment of All Triumphant Buddhas,
Supreme Protector of the Dharma,
and Everlasting Refuge, Pema Ledrel Tsal—
pray, remain as Lord of the Family until I awaken
and bless me to mingle my mind with the Dharma.

Listen deeply, wise and intelligent one.
The ways of entering the vehicles of Dharma
such as the scriptural tradition and more
contain inconceivable viewpoints and tenets.
How could someone as ignorant and blind as me
understand the meaning of their eloquent explanations?

However, due to pure aspirations and merit from past
    lifetimes,
I met an awareness-holding lineage lama,
and the light rays of his compassionate blessings
cleared all the darkness from my mind.

Then, I studied a little bit about
the extremely profound and secret path
of the definitive meaning,
the way to actualize buddhahood in a single lifetime.
Based on that, I will offer a bit of explanation
on positively developing the secret key points
of the exalted state of primordial liberation.

The basic space of the ground is unchanging and luminous.
It is self-existent awareness,
the dharmakaya beyond the dualistic ideas of conceptual mind.

Mind and all its thought activity are primordially liberated
and cleansed within this ground of equality,
where kayas and primordial wisdom are perfected as the vase kaya.

Through deep faith that sees the lama as an actual buddha,
the true nature of this lucid, empty awareness is recognized,
and without reliance upon words or indications,
self-abiding primordial wisdom becomes evident.

In this approach, one doesn't become accomplished
through engaging the two accumulations of merit and wisdom
    separately,
as is the case in the *paramita* vehicle.
Instead, awareness abiding as the three kayas
actualized at the time of the ground
is the dharmakaya, utterly pure from the beginning.

That is the key point of the result
to arrive, instantaneously,
at the royal kingdom of Samantabhadra.

These three crucial features are not found
in the causal scriptures about mind
but are subsumed within the special qualities of the ground.

The primordial ground is unchanging, like the sky.
Transparent and beyond conceptual construct,
it is a pristine openness,
free from unawareness,
just like the light of the sun.

It is completely clear and luminous without any
   obscuration,
like a mirror where anything can appear,
but there's no fixation,
just a comprehensive knowing.

The ground is stainless, like mercury.
It is wide awake, naked primordial wisdom.

This, a naturally occurring and uncontrived state
endowed with these four qualities,
abides within.
These are the special feature of awareness.

In terms of separate conceptual distinctions,
the primordially pure original ground,
based upon the aspect of its essence,
ultimately is not a thing with truly existent characteristics.

Self-knowing awareness is baseless and rootless.
It is uncontrived, unchanging, and beyond the reach of words.

No effort is needed—
it transcends all intellect.
It is beyond conceptual construct
and endowed with the three gateways to liberation.

Ultimate reality is uncreated.
It is a primordially empty sphere
where the perfection and equality
of samsara and nirvana is the dharmakaya
naturally appearing to itself.
It's utterly amazing!

That skylike experience is naturally liberated
and without fixation;
it transcends all effortful accepting and rejecting.

Within this, inconceivable ultimate reality,
primordial wisdom arises, but not as a meditation.

When the true meaning of ineffability is directly seen,
you will discover the result of nothing to attain.

Like tributaries from a great ocean,
all phenomena emanate from the ground's vast expanse.
Whatever arises is arising as the dharmakaya's dynamic energy.
Whatever appears is appearing within primordial wisdom.
Whatever there is exists as the natural state of awareness.
Whatever concepts there are exist as unconditioned thinking.
Everything, everything is great primordial wisdom,
unwavering from the ultimate expanse.
The exalted state of Samantabhadra is incredible!

In this way, the supreme essence of Dharma
is this secret of your own mind,
completely understood through profound insight.

Even though you may have skillfully expounded the meaning
of the eighty-four thousand Dharma teachings,
the ultimate way to achieve realization
is understanding the single unique sphere of your own mind.

This is the unsurpassed result
of becoming indivisible with Samantabhadra.

Furthermore, even if I lack eloquent explanations from skilled
      orators
about the way that awareness abides as the ground,

according to the oral tradition of the lineage awareness-holding
    lamas,
these profound key points are like children jumping onto their
    mothers' laps.
They are an elucidation of quintessential heart advice
for the noble incarnation of the Dharma King Namnying.

A non-Dharmic wandering beggar lady
who is neither nun nor common wife,
Dechen Dewai Dorje, a liar and confused person
who holds the name of a treasure revealer
virtuously wrote down in words whatever came to mind
as a substitute for her speech,
from the pleasure grove of Sera Monastery.

May the power of this positively increase his noble commitment
to attain the glory of total liberation in this life and body
and spontaneously enact deeds that benefit all!

Sukha Vajra [Dewai Dorje] devotedly offered this with a silken scarf on
the fifteenth day of the sixth month from the retreat at Sera Monastery.

A Spell of Crazy Advice

Oh dear! How very sad!

Embodiment of all triumphant buddhas,
Protector of the Dharma, Pema Ledrel Tsal—
consider me with your compassion from the invisible sphere of
    space
and lovingly protect me, inseparable from you, until I awaken.

"Through the power of pure intentions from prayers made long
    ago,
method and wisdom will remain beyond meeting or parting
throughout all their lifetimes."
So, the vajra prophecies declared and repeatedly eulogized.

Yet now, due to the force of karmic winds,
you, Sublime One, dissolved into space
and are no longer seen or heard.
There is no greater "beyond meeting and parting" than this.

Since I have no other hope besides you,
I pray that as long as I remain circling
in the wheel of positive and negative actions,
you won't forsake me with the force of your great love,
even pitiable as I have now become.

Please, show me your true, joyous face
and don't ever leave me.

From this life throughout all my lifetimes,
may I never be apart from you, Lama and Glorious Protector!

Undaunted by obstacles and the forces of negativity,
may we bring to completion the infinite activities of method and
    wisdom
and open the doorways for vast enlightened deeds
through profound Dharma teachings.

Once we have fully emptied the most unfortunate abodes
within samsara's three realms,
may we actualize nondual awareness kayas
and attain actual buddhahood
within the youthful vase kaya of original space.

Dewai Dorje offered this,
a spell of crazy advice,
to the ears of Shila Vajra.

May virtue prevail!

Instructions for Noble Senge

Luminous self-knowing awareness is the ultimate heruka
residing as Pema Ledrel upon my crown chakra of great bliss.
To you I pray—ripen my mind that it be freed.

Awareness is pure from the beginning,
beyond the reach of thought and word.

No matter what arises, just rest without attachment and fabrication
and the ties of mind's dualistic and deluded perception will come
undone.

This exalted state of great primordial wisdom abides within.

It is your own uncontrived awareness,
groundless and without any basis.

Don't fixate on outer objects,
but sustain everything that arises in its expanse.

Mind's inner thinking is the natural face of the dharmakaya,
the sphere of primordial wisdom, fresh and innate.

Sustain its expressiveness within unchanging space and awareness
beyond all conceptual constructs.

Samantabhadra's exalted state of awareness is direct liberation!

These words, per the request of Senge,
were written by the carefree wanderer named Sukha [Dewai Dorje].

May they be virtuous!

ADVICE FOR KUNZANG NANGDZE

Listen up, my sublime Dharma friend.

Empty advice, you don't need.
It will tire you out.
Deceitful thoughts, you don't need to track.
Just sustain the unchanging vajra essence of your own mind
and seize, right now, the kingdom of the dharmakaya.

What's the use in knowing many philosophical assertions and
    beliefs?
You won't become enlightened through relative, childish
    teachings.
Ours is the tradition of the ultimate!
Practice the essential Great Perfection
with a resolute intention to remain in isolated mountain retreat.

The essence of self-knowing awareness is pure.
It is like a stainless sky.
The meaning of the luminous Great Perfection
is beyond the reach of intellectual ideas.

You must strive to practice this peerless path unmistakenly
by leaving your mind free, unfabricated, and relaxed.
Then you will behold the primordial wisdom
of luminous awareness from within.

The view has no focal point.
It is beyond objects of dualistic perception.

Meditation has no fixation.
It is the state of the luminous dharmakaya.

Conduct is a naturally liberated expanse,
beyond the duality of acceptance and rejection.

The result is the actualization of self-knowing awareness,
   Samantabhadra.
Effortlessly seize this: the royal throne of the dharmakaya!

These words are for my student Kunzang Nangdze,
who said some spiritual advice was needed.

Faced with such a clear request,
the lowly wanderer, the misguided Dewai Dorje
offered whatever came to mind
as a reminder of practice.

May virtue prevail!

ADVICE FOR ATRAK

Universal embodiment of triumphant buddhas
gone before, present now, and still to come,
Heruka, Everlasting Protector and Refuge, Pema Ledrel Tsal—
pray, remain as Lord of the Family until I awaken
and merge my mind with the Dharma.

Listen, fortunate one who made pure prayers long ago—
if you are interested in embarking upon the perfectly pure path,
you must rely upon fully qualified and virtuous spiritual
    friends.

Study such teachers' realization and behavior while pleasing
    them
through three ways of service.[28]

Train your mind with the four thoughts
to turn away from samsara,
and be smart about what to avoid and engage.

One's homeland is like an isle of cannibals:
whatever is done there amounts to nothing
apart from causing rebirth in the lower realms of samsara,
purchased by the price of one's own unhappiness and suffering.

Like a lair of poisonous snakes that brings ruin,
karmic results are undeceiving. They ripen on you.
Therefore, remember that all samsaric doings
ultimately have no essence.

If you can practice just one Dharma teaching from the depth of
    your heart,
in a place free of distractions where the qualities of wisdom well
    forth,
such as an uninhabited and isolated mountain abode,
I think you will understand the essential meaning
of luminous and uncompounded self-knowing awareness.

Without intellectually fabricating or changing awareness,
rest in its indescribable empty cognizance.
This is the key point for great actualization of the view.

Profound and luminous, ultimate reality has no direction or
    limit.
In its ground, kayas and primordial wisdom are complete and
    perfect.
It is the natural state of awareness,
where all the things of samsara and nirvana
are beyond the reach of effort and conceptual construct.
The key point for meditation is just this great primordial
    wisdom—
the unity of emptiness and luminosity—
totally beyond all fixation on meditation.

Within the state of awareness,
all that appears is beyond something to accept or reject.
Everything dawns as the manifestation of great primordial
    wisdom,
and dualistic perception dissolves into space.
The key point for conduct is to rest in this uncontrived state,
which ultimately is self-existent wakefulness itself.

Great primordial liberation is beyond the mind of conceptual
    ideas,
as well as the words view, meditation, and conduct.

It is the luminous expanse of three-kaya equality.
The key point of the result is to actualize this,
self-knowing awareness.

Try to practice continuously in this way,
and I have no doubt that you will arrive in this very lifetime
at the everlasting kingdom of awareness,
which abides neither in samsara nor in nirvana.

These words, coming from a profound request by the faithful Atrak,
were composed by the lazy Dechen Dewai Dorje.

May they be virtuous!

A Teaching on View, Meditation, Conduct, and Result for Chatral Sherap Ozer

To my peerless guide Pema Ledrel,
indivisible with Samantabhadra,
I pray—look upon us with compassion,
and bless my mind that it ripen and become free.

Now then, fortunate one, please listen.
Self-occurring awareness is the awakened mind.
It is beyond conceptual construct
and endowed with the three gateways to liberation.
It is the glorious great nature of kayas and primordial wisdom,
the all-encompassing, nondual expanse of samsara and nirvana.
To realize that, just as it is, is the view.

This uncontrived relaxed knowing
is an unimpeded and effortless state
free from the ideas of conceptual mind,
where everything appears as the nature of great primordial
      wisdom.
To actualize that natural "letting-be" is the meditation.

Whatever arises is left as it is in this innate expanse
where accepting and rejecting are primordially exhausted
and dualistic thought is gone.
Relax therein with the naked encounter of perceptual objects,
and take their appearances as the path of wisdom—
a great skylike experience of natural liberation of attachment and
      clinging.
To rest in this uncontrived state is the conduct.

An inner luminosity,
where essence, nature, and capacity are gathered inward yet not
    dulled,
is the dharmakaya, self-occurring awareness.
It is a state of primordial wisdom that is unchanging,
abiding neither in samsara nor in enlightenment.
This is the result, beyond the reach of anything to abandon or
    attain.

These key points of view, meditation, conduct, and result
are just conceptual distinctions of one thing.
Chatral Sherap Ozer requested this with a mandala,
and the daft and frivolous wandering beggar
Sukha Vajra Tsal [Dewai Dorje] composed it.

May virtue prevail!

Spontaneous Advice Mingling Joy and Sorrow

Kye ma! Kye hu! Oh my! Oh dear!

The things of the world,
everything I think about,
just make me sad.

Impermanent, fleeting things,
whatever I consider,
are like guests gathered at a family reunion long ago.
Look at how everything gathered separates at last.

Wealth and possessions are just like dew on grass—
look at how everything collected runs out at last.

My beloved soulmate is just like a rainbow in the sky—
look at how partnerships end in parting.

My precious son is like mist in the sky—
look at how finally, we lose everything we've protected.

Joyful Dharma friends are like summer flowers—
look at how all that comes together finally falls apart.

We, mother and son, came together through earlier karma.
Look at us here—we have no idea what will happen.

Now, in any event, there's no essence to samsara.
We must practice the sublime Dharma,
which is what is essential and meaningful.

You've heard the instructions for realization of self-knowing
    awareness as the lama
through the great kindness of the sole father, our realized master.
Don't waste them now. Put them into practice.

Align the rest of your life with these essential teachings
and practice the glorious Dharma to benefit all.

When the blessings of the lama's wisdom body enter your body,
you receive the instructions for ripening your ordinary body
as the wisdom form of the deity.

When the blessings of the lama's wisdom speech
penetrate your own ordinary speech,
the inhalation and exhalation of your breath
will dawn as the manifestation of sacred syllables.

When the blessings of the lama's wisdom mind
infuse your own ordinary mind,
you will realize the meaning of ultimate reality,
and then, with your mind aligned with the lama's wisdom,
you will gain confidence in the great purity and equality of
    samsara and nirvana.

These words are spontaneous advice mingling joy and sorrow.
They were written by a heartbroken girl, Dewai Dorje,
and offered to her heart son Shila Vajra
as heart advice and as a lament.

May virtue prevail!

Words of Despair

Most compassionate master and guide of beings,
omniscient Pema Ledrel Tsal—
think of me and my unfortunate karma with compassion.

As I think more and more, sadness grows.
As I reflect and remember, my tears fall.

I met you through karma from past lives,
and you cared for me lovingly for so long.

At present, due to evil karma and my negative and lowly physical
      form,
I have little opportunity to be with you, Father.

Though I possess the most profound teachings of your wisdom
      speech,
my low intelligence makes me a poor vessel for them.

Though all my beloved Dharma siblings still remain,
I alone have been exiled to the unknown ends of the earth,
where I don't recognize anything apart from grass, trees, and
      water.

The beaming face of the lama, the exceedingly kind father,
has disappeared.
Now my expectations for direct teachings goes to texts—
I don't have a single lama to teach me the path.
My own mind has to take care of itself.

I have no one with whom to share the experiences of love in my
    heart,
and must cry out with longing to your invisible wisdom body.

I have no one from whom to request the ripening and liberating
    instructions,
and must rely on my own mind as the lama.

I have nowhere to make material offerings
and must offer with my imagination.

I have no more the fortune to gaze upon the mandala of your face
and must rely on sleeping Buddhalochana.

I am without the touch or sight of your splendid wisdom body
and must rely on the meditations and dreams of my cloudy mind.

I have no place to receive the nectar of your kind words of
    wisdom
and must compose texts based on your oral teachings.

I have no way to request the experiences and realization of your
    loving wisdom mind
and must rely on intellectually asserting twofold emptiness
    (posited as the indivisibility of the emptiness of the
    nonconceptual primordial wisdom of the lama's enlightened
    mind and the primordial wisdom of the emptiness of my own
    awareness, the fourth part without the three).[29]

I have no one to ask about what to do
in thought, word, and deed
and now must take care of everything myself.

I have no one with whom I can actually share the foods I have
and must rely on offering the first portion of the feast.

Now, in all my thoughts,
I just remember my sublime master.

Even if I have nice clothes,
there's no place to wear them.
Even if I hear nice words,
there's no place to share them.
Even if experience and realization dawn,
there's no one to tell.
Happy and sad karma unfold,
and there is no one to whom I can ask questions.
I am oppressed with grief and feel hopeless.

Anything I can think about doing
only increases my suffering.
I have no control over death,
that much is sure,
but I think it best to go far away
since I have no protection.

Since my beloved Shila Vajra and your Dharma brother
[Natsok Rangdrol] don't intend to abandon me,
it falls to me to end my pain.

At present, when I think more and more,
all I can do is remember my lama.
I recall my Sublime Master, Buddha of All Time,
the Ever-Excellent Sublime Master Pema Ledrel Tsal.

With your great loving heart,
please, Father—hold me inseparably with you
from now throughout all my lifetimes
in the treasury of your exalted state of realization.
Then in whichever sublime pure realm is fitting,
may I be reborn first among your retinue.

If you don't welcome, teach, and guide me there,
there will have been little use for our connection of thirteen
    years.
So, now by the power of the undeceiving two truths,
may I become spiritually accomplished
indivisibly with you, Sublime Master!

I became unbearably sad at one point
from having witnessed the pain in this life
and future lifetimes for sinners like me.
Out of my senses, I, the orphan Dewai Dorje
wrote down my despair in words
and offered them to Shila Vajra.

May this be virtuous!

A Letter of Foolish Advice, a Mask of Awareness[30]

This letter, "A Mask of Awareness," offered as foolish advice, is for Chogtrul Dondrup Dorje, a Dharma master of scripture and realization. Due to the extreme difficulty of decoding the profound key teachings of the dakinis, it's obvious that I can't clearly explain the meaning of their oral instructions. Nonetheless, I will say a little something as just a mistaken reification, a mask of realization.

The original, fundamental nature of reality is the great entity of the three: essence, nature, and capacity. Therein, the aspect that makes up the ground of both liberation and confusion is called the general ground. However, the aspects of liberation and confusion are just conceptual distinctions since the ground and the appearances of the ground are one in essence.

From within the nature of the ground that is like that, the power of an extremely subtle aspect of awareness moves the essence of the wisdom winds. (These fivefold lights, or life-force winds, are by nature the primordial wisdom of the ground.)[31] Then, the appearances of the ground, manifestations of spontaneously present wisdom, arise in eight ways.[32] In their arising is consciousness, naturally occurring as an unobstructed openness through the dynamic energy of awareness's capacity.

Samantabhadra, from the very first instant, gave birth to awareness without losing consciousness to external objects. Then, through recognizing that all spontaneously present kayas and wisdom—which are the natural complexion of the primordial ground, a space beyond all conceptual construct—are self-appearing, Samantabhadra saw the way that awareness is in its true nature, as well as how it abides as the ground (the dividing line between awareness and ignorance). From then on, Samantabhadra remained in the great luminous state of unimpeded primordial wisdom, in the true nature of the ground itself, completely beyond resting or not resting in meditation.

All path appearances of the spontaneous presence of the ground's primordial expressiveness are naturally perfect and complete (within it). Therefore, for Samantabhadra, separate phenomena of a path and a result, which must be newly accomplished, have no reference whatsoever. From that perspective, path is simply a conventional designation. (Resting in the nature in the second instant,) Samantabhadra didn't need to rely upon any progression through the paths and levels of the buddha fields, endowed with the twenty-five glorious powers. These are the phenomena of the result.

In the great primordial wisdom of the natural state of meditation, Samantabhadra (Kunzang) is *ever* (*kun*) unmoving, unwavering, and unchanging throughout past, present, and future. Samantabhadra—as the very nature of unconditional space beyond conceptual construct that never abided in confusion and cannot possibly engage in confusion later—is *excellent* (*zang*).[33]

In sum, having instantaneously perfected all sublime qualities of the nature of the ground (once the spontaneously present, everlasting, and all-pervasive activities are complete, liberation within inner pure space occurred in the third instant), Samantabhadra discovered the sixfold resultant phenomena and then, like a mirage, demonstrated becoming liberated within the original ground. This is simply my understanding. I am unable to clearly say with conviction that this is the inner meaning of primordial wisdom based upon study and contemplation.

I've made the meaning of this easy to understand for those who, like me, don't have comprehension from study. Based just on the distinction between awareness and unawareness, there are no outer and inner dimensions to the ground, but it's taught as if there are. For an individual person, recognition of the fundamental nature of mind, just as it is, is the ground of liberation. Whereas, through solidification of perception, the mere aspect of mind and its not knowing are the ground of confusion.

Based on these distinctions, which come from the oral instructions (on differentiating mind and awareness) of sublime lineage lamas, what is correctly seen as the fundamental nature of ultimate reality free from arising, ceasing, and dwelling is the *ground*.

Until realization is actualized through analysis and familiarity, meditate by practicing view and conduct as a unity without laziness and distraction. Practice must be the antidote for ignorance and the afflictions. It must sever dualistic perception and concepts about the self.

What needs to become liberated? Your own mind must become liberated. When it isn't, it's the thread stringing dualistic perception. Ways to subdue the mind must be established through three valid modes of knowledge: the teachings of the Buddha, the transmissions of the lama, and your own self-knowing awareness. Until you arrive at the level of extinguishment within ultimate reality, practice untiringly and give up everything that you do, say, and think that isn't in harmony with the Dharma. The *path* is what brings the natural state of the ground to completion.

When you practice in this way and actualize the unchanging dharmakaya, the pure space of the three-kaya equality, without any intellectualization, it'll be like the ocean without any differentiation or exclusions, once drops of water have mixed into it. What are called path awareness and ground awareness are not separate. Like space dissolving into space, they are nondual and of a single taste within the dharmakaya expanse of the primordial ground. The attainment of stability there is simply designated as the *result*.

Ultimately, however, according to individual minds there are various ways—more and less sublime—that this appears from the purview of dualistic perception. It isn't definite as one thing. For example, since I don't have many inner and outer qualities, there is no beginning nor end to all the explanations on these topics.

Though you may not know the long-term possibilities of these oral instructions, simply because you have not broken Rinpoche's command, I, a deluded one, have shared how ultimate reality is to my mind, simply through having intellectually examined it. I hope you will keep this in the precious expanse of your wisdom mind.

Composed by Kunzang Dekyong Chonyi Wangmo [Dewai Dorje].

May virtue prevail!

A LETTER OF ADVICE FOR MY NOBLE STUDENTS
AT THE RETREAT CENTER OF TSANGAR[34]

All you students, high and low, don't just sit around on your beds occupying yourselves with enjoying meat, butter, cheese, and whatever you like, all the while proudly saying you are doing the highest practice. Try your best to become independently proficient in the practices of primordial purity and spontaneous presence. As you know, there's nothing reliable about changing objective perceptions. All appearances of confusion and its distorted forms are teachers who show their own illusory and unreal nature. Right there is where you need to seize the throne of awareness. Otherwise, if you don't understand that but say "Everything is illusory, dreamlike, and my own perception," it is the same as being sure that drawings of horses and oxen are the real thing. Since the appearances to come in the bardo are like that, it'll be difficult for you to cut through them.

Therefore, like I already told you earlier when giving the oral instructions, once you attain confidence in primordially pure awareness and recognize its spontaneous presence to be self-appearing, you must perfect that training. That is how you will attain stability in these as a unified path and will later actualize the confidence and warmth of realization.

Don't depart from the view, during meditation, post-meditation, and daily activities, no matter what positive or negative circumstances, happiness, pain, joy, or sorrow arise. Never separate from the confidence of your meditation. Don't stray for even a single second from being conscientious about your conduct, and familiarize yourself with the true nature of reality, your own awareness.

As I told you, you must reach the extent of relative phenomena becoming liberated as ultimate reality. All of you, high and low, must maintain this practice to the utmost and totally reject—in thought, word, and deed—everything that isn't the pure Dharma. I request you to practice for not less than one hundred days, keeping harmony and pure ethical discipline.

Dewai Dorje offered this while watching the sunrise on the Riwoche Zhapdrung's golden temple on the seventeenth day of the twelfth Rabbit month.[35]

May virtue prevail!

A Letter of Advice for the Students of Jigdral Chokyi Lodro

I pray to Pema Totreng Tsal,
who embodies all three kayas and buddha families
and is indivisible from Rigdzin Jigdral Chokyi Wang—
please, bless our minds.

How amazing! Listen up my sublime friends.
Worldly activities of samsara have no essence.
The sacred Dharma is what is essential.
Diligently practice it in this lifetime, Dharma friends.

Make aspirations six times throughout the day and night
to be inseparable from the actual emanation of Orgyen—
Jigdral Chokyi Wang—
and you will recognize your true nature of primordial wisdom,
Dharma friends.

Don't be sad, thinking you won't see me again.
How could we ever be separate?

Unborn and uncontrived,
an utterly open expanse beyond all conceptual construct
is me, Kunzang Wangmo—primordial emptiness.
In this unfathomable and inexpressible state,
you will see who I really am.

Unblocked and self-occurring,
its manifest displays of spontaneously present wisdom

are me, Dewai Dorje: empty awareness.
Within the expanse of this unconfined empty lucidity,
you will see who I really am.

From the magical manifestations
appearing as the dynamic energy of its capacity,
I, Dekyong Wangmo, am limitless.
You will meet me in this domain of unchanging ultimate reality.

The appearance of the ground—
spontaneously present, unconditioned great bliss—
and the experiences of the path,
are invisible from me, Khacho Wangmo.
You will meet my true nature as this primordial great perfection.

We are never separate, Dharma friends!

Nonreligious and unvirtuous,
I, Dewai Dorje, deeply wish to align
the rest of my life with the Dharma.
With my life and practice one,
I am completely happy.

Poor and hungry,
I, Dewai Dorje, deeply wish to focus my life
on asceticism just like a beggar.
Without social or Dharma skills,
I am completely happy.

Unknown and unrecognized,
I, Dewai Dorje, intend to establish my practice
in unfixed mountain retreats.
I am completely happy,
regardless of what people say about my actions.

Neither single nor coupled,
I, Dewai Dorje, deeply wish to meditate in ease,
all by myself.
I am completely happy,
even if people say my living isn't proper.

It would be fine if I thought I were a qualified consort
for a regent of the Lotus Born,
but since my merit is less, I have become contentious.
I have little need for a nasty life partner
who fights and competes with me.

My consort is the hero of appearances as great bliss,
and even if people gossip that I'm single and unpartnered,
I am completely happy.

Without Father to protect me, Mother to guide me,
or a romantic partner, I, Dewai Dorje,
haven't any heroes I'm attached to.
My deepest desire is to journey to the Lotus Light Palace of Great
    Bliss.
Though I lack the power of having my father's title,
I am completely happy.

Of course, this is a joke my dear Dharma friends!
There's no one happier than me,
happy, happy girl that I am.
Paying attention to others, taking care of attendants and such—
I don't want any of this.
Watching out for myself is enough.
Benefiting myself and everyone else
is happening right here where I am.

There's no one sadder than me,
sad, sad girl that I am.

My partner rose up as an enemy
and led me into things I didn't want.
Through various means, he expelled me
without any power of my own to another place.
I don't even have legs that can walk
and move around like an arthritic.

Wretched as well are my orphaned children,
cut off from the fortune of having their father's wealth
and incessantly scolded.
We're pathetic, anxious, and utterly stressed.
Who could bear our suffering, mother and children?

Both my son, precious as life itself,
and my equally cherished daughter
wander uncertainly in unknown lands like dogs.
They are shamed in the footsteps of their heartless father.

These appearances surely are just illusions, dreams.
Later, the infallible results of this karma will be very difficult.

To the ears of some beloved Dharma siblings,
Dewai Dorje offers some sad advice in a letter.

I pray before long we will *truly* meet each other.

When the clear request of the actual sublime students of the great awareness holder Jigdral Chokyi Lodro landed upon my crown, I, Dechen Dewai
Dorje, sang a sad song of whatever came to mind.

May virtue prevail!

Collapsing Outer, Inner, and Secret Confusion

Destroy outer confusion
by separating from attachment to the six senses,
and become liberated without sullying anything
by mental antidotes.

Destroy inner confusion
by separating from fixation on development practice,
and become liberated through experiencing all thought and
    perception
as illusory wisdom deities.

Destroy secret confusion
in the primordial ground, pure from the beginning,
and become liberated within the vajra chain,
the essence of primordial wisdom.

Ongoing confusion is confusion
within the ultimate expanse.
Its destruction is destruction
within the ultimate expanse.

Without moving from the ultimate expanse,
all phenomena become liberated.
I, a destroyer of confusion, am Vimamitra.
Ah . . .
Phet!

My outer yoga is taking the dynamic energy of awakened mind—
the universe and all it contains—
as the mudra of wisdom deity.

My inner yoga, the wisdom body of unified bliss,
is the practice of union and liberation with a consort.

My secret yoga is the practice of nondual primordial wisdom,
the vajra essence free from any basis.

I, a yogi, am Vimamitra.
Ah . . .
Phet!

Written by Sukha Vajra [Dewai Dorje].

8. Pronouncements before Passing

For Buddhist practitioners, death is an extraordinary opportunity. For it is that moment, when consciousness separates from the confines of physical form, that luminosity dawns and blazes as never before. Those who can seize the moment, by recognizing what is, are liberated on the spot. For others, subsequent events present further portals for recognition as the phenomena of the bardo unfold. Given the potency of the death experience for awakening, the Tibetan tradition as a whole, and especially the Dzogchen tradition, offer a plethora of skillful supports for the dying.

It is a natural inclination for those sensing into their own deaths, whether imminent or not, to want to say what is most important before the opportunity to do so is gone. To fully internalize the truth of death leads to speaking the truth, however and whatever that may entail for an individual. In this context, the tradition of final testaments (*zhal chems*), teachings and advice offered as the most essential by masters to disciples, enriches Tibetan Buddhism as a whole and especially the world of shaldam. Dewai Dorje's writings contain several such selections, two of which conclude this final chapter.

"Heart Advice, A Final Testament," written for Drime Ozer, covers with deeply felt earnestness crucial instructions on practicing most aspects of the path. Combining spiritual and practical advice, Dewai Dorje holds nothing back in telling her beloved exactly what she thinks he should and shouldn't do. The intimacy between them is revealed in the moving and genuine pronouncements of what she sees would be dangerous for him. This degree of comfort and familiarity speaks to a relationship between heart Dharma friends, stripped of the formalities that otherwise could color communication between individuals of differing status within the tradition. Dewai Dorje taught Drime Ozer as an equal in a relationship of loving mutuality.

The final piece, "A Beggar Lady's Final Testament," combines the highest Dzogchen instructions with foundational Dharma advice. Written for monastics, it synthesizes Dewai Dorje's indispensable counsel. For those who need something concise and easy to implement, this can be taken everywhere. It is as relevant for Dharma practitioners today as it was for her community one hundred years ago.

While neither of these final testaments is dated, Dewai Dorje might have written them at any time over her decades of life in eastern Tibet. From its language, the first likely was written before the passing of Drime Ozer in 1924. It's not unusual for teachings labeled as final testaments to be composed well before a master's actual passing. Genuine practitioners are steeped with the truth of impermanence and know that death can arrive at any moment. The urgency therefore to say what is most crucial is always upon them. What would be possible if such were the case for all of us?

Heart Advice, A Final Testament

How wondrous!
Superb Heir of All Victorious Buddhas,
gone before, present now, and still to come,
Secret Consort throughout All Lifetimes,
Great Hero—please, hear me.

I have little freedom,
since my past accumulation of merit and wisdom was weak.
I have fallen under the control of others,
and as I am forced to wander in faraway places,
my despair never lifts.

I have no desire to leave you, dearest partner,
equal to my heart, eyes, and very life.
But when negativity forces us apart for a little bit,
please, listen to this heart advice,
a final testament of what I am thinking.

Transmitting the *mani* mantra to the Great Compassionate One,[1]
or teaching sentient beings in the presence of Buddha—
this is not what I am doing.
Since our hearts are harmoniously intertwined
and we have great love and pure samaya between us,
I am just telling you what I think,
without hiding or changing anything.

Visualize your father and lama,
the actual buddha of triple time,
Dudjom Dorje Drolo Tsal [Dudjom Lingpa]
constantly upon your crown.

Since he's unrivaled among hundreds of lamas,
you don't need to rely on others,
as there is the danger of breaking samaya.

Yidam deities, empty in their appearing, arise as the lama
and are perfected as an expanse of self-arisen supports and
    supported manifestations.
You don't need development practice that fixates on these
    appearances.
This brings the danger of falling into perpetual reification.

Mantra's speech is the language of the unborn, emptiness.
Breathing in and out is the wheel of mantra.
You don't need to count mantra recitation conceptually.
You risk breaking its continuity with pointless chatter.

Self-arisen mind, beyond causes and conditions,
is spontaneously present as an exalted state of primordial
    perfection.
You don't need to use antidotes of accepting and rejecting.
These carry the danger of obscuring the twofold radiance of
    wisdom.[2]

Present in and of itself and uncompounded,
the dynamic energy of space and awareness
appears as kayas and orbs of five-colored light.
This is the actualization of the natural radiance of the four
    visions and six lamps.
You don't need to rely upon mere relative interdependencies.
These bring the danger of temporary visual experiences of light
    rays.

In the illusory displays of dakinis, mind's magical manifestations,
connate primordial wisdom arises as the dakinis' creative power.

You don't need to hold these as separate and distinct.
Doing so risks inviting unwanted punishment.

The miraculous display of the haughty protectors' wrath
steals the life force of any enemy that is visualized.
Killing for meat and beating drums is pointless.[3]
Misunderstanding the messengers risks harming yourself.

Wrathful, supreme method, the body of the vajra king
penetrates the *bhaga* of the queen of unchanging space.
You don't need beautiful human seductresses.
They bring the danger of losing the potency
of your channels, winds, and vital essences.

Supreme accomplishment is evidenced by the power to reveal
    profound treasures,
which are to be held as precious as life itself without any
    disrespect.
You don't need to compose teachings using the conventional
    language of intellectuals.
Doing so risks profound teachings falling into the hands of
    transgressors.

Upon the face of the clear mirror of self-arisen phenomenal
    existence,
the symbolic writing of the mother-dakinis appears in images.
Practice these, the dakinis' oral instructions, precisely as they
    should be.
You don't need to seek divination about the chaotic appearances
    of delusion.
That brings the danger of being deceived by evil spirits.

Through powerful and persistent prayers, genuine Dharma holders,
endowed with spiritual wealth yet humble in appearance,

will come to your door.
View them wisely, protect them,
and give them ripening and liberating instructions.
You don't need to live according to others' ethics.
Doing so puts you in danger
of wrong intentions, obstacles, and negative circumstances.

The spread and supervision of profound Dharma teachings
are controlled by the dakinis of ultimate reality.
You don't need to cater to the wishes of ordinary humans.
That carries the danger of mistaking the timing of Dharma
    teachings.

When the father's riches are mined by the son,
empty awareness, the best wisdom-dakini partner,
is taken as the siddhi beyond method and wisdom.
You don't need human ladies as consorts.
This risks entanglement with one who isn't your destined partner.

The sole heart son Natsok Rangdrol
will rely on only you as refuge, now and in the future.
Protect him lovingly, and kindly give him the profound
    teachings.
You don't need to go to Gangri Tokar.[4]
There's the danger of getting sick and dying.

When you instruct students in both worldly and spiritual
    matters,
some cannot be tamed by gentleness and need wrath,
and some cannot be tamed by wrath and need gentleness.
Care for all beings with fearless conduct.
You don't need to hope, fear, or pretend anything.
Pandering to others risks giving them control of your mind.

For transgressors untamed by either wrath or gentleness,
incite the powerful display of the haughty protectors as
    opponents
who will wipe them out until nothing, not even their names,
    remain.
You don't need to talk idly with transgressors.
Doing so risks getting lost in their wildness.

Food taken and clothing worn
are the wheel of the two accumulations,[5]
enjoyments to be invested as ornaments.
Don yourself with nice clothing and enjoy special foods!
You don't need to eat and dress like a beggar.
Doing so risks offending the wisdom deities in your body's
    mandala.

When enacting great deeds for the teachings of the Buddha and
    beings,
if you stay in retreat, you will accomplish benefit for self and
    other.
You don't need to run around on horseback doing village rituals.
Doing so risks being affected by obscurations of ripened karma.

Trust only yourself.
You don't need the competition and conflict of friends and
    enemies.
Sweet talkers with hearts of black smoke
bring the danger of losing your freedom to others.

Without feeling discouraged by all these faults,
focus on serving the Buddha's teachings and sentient beings.
The word *death* is just a bubble.
Your own perception will dawn as a buddha field,
present in and of itself.

You mustn't focus on death.
This risks both of us breaking our sacred commitments.

Always be confident in your own decisions.
Losing freedom to others buys your own suffering.
Forget about keeping up appearances and pandering to peoples'
    wishes.
Be aligned within and hold your own ground.
You mustn't lose your attention by cleverness.
Doing so risks mistaking evil intentions for positive ones.

To have your own freedom is to be like a king
with nothing but blue sky below.
If you lose your power to others,
you make your own pain
and there's nothing except the lowest place of all.

Be confident in whatever you think.
Since you're not an ordinary person,
the mother-dakinis are protecting and supporting you.
You don't need to ask random people what to do.
Doing so risks forsaking your great purpose.

This heart advice comes with pure intentions.
I don't know much about worldly or spiritual endeavors,
but I am just saying what I think.

If these words are senseless, I regretfully confess.
Please, if I have upset you, forgive me.
My superb hero, keep this in mind.

I thought, "I will go and wander lands unknown,"
but the unceasing power of the awareness holder Pema
has indivisibly connected method and wisdom for lifetimes.
When the natural form of vajra wisdom shows,

the compassion of the supreme hero will reverse,
being led by iron hooks of great craftiness and skill.

I don't need to pursue fame and the eight worldly concerns.
My mind is singularly aligned with four aims.[6]

I don't need riches. I can't carry even a tiny sesame seed.
The seven eternal riches of the noble ones are the best wealth.[7]

I have no need for nice food and clothes.
They just increase confused perception.
Alone, I rely solely on the greatest food
of the immaculate five elements.

I don't want companionship.
It's hard to have it when needed.
Alone, I rely for friendship on dakinis,
the dynamic energy of awareness.

I don't need to make children.
They just increase attachment and aversion.
My beautiful young child is awareness,
self-existent wakefulness.

I don't need to engage with consorts.
They're the basis for breaking samaya.
You, my hero, are the support for what appears to my mind.
On the path of luminosity, the best is to never part from great
    bliss.

I don't need a retinue and students.
They just cause anger.
Intangible deities and demons are my retinue and disciples to
    tame.

I don't need anything!
Everything is ruined by needs.
Not needing a single thing is best for sleeping in ease.
Whatever manifests is my wealth, present in and of itself.
Food and clothes amassed through stinginess—how pathetic.

I'm going, going to Lhasa in Central Tibet,
with aspirations made long ago at Gangri Tokar.
Incorporeal dakinis, please befriend and help me.
I will journey without any weariness in body or mind
together with a retinue of dakas, so don't worry.
We'll meet again in actuality at a feast celebration.

May there be auspiciousness for us, method and wisdom
united through powerful prayers, to meet again and again.

Thoughtlessly, I roam like a dog far away,
but this well-meaning heart advice, offered as a final testament,
I give to you, my noblest hero,
as dear to me as my heart, eyes, and very life.
I request again and again your great kindness
to pray that we shall never be apart!

This was written by a simple and frivolous beggar lady who just eats, sleeps,
and defecates.

May virtue prevail!

A Beggar Lady's Final Testament

Self-occurring awareness has always been utterly pure,
without any origin or basis.
Unconstricted by fabrication and fixation,
it is a natural state of letting-be.

Sustain its inseparable emptiness and lucidity
as the experience of primordial wisdom,
and display the innate glow
of your pristine true nature—Samantabhadra.

The exalted state of the Great Perfection
is beyond the reach of words, thought, and expression.
Rest in that experience,
without fabricating it by dualistic mind.

These words for faithful and pure monastics,
from the silly and unspiritual Dewai Dorje,
were written as illuminating advice.
Don't be indifferent to them.
Practice this single-pointedly.

Apart from self-knowing awareness,
the existence of buddha is impossible!
The supreme state of Samantabhadra is amazing.

There's no point in activities of the eight worldly concerns.
Nothing comes from them except ruin for yourself and others,
so avoid them like poison,
and keep to the isolated solitudes of the mountains.

Practice the instructions of the lama, the sole father.
Maintain mindfulness about what you shouldn't do.
Meaningless sloth squanders the freedoms and advantages
of your precious human rebirth.
Keep this in mind and you will gain understanding.

A carefree beggar lady wrote this as a final testament.
I pray that we shall meet again later.

May virtue prevail!

Notes

Translator's Introduction

1. Holly Gayley and Joshua Schapiro encapsulate the meaning of shaldam as follows: "Etymologically, the Tibetan term *shaldam* suggests pith instructions received directly from the mouth of a master. Works of shaldam convey an aura of intimacy and immediacy, as in an oral transmission from tantric master to disciple. As such they often carry the presumption of a lived encounter with instructions tailored to a specific individual." *A Gathering of Brilliant Moons: Practice Advice from the Rime Masters of Tibet* (Boston: Wisdom, 2017), 8.

2. *Love and Liberation: Autobiographical Writings of the Tibetan Buddhist Visionary Sera Khandro* (New York: Columbia University Press, 2015).

3. See Sam van Schaik, *Tibet: A History* (New Haven, CT: Yale University Press, 2013), 169–79.

4. The mantra of Avalokiteshvara, the deity of compassion is *om mani padme hung.*

5. Ngawang Zangpo, trans., "The Excellent Path of Devotion," in *Refining Our Perception of Reality: Sera Khandro's Commentary on Dudjom Lingpa's Account of His Visionary Journey* (Boston: Snow Lion, 2013), 272.

6. *Dbus bza' mkha' 'gro gsung 'bum*, vol. 1 (Chengdu: Si khron dpe skrun tshog pa, 2009).

7. The practice of Troma Nagmo lies at the heart of the Dudjom tradition. This is a chod, or severance, practice. It features the three-kaya dakinis—Samantabhadri, Vajravarahi, and Troma Nagmo—and is composed of infectious melodies and concept-shattering liturgies that enrapture practitioners while stripping away egoic confines to catapult them into realization. It is, without doubt, a complete path to enlightenment in and of itself.

8. In the years after Drime Ozer's passing, Dewai Dorje's Dharma activity blossomed. One of her most important deeds was to collect, edit, and transcribe Dudjom Lingpa's entire treasury of teachings in her thirty-

eighth year, a collection that included over twenty volumes. Doing this required her to return to Dartsang Kalzang Monastery, a place that held some of the best and hardest memories of her life. The insistence from Drime Ozer's heart students, and in particular from Sotrul Natsok Rangdrol, that Dewai Dorje was the person to carry out this crucial act of textual preservation convinced her to do it despite the challenges of returning to the Dudjom seat at Dartsang. Akyongza, Drime Ozer's main consort and the sister of a powerful lord from the Akyong clan, still resided at Dartsang, and Dewai Dorje had good reason to wonder about her reception there after having been expelled. Nevertheless, she was determined to complete the task, and she went with her daughter and two attendants, Tupzang and Tsultrim Dorje, back to Dartsang. The party was greeted by some direct disciples of Drime Ozer, who were as thrilled to see her as if greeting someone who had risen from the dead. She then found a willing and supportive ally in Tulku Dorje Dradul (1892–1959), Dudjom Lingpa's eighth son, who lent her the texts and played a crucial role in helping her succeed with the task. For more information, see Jacoby, *Love and Liberation*, 314. Dewai Dorje would also have been in possession of all the volumes of Drime Ozer's treasures. Combining these two collections—the treasures of the father, Dudjom Lingpa, and his son Drime Ozer—would have numbered around forty volumes of texts.

9. From Chatral Sangye Dorje's private manuscript of addenda to the biography of Dewai Dorje, the Lady from Central Tibet, titled *Turquoise Jewels*.

1. Prayers

1. This text, the *Essence of the Profound Meaning: Instructions for Realizing the True Nature of the Natural Great Perfection, a Commentary on the Meaning of "Buddhahood without Meditation,"* was completed by Drime Ozer at the behest of Dewai Dorje. A private manuscript, its colophon states, "Based on requests, I was close to finishing this when, due to circumstances of various kinds of lethargy, I left it incomplete. During that period, the strict command to finish it from the Mistress of Space, the Bliss-Sustaining Lady [Dewai Dorje], landed upon me. Unable to refuse her, I, Longchen Drime Ozer, or Pema Ledrel Tsal, created the supportive conditions for the concluding words, which were written down by the yogi Shila Vajra [Tsultrim Dorje]."

2. The title of this biography is *An Utpala Garland of Blooming Flowers to Ornament the Ears*, and *A Chariot of Devotion to Enlighten the Heart: The*

Story of the Liberation of Pema Dodrul Sangak Lingpa, the Omniscient Refuge Lord, Master of Accomplished Ones, and Precious Keeper of Infinite Profound Treasures.

3. For more information, see *The Hundred Tertöns* by Jamgon Kongtrul Lodro Taye.

4. The Sanskrit word *kaya* (*sku*) is rich with a plethora of meanings found within the teachings of Buddhism in general and in Dewai Dorje's writings in particular. With respect to the latter, she uses the word *kaya* to refer to the dimensions of wisdom, as in the three kayas just explained, as well as to refer to the actual bodies, or forms, manifestly present, of people, most often Drime Ozer. Indeed, the Tibetan word *sku* when combined with the word for "body," *gzugs*, makes it honorific. She also uses the term in the context of the Dzogchen practice of Togal, where practitioners' visionary experiences include seeing the forms of the wisdom deities. While this is not an exhaustive list of how the term is and can be used, it covers some of the principal ways it is used and should be understood in different contexts.

5. Here as well Drime Ozer is referring to Dewai Dorje.

6. The central subtle energy channel, the avadhuti, runs through the center of the body and is flanked on either side by the left and right channels. Practitioners working with the energies of the subtle body use visualization and other tantric techniques to remove constrictions or knots at the key junctures of the central channel and thereby facilitate the free flow of wisdom winds and the corresponding unfoldment of realization.

7. The five poisons, also referred to as afflictions, are ignorance, aggression, attachment, jealousy, and pride.

8. Development- and completion-stage practice are the two main approaches of the path of Secret Mantra. The former is emphasized in the inner Mahayoga tantras, which present techniques for experiencing the world and beings as a buddha field filled with wisdom deities. The approach involves conceptual meditation. The latter, completion-stage practice, in the Mahayoga context, induces luminous and empty nonconceptual primordial wisdom through various techniques including refining the five winds in the central channel.

9. In his commentary on Jigme Lingpa's *Treasury of Precious Qualities*, Kangyur Rinpoche, Longchen Yeshe Dorje describes the seven qualities of union as follows: "First, all aspects of the enlightened body arise as the manifold illusory appearance of phenomena—this is referred to as *union*. Second, all aspects of enlightened speech, free from the obscuration of

sounds and words, are *perfect enjoyment*. Third, all aspects of the enlightened mind are free from dualistic thoughts and enjoy immutable *great bliss*. Fourth, the enlightened mind subsists *without inherent existence*. It is not a mere nonaffirmative negation established by analysis but is characterized by self-cognizing awareness. These first four aspects perfect one's own aim. Continuing with the seven qualities of union, there is, fifth, the effortless accomplishment of the aims of others through *nonconceptual great compassion*. Sixth is the *unceasing constancy* of this compassion. And seventh is the *unobstructed arising* of form bodies and infinite methods of Dharma according to the aspirations and faculties of beings. With these last three aspects, the aim of others is automatically accomplished." *Vajrayana and the Great Perfection*, Treasury of Precious Qualities, vol. 2 (Boulder: Shambhala, 2020), 229.

10. Tsari is an important pilgrimage destination and sacred abode in southeastern Tibet. See Toni Huber, *The Cult of the Pure Crystal Mountain* (Oxford: Oxford University Press, 1999).

11. Twofold omniscience (*mkhyen gnyis*) refers to the primordial wisdom that sees the nature as it is and simultaneously sees its multiplicity.

12. In general, obscurations veil the mind's true nature—the buddha nature, or awakened mind—from every individual. Omniscient Longchenpa tells us, "And *The Hevajra Tantra in Two Sections* says, "Sentient beings are truly buddhas/ and yet are stained by adventitious obscurations./ When these are removed, indeed they are truly buddhas." *Finding Rest in the Nature of Mind* (Boulder: Shambhala, 2017), 208. Obscurations fall into two main categories: those deriving from defilement (*nyon sgrib*) and those that are conceptual (*shes sgrib*). Mahayana practice and Vajrayana empowerment and subsequent practice guide followers along paths that remove these obscuring veils to enable the unfiltered sunlight of the buddha nature abiding in every sentient being to shine forth.

13. The youthful vase kaya refers to the actualization of awareness abiding in its inner radiance. See the introduction to chapter 2 for more information.

14. The five female buddhas begin their appearance here, starting with Dhatvishvari, the consort of Buddha Vairochana.

15. According to the Early Translation Nyingma tradition, the approaches of the spiritual path are categorized in a ninefold manner. First are the paths of hearers, solitary realizers, and the vast approach of bodhisattvas, the Mahayana. These are followed by the three outer tantras—kriya, charya, and yoga—and then by the three inner tantric approaches of maha-, anu-, and atiyoga. All these approaches lead to the same result of fully enlight-

ened buddhahood, but their methods become increasing more refined, efficacious, and potent as one traverses from the first approaches to the higher ones. The culmination of all spiritual paths is found in the teachings of atiyoga—the Great Perfection, Dzogchen—from the purview of Nyingma practitioners.

16. Adopting the behavior of dogs and pigs can have both a positive and negative sense. Here Dewai Dorje is using this analogy to highlight the negative. See chapter 7, note 24 for the positive connotation in the context of Dzogchen practice.

17. The five chakras are five energy centers in the subtle body located at the crown, throat, heart, navel, and secret centers.

18. These refer to meditation on the emptiness of the corporeal body, its channels, and the mind.

19. The four chakras are the energy centers at the crown, throat, heart, and navel centers. The teachings referred to here work with the upper door on the path of method whereby practitioners train to induce the wisdom of bliss using the subtle energies in their own body. The instructions on the five chakras work with the lower doors and equip practitioners to engage in qualified practice with the body of another. See *Vajrayana and the Great Perfection*, 178.

20. A literal translation of the Tibetan for Golok could be rendered as "wrong-headed" or "rebel."

21. This is Secret Mantra terminology to be explained by a qualified teacher.

22. The five primordial wisdoms are dharmadhatu, mirrorlike, evenness, discriminating, and all-accomplishing.

2. Poems

1. This refers to the *mani* mantra: *om mani padme hung*.

2. The six consciousnesses are the five sensory consciousnesses and the mental consciousness.

3. The four maras as presented in this poem—and as commonly appear in the practice of chod, or severance—are the maras of the afflictions, the aggregates, the godly son, and the Lord of Death. Sarah Harding elucidates these as "1. The mara of the aggregates: the five aspects of embodied experience—form, feeling, sensation, formation, and consciousness. Just having a body with perception and consciousness can act as an obstacle to full awakening. 2. The mara of the afflictive emotions, the emotional reactions in response to the pleasure, pain, and neutrality of perceptions.

3. The mara of the "child of the gods"—that is, being spoiled and indulgent to the extent that any spiritual development is precluded by complacency.
4. The mara of death, or "the lord of death," an obstacle that needs no description." For more information, see *Machik's Complete Explanation* (Boston: Snow Lion, 2013), 36.

4. The eight worldly concerns are gain and loss, fame and disgrace, praise and blame, and pleasure and pain.

5. Dewai Dorje's treasures include a synopsis of four characteristics of the uncontrived state, which draws from the Dzogchen practices of both Trekcho and Togal. She describes these four as experiences of (1) utter clarity, when awareness abides unwaveringly in the expanse of space and bindus (*thig le,* spheres of light); (2) open spaciousness, when all arising thoughts, the natural energy of great penetrating knowledge, are recognized as not being beyond primordial wisdom and ultimate reality; (3) vivid brightness, when, without blocking or establishing everything arising as space and bindus, all is fully encompassed within the sphere of space and bindus, the expression of awareness; and (4) alert wakefulness, when awareness—the three kayas beyond meeting and parting, endowed with the special features of the inwardly radiant youthful vase kaya—is actualized as kayas, primordial wisdom, and bindus. In chapter 6, Dewai Dorje also elucidates a fourfold mode of remaining uncontrived in "Four Qualities of the Uncontrived State," p. 205.

6. The ten paramitas, or perfections, are generosity, diligence, ethical discipline, patience, concentration, sublime insight, skillful means, power, aspiration, and primordial wisdom.

7. Rameshvara, according to the Queen of Great Bliss sadhana from the Longchen Nyingtik tradition, is one of the celestial abodes (*mkha' spyod*), identified at the hair at the center of the forehead (*urna*) of the vajra body, or sacred dimension of the bodies of sentient beings. See Matthieu Ricard, *The Life of Shabkar: The Autobiography of a Tibetan Yogin* (Boston: Shambhala, 2001), 593.

3. Prophecy

1. Drime Ozer was born in the year of the Snake (c. 1881).

4. Proclamations of Realization, Wonder, and Despair

1. Gyalsen (*rgyal bsen*) is a class of nonhuman spirits, while Vajradhara is a buddha. Here Dewai Dorje plays with labels of spirits and names of

buddhas, combining them to challenge ordinary thinking about helpful and harmful influences.

2. Gaga is mentioned as a prophetic name for a glorious incarnation of Yeshe Tsogyal in Dewai Dorje's long autobiography.

3. In the Vajrayana tradition, the three ways that a lama is said to express kindness are offering ripening empowerments, reading transmissions, and liberating instructions. Those from whom a disciple receives all three can be considered "root" lamas.

4. In the practice of Tibetan medicine, golden needles have been used to extract fluid from the heart. If used improperly, there is the danger of harming the patient. Thus, it is an instrument that must be used with exceptional precision.

5. This equates to c. 1925, the year after the death of Drime Ozer.

6. The reference to the sole father here is Dudjom Lingpa, Drime Ozer's father.

7. The month of sagadawa corresponds to the fourth month of the Tibetan lunar calendar and marks the beginning of summer, a time when change is apace. It is also the month when the Buddha's enlightenment and mahaparinirvana are celebrated.

8. In the colophons of her shaldam, Dewai Dorje frequently mentions the three perceptions. This is often a way of referring to a mendicant's unelaborate lifestyle, which boils down to eating, sleeping, and defecating.

5. Pure Visions

1. For example, Omniscient Longchenpa blessed Jigme Lingpa in pure visions, which served to catalyze the latter's revelation of the treasures of the Longchen Nyingtik tradition.

2. Dewai Dorje meticulously captured the teachings given by Drime Ozer on Dudjom Lingpa's *Nang Jang*, and this, her commentary based on his instructions, comprises an entire volume of her Collected Works. Two English language translations of this commentary are available. Ngawang Zangpo's translation of this commentary has been published as *Refining Our Perception of Reality: Sera Khandro's Commentary on Dudjom Lingpa's Account of His Visionary Journey*. Alan Wallace's translation has been published as *Garland for the Delight of the Fortunate*, which is included with his translation of Dudjom Lingpa's *Nang Jang*, titled *Buddhahood Without Meditation* (Somerville, MA: Wisdom, 2015). For more information on Dewai Dorje's special connection to this text, see pages 1–2 of Wallace's introduction to *Buddhahood Without Meditation*.

3. For further explanation of Mahottara Heruka, see *Vajrayana and the Great Perfection*, 288–89.

4. See chapter 1, note 6.

5. This refers to the heart chakra, that which gathers thought. In her extensive explanation of the stages of completion practice for the deity Vajravarahi, Dewai Dorje teaches that the heart chakra has eight branch channels that blaze with shimmering blue light.

6. Most likely this was the year 1935, which was the year of the Bird according to the Tibetan calendar.

7. A mantra of Padmasambhava, Guru Rinpoche.

8. These four levels of awareness holders mark progression upon the path of Secret Mantra.

9. For more information on what is considered to be half nirmanakaya and half sambhogakaya, see *Vajrayana and the Great Perfection*, 293–94.

6. Pith Instructions

1. *The Princeton Dictionary of Buddhism* lists the eight conceptual limitations under the heading of the "eight extremes" as follows: "The antinomies of production and cessation, eternality and annihilation, sameness and difference, and coming and going, which constitute the eight deluded views of sentient beings." The three gateways to liberation are three avenues for accessing the ultimate nature. They are emptiness, wishlessness, and an absence of characteristics.

2. The Tibetan for "wish-fulfilling jewel" is *yid bzhin nor bu*. In this explanation, Dewai Dorje explains each individual term in the phrase. The first term, *yid*, is one of Tibetan language's many terms for "mind," commonly translated as "intellect," and here as "wish." The second, *bzhin*, quite literally means "like" or "as." Thus, the first two taken together, literally, are close to "as wished" and in this pairing most often are translated as "wish-fulfilling." The second word, *nor bu*, usually translated as "jewel" or "gem," Dewai Dorje has here broken into its two distinct parts. She uses the verbal meaning of the first, *nor*, "to mistake" or "err," and the nominative meaning for the second, *bu*, "child" or "son." Throughout her writing she refers to Drime Ozer as Wish-Fulfilling Jewel.

3. While the four special features that Dewai Dorje mentions here may not be exactly the same as those she elucidates in other shaldam, readers will benefit from consulting chapter 2, note 5 for greater context.

4. The Tibetan *'dud po lag ring* refers to a particular demon or mara.

5. This refers to the practice of chod, or severance.

6. These are exercises of yogic breathing similar to pranayama.

7. Dewai Dorje employs the metaphor of a child jumping onto its mother's lap in her teachings on the dawning of the luminosity at the time of the bardo of death. This metaphor is found widely in instructions on the bardo of dying to support practitioners in recognizing the luminosity of awareness that arises in the dying process. The "child" luminosity refers to the recognition of awareness that the practitioners have cultivated during their lifetimes. The "mother" luminosity is the appearance of primordial purity that arises at the moment of death. It is taught that when this is recognized to be what it is, like a child recognizing its mother and bounding onto her lap, mother and child luminosities will become mingled indivisibly, and liberation will be achieved.

8. Here Sera Khandro is referring to practices that involve working with the subtle energy channels, winds, and vital essences in the body.

9. See the introduction to chapter 6 for a more detailed explanation.

10. The syllable *ah* in the Tibetan alphabet, which is the first vowel, is often used to indicate the empty unborn nature of all phenomena. It is also taught to be the *Perfection of Wisdom* in one syllable, the shortest of the "child" *Perfection of Wisdom* sutras.

7. PERSONAL ADVICE AND LETTERS

1. See the introduction to chapter 5. *Nang Jang* and Dewai Dorje's commentary on it expand the pithy introduction Dewai Dorje provides in this concise advice within the larger context of the teaching.

2. See Ngawang Zangpo, trans, *Refining Our Perception of Reality*, 65.

3. Ibid., 165.

4. A thorough explanation of the latter example also appears in Kangyur Rinpoche's explanation of Jigme Lingpa's *Vajrayana and the Great Perfection* (259): "'Awareness manifests in objects of the senses' (*rig pa yul la shar*) means that the creative power of cognitive potency (*thugs rje'i rtsal*) manifests unceasingly. However, because the nature of awareness and the manifestation of its creative power are not distinct and separate entities and because, in the state of awareness, thoughts do not chase after sense objects (for their root or basis has been recognized), there is no examination or scrutiny either of the outer objects of the six consciousnesses or of the inner mind. There is not even any fixated settling in the unborn ultimate nature. When stripped to its naked state [when, in other words,

it is divested of all concepts], mind-transcending awareness, the ultimate nature of things, is beyond change. It cannot be overwhelmed by appearances. It is like mercury, which does not mix with the dust when it falls on the ground. By contrast, the ordinary mind fails to recognize the actual nature of the apprehended objects, and thus it clings to them. It merges with the various dualistic thoughts of subject and object that follow each other continually, and thus it perpetuates phenomenal existence, and karma is accumulated."

5. A concise explanation of this is given by Kangyur Rinpoche in *Vajrayana and the Great Perfection* (296): "These primordial wisdoms may be summarized as follows. The primordial wisdom of the dharmadhatu refers to the knowledge of the nature of things. The remaining four wisdoms refer to the knowledge of phenomena in all their multiplicity."

6. "As corresponding to the wish to go,/ And then to setting out,/ The wise should understand respectively,/ The difference that divides these two." Śāntideva, *The Way of the Bodhisattva: A Translation of the Bodhicaryāvatāra*, translated by Padmakara Translation Group (Boston: Shambhala, 1997), 55.

7. Dewai Dorje writes about Dzirong Sanglung Monastery and the mountain retreat center of Sanglung at a place called Dzika and identifies Sanglung as a "branch" of Tsangchen (Dzogchen) Monastery.

8. See the introduction to chapter 7.

9. This title was given by Dewai Dorje.

10. This title was given by Dewai Dorje.

11. Guru Yoga lies at the heart of all Secret Mantra practice and especially Great Perfection practice, which depends upon an unshakable devotion endowed with the insight that externally appearing teachers are the manifestation of the ultimate guru, indwelling wisdom awareness. Guru Yoga practice takes many forms but in essence is a process of saturating one's ordinary way of being with the noble qualities of the wisdom guru's form, speech, and awakened mind.

12. These are specific references to details of the path of Togal, to be clarified by a lineage teacher.

13. Bindu (*thig le*) is a Sanskrit word that has myriad meanings based on its use in different contexts. In my translation of Dewai Dorje's writings, I have chosen to render *thig le* as "vital essence" when it is used in the context of the body's subtle energy network of channels and chakras (energy centers). In other contexts, such as the verse here, bindu (*thig le*) means "sphere or orb of light," and this usage is widespread in Dzogchen teach-

ings on the practice of Togal. The word is also used to refer to mind's essential nature in yet other contexts.

14. These include psychic powers, "the divine eye," "the divine ear," knowledge of other's minds, and knowledge of past lives. See *Princeton Dictionary of Buddhism*, s.v. "buddhacakṣus."

15. This refers to practitioners whose realization allows them to control what happens when they die and specifically whether they remain in their previous bodies (*kayas*) to benefit beings or dissolve into the ultimate expanse.

16. The four types of fearless confidence are not having hope to attain buddhahood or disappointment at thinking it won't be attained and not fearing rebirth in the lower realms or having hope not to be reborn there.

17. The four thoughts are contemplations on a precious human rebirth, impermanence, the sufferings of samsara, and karma, the law of cause and result. The eight worldly concerns are attachment to gain, praise, fame, and pleasure, and aversion to loss, blame, disgrace, and pain.

18. For an extensive explanation of the different levels of vows, see Panchen Ngari Pema Wangyi Gyalpo and Dudjom Rinpoche Jigdral Yeshe Dorje, *Perfect Conduct: Ascertaining the Three Vows*, translated by Samdrub Gyurme and Sangye Khandro (Somerville, MA: Wisdom, 2014). This work is a thorough explanation of the vows of individual liberation, bodhisattvas, and Secret Mantra and contains a commentary on the same by His Holiness Dudjom Rinpoche.

19. For an explanation of the samayas, see *Vajrayana and the Great Perfection*, 199–201.

20. The garuda, a mythical bird, is said to emerge from its egg fully mature, without needing to go through any processes of growth and development to be able to fly through the sky. In this context, the garuda is used as an example for a practitioner who is free from ordinary ways of being and doing based on the afflictions, especially in the face of obstacles and challenges. This is in fact what "secret conduct" means.

21. The textual notations found in Dewai Dorje's manuscript tell us that this quotation is found in the fifth volume of the one hundred thousand tantras of the Kangyur.

22. See chapter 6, note 1.

23. In her long autobiography, Sera Khandro identifies Gara Terton (1857–1910) as Dudul Wangchuk Lingpa. Gara Terton was a powerful treasure revealer and the abbot of Benak Monastery with whom Sera Khandro had a prophesized connection that never came to fruition due to various obstacles. However, her connection with him led to her relationship with

his son, Gara Gyalse, and the many years of their vexed and challenging partnership.

24. In his seminal Dzogchen treatise *Yeshe Lama*, Jigme Lingpa gives instructions on what conduct should be like for a Dzogchen practitioner. There, he describes it as behavior that is like dogs or pigs, who have no concepts of purity or filth, showing that the practitioner has eliminated concepts based on things being clean or dirty.

25. The six collections are the five sensory consciousnesses along with the mental consciousness.

26. Lungs, when boiled, stay on the surface of soup. Here, Sera Khandro is using this example to illustrate those who pay lip service to the teachings on mindfulness by saying they understand them but who do not actually practice them. In the dramatic tale of two bees in *A Drama in the Lotus Garden*, Paltrul Rinpoche uses the example in a similar way: "Affections are like a dish of lung. There is something in the mouth but nothing substantially satisfying." See Tulku Thondup, trans., *Enlightened Living: Teachings of Tibetan Buddhist Masters* (Hong Kong: Rangjung Yeshe, 1997), 87.

27. At the end of her long autobiography, Dewai Dorje talks about the circumstances surrounding its composition. She writes about an extremely intelligent scholar who was a holder of the vinaya and an incarnation of both the Dharma King and Namkhai Nyingpo. This person, Norbu Wangyal, offered her silver and gold, a white Benares silk scarf, and his body, speech, and mind to be of service. She describes him as someone who had totally renounced all activities that were not in line with the Dharma and then applied himself single-pointedly to study and practice. He made Dewai Dorje the best offering, the offering of the very essence of that practice, and then earnestly requested her to write her life story. This Norbu Wangyal most likely is the same Khenpo Norbu Wangyal mentioned in several other places as Ase Norbu Wangyal.

28. The three ways of service to one's guru are to provide material support, offer physical service, and offer one's own practice. The third is considered to be the very best kind of service and offering.

29. The textual notes here were handwritten by a disciple in one of the original manuscripts that were used as a basis for the unpublished computer input version of her Collected Works.

30. This title was given by Dewai Dorje.

31. All text in parentheses are annotations in the original Tibetan manuscript.

32. The eight gateways of spontaneous presence are a crucial Dzogchen teaching for understanding how the original ground manifests itself.

33. "Ever-Excellent" is an English translation of the Tibetan Kuntuzangpo (Kun tu bzang po), or Kunzang, for the Sanskrit Samantabhadra.

34. This title is given by Dewai Dorje. Dewai Dorje visited the retreat center of Tsangar several times when she was around forty. She offered the entire transmission of Dudjom Lingpa's Collected Works to the retreatants there.

35. Dewai Dorje passed away in Riwoche, in Kham, eastern Tibet in 1940. It was the only time she visited there, and thus it is fair to assume that this letter was one of her final offerings of advice to her students.

8. Pronouncements before Passing

1. Avalokiteshvara.

2. Knowing the nature as it is and seeing the variety of all things.

3. What is pointless is killing animals to get meat for ritual ceremonies done, usually with drumming, for the Dharma protectors.

4. Gangri Tokar is a sacred place in Central Tibet, to the south of Lhasa, where Omniscient Longchenpa composed several of his major Dzogchen treatises. Drime Ozer had already made pilgrimage to this spot on his early trip to Central Tibet when Dewai Dorje first encountered him

5. This refers to the accumulations of merit and wisdom.

6. The four aims are to live as a beggar, in a state of poverty and inconsequence, focused on dying, and alone in a solitary place.

7. These are described as the richness of faith, ethical discipline, study, giving, knowing shame, conscientiousness, and sublime knowledge.

BIBLIOGRAPHY

THE SOURCE TEXTS

Sera Khandro Dewai Dorje. *Se ra mkha' 'dro bde ba'i rdo rje* [The Collected Works of Sera Khandro Kunzang Dekyong Wangmo]. 7 volumes. Unpublished manuscript.

———. *Dbus bza' mkha' 'gro gsung 'bum* [The Collected Works of the Dakini from Central Tibet]. Chengdu: Si khron dpe skrun tshog pa, 2009.

———. *Se ra mkha' 'gro bde chen bde ba'i rdo rje'i gsung 'bum* [The Collected Works of Sera Khandro Dechen Dewai Dorje]. In *Gangs can skyes ma'i dpe tshogs* [A collection of printed works of Tibetan women], vol. 15. Sichuan: Si khron bod yig dpe rnying bsdu sgrig khang, 2015.

REFERENCE WORKS

Barron, Richard, trans. *Buddhahood Without Meditation: A Visionary Account Known as Refining Apparent Phenomena (Nang-Jang)*. Junction City, CA: Padma, 1994.

Chonam, Lama, and Sangye Khandro, trans. *Jigmed Lingpa's Yeshe Lama: An Extensive Oral Commentary by Khenchen Namdrol Rinpoche*. Ashland, OR: Berotsana, 2023.

Gayley, Holly, and Joshua Schapiro. *A Gathering of Brilliant Moons: Practice Advice from the Rime Masters of Tibet*. Boston: Wisdom, 2017.

Harding, Sarah, trans. *Machig's Complete Explanation*. Boston: Shambhala, 2003.

Huber, Toni. *The Cult of the Pure Crystal Mountain*. Oxford: Oxford University Press, 1999.

Jacoby, Sarah H. *Love and Liberation: Autobiographical Writings of the Tibetan Buddhist Visionary Sera Khandro*. New York: Columbia University Press, 2014.

Jigme Lingpa and Kangyur Rinpoche, Longchen Yeshe Dorje. *Vajrayana and the Great Perfection*. Treasury of Precious Qualities: The Rain of Joy, vol. 2. Boulder: Shambhala, 2013.

Longchenpa. *Finding Rest in the Nature of Mind*. The Trilogy of Rest, vol. 1. Translated by Padmakara Translation Group. Boulder: Shambhala, 2017.

Ngawang Zangpo, trans. *Refining Our Perception of Reality: Sera Khandro's Commentary on Dudjom Lingpa's Account of His Visionary Journey*. Boston: Snow Lion, 2013.

Panchen Ngari Pema Wangyi Gyalpo and Dudjom Rinpoche Jigdral Yeshe Dorje. *Perfect Conduct: Ascertaining the Three Vows*. Translated by Samdrub Gyurme and Sangye Khandro. Somerville, MA: Wisdom, 2014.

Ricard, Matthieu, trans. *The Life of Shabkar: The Autobiography of a Tibetan Yogin*. Boston: Shambhala, 2001.

Śāntideva. *The Way of the Bodhisattva: A Translation of the Bodhicaryāvatāra*. Translated by Padmakara Translation Group. Boston: Shambhala, 1997.

van Schaik, Sam. *Tibet: A History*. New Haven, CT: Yale University Press, 2013.

Tulku Thondup, trans. *Enlightened Living: Teachings of Tibetan Buddhist Masters*. Hong Kong: Rangjung Yeshe, 1997.

Wallace, B. Alan, trans. *Buddhahood Without Meditation: Düdjom Lingpa's Visions of the Great Perfection*. Somerville, MA: Wisdom, 2015.

INDEX

Index of Text Titles